PEAKS
AND
TROUGHS

PEAKS
AND
TROUGHS

IN AT THE DEEP END, HIGH IN THE HILLS

Nick Perry

Illustrations by Rosalinda Monteiro

First published in Great Britain in 2016 by Polygon, an imprint of Birlinn Ltd.

West Newington House
10 Newington Road
Edinburgh
EH9 1QS

www.polygonbooks.co.uk

A CIP catalogue reference for this book is available from the British Library.

ISBN 978 1 84697 365 9
eBook ISBN 978 0 85790 912 1

Design and typesetting by Studio Monachino

To my children, Sam, Lysta, Seth and Belah

Most of what follows is true.
Some names, dates and locations have been changed
to protect the innocent, the guilty and the insane.

1

The Gift and
a Journey

As we sat in the offices of Huggett, Bellows & Wilde, a firm of solicitors just down from West Hampstead Tube station, I could hear the dull hum of the Underground rumbling through the bowels of the building. It could have been mistaken for a recurring stomach complaint for it came and went every couple of minutes, then settled down until the next train passed beneath us. We had dressed for the occasion: my brother Jack and I were both wearing ties, and had even polished our shoes. This was not a natural look, and neither was Jack's hair, flattened down with Brylcreem. It was an attempt at smartness that didn't suit us. No matter how hard we tried, neither of us could ever achieve the appearance of someone well groomed.

Eventually Mr Bellows came in and sat down: wispy white; unlike us naturally neat. With a tight-lipped smile he looked at us benignly, opened the file, and in ecclesiastical tones told us we had each inherited £6,000. It did feel as if we were receiving a divine gift. We had only met this generous spinster aunt Elsie as children. She had lived on some outer branch of the family tree; I couldn't remember her name being mentioned, recognising her only in faded photographs in the family album. I suddenly felt a tremendous warmth for her, regretted that I could not express my thanks. For little though we knew it then, she had changed our lives.

Jack and I didn't speak about it, not at first, as we walked along the Finchley Road. The money, what we were going to do with it.

That's what I was thinking about when we got to the Cosmo, a café run by a rotund Italian called Giuseppe who operatically shouted orders back to the kitchen where his wife and children slaved. He knew us well; since he was still open at midnight, we would often end up there after the late night film in Swiss Cottage. He slid two plates of baked beans across the table in front us.

'Grazie.'

'You boys, you're so Italian.'

We buttered our toast without speaking, turning over in our minds the possibilities that now presented themselves.

For the past year I'd been drifting from job to job. The lowest point had resulted from replying to an advert in the *Evening Standard*, filling a vacancy to work in the warehouse of a sausage skin factory. I lasted three months.

I was twenty-three, married to Ros, a Welsh girl, once a children's nurse, now bringing up our six-month-old twins, Sam and Lysta. Jack, fifteen months younger than me, worked for our uncle, a film producer. I never knew quite what he did apart from running around all over the place picking up people from airports and taking them in taxis to various locations.

'I want to leave London, get out into the countryside. Start a new life. Jack,' I said, while he seemed to be counting the baked beans on his toast, 'this is what they call a karmic moment.'

'You sound like a hippy.'

'Can you finish your baked beans? It's annoying watching you eat them one by one.'

Since meeting Ros I'd become involved with the followers of Rudolf Steiner: 'anthroposophists', they called themselves. They cared about the earth, practising farming methods free of chemicals and pesticides. I started to attend seminars, and the more I heard the more I wanted to know. So in the summer I went to work on a Steiner farm down in Sussex, going home to Ros at weekends. I absorbed it all: phases of the moon, companion planting, the waxing and waning of everything. I lived in a sun-swung zodiac believing I'd found the answer. We even played Beethoven symphonies to a herd of milking cows, convinced it would increase their milk yield.

'I wouldn't mind being a shepherd,' said Jack, spearing a couple of baked beans with the end of his fork. 'But what I'd really like is a dog. A Border collie.'

'Let's buy a farm . . . Yes, let's buy a farm!' I shouted, bringing my fist down on the table. After all, we were country boys at heart, brought up in Dorset. Ten minutes later we realised what a ridiculous idea it was. After all, we only had £12,000. That wasn't going to buy us a farm.

'It would up in the hills of North Wales,' Ros told me later.

Her enthusiasm about it all, and her parents in Caernarfonshire, made it a real possibility.

A few days later, Jack and I made a pact to put our money together and get out of London. We washed it down with a bottle of Niersteiner, a cheap German wine. Ros was delighted; she would be returning home, and Sam and Lysta would be growing up close to their grandparents.

Jack bought books on sheep farming, absorbing himself in the shepherd's way of life.

'What have you discovered, Jack?' I asked.

'Looks like it's seven days a week, three hundred and sixty-five days a year.'

'You can say goodbye to your weekend lie-ins, then?'

Not once did it occur to us that knowing the theory is one thing, putting it into practice quite another.

Gwyn, Ros's father, rather than saying, 'You don't know anything about farming,' was right behind the idea. A consultant paediatrician at Bangor hospital, he was a kind-hearted Quaker whose generosity showed itself in every act. Estate agents' leaflets of hill farms and smallholdings began arriving in the post. Every day Gwyn was out in his VW Beetle to take a look.

A month later we drove to North Wales to stay with my in-laws in Caernarfon for the weekend. By Saturday afternoon we had put in an offer on Dyffryn, a remote hill farm of forty-eight acres above the village of Penygroes, exchanging contracts within a month. We had bought it for six thousand quid!

Through the weeks that followed we talked about nothing else. Ros wanted to grow vegetables, Jack was going to have a flock of sheep, I would look after pigs. Gwyn bought us a Morris Traveller, and I started to learn to drive around the streets of London. I said to Jack that as soon as I passed my driving test we should buy a Land Rover. 'We're farmers now.

Straw bales in the back, a sheep dog sitting between us on the front seat.'

'Yes, wearing braces and a flat cap.'

'What, the dog?'

'No, us.'

Jack watched *One Man and His Dog* every Sunday. I had to endure his endless attempts at getting the whistle just right, the one where you stick two fingers in your mouth and a piercing shrill rips through the air. He couldn't master it, but unfortunately never stopped trying.

Jack grew a beard, wore collarless shirts and combat jackets. He got rid of his denim cap. We both bought waistcoats in the Portobello Road, and those old leather braces, the sort farmers wear. Shirt-sleeves rolled up, we were dressed to fill the part.

We counted down the days, making plans, and decided to make the move on the first of January 1970. What better time to begin a new phase in your life?

Every night after the twins had gone to sleep I told Ros what we were going to achieve in that first year. I couldn't wait for it to be haymaking time, me driving a tractor and trailer and stacking the bales in the barn. It was left to Ros to put a spoonful of reality into the mix. 'You're flying too high, the both of you.'

'What do you mean?' I said, aghast.

Ros gave us her assessment of the practicalities involved in beginning a new life. She turned our attention to the not insignificant fact that the farmhouse at Dyffryn needed to be made habitable. Had we not noticed that it was no place for the twins to live? Had we not considered that she would probably not be moving in for several weeks?

'You two are actually going to be camping in the house. Why do you think we got the place for just six thousand pounds?'

Jack and I looked at each other as if to say well of course we'd thought of all that. We hadn't, not for a single moment.

'There's a lot of work to do,' she said. 'It's more than just painting and putting up wallpaper.'

I gave her a kiss then, a reassuring one. 'Don't worry, Ros,' I said. 'I realise you haven't seen it yet, but I'm a practical man around the house.'

'Me too,' said Jack. 'We can turn our hands to most things.'

'Or if we can't we can pick them up pretty damn quickly.'

'You're going to need to.'

I'd never put up a roll of wallpaper, though I had painted a friend's back door once. I wasn't going to tell Ros that.

'Everything is in the planning,' she said, 'and I'm leaving in two days.' That's what was worrying her. She was going to be staying with her parents in Caernarfon seven miles north of Dyffryn while Jack and I got on with turning the house into a home.

Then Ros let it be known that she didn't like the idea of me driving the Traveller to North Wales. We had a bit of a row about it but I was determined it was a risk worth taking.

'If the police stop you, you'll have to pay a huge fine.'

'There's nothing wrong with my driving,' I told her. 'I drive the Traveller around London every day.'

'That's not the point, is it?' We never resolved the matter.

I was awake most of the night before Ros was leaving with the twins. Those slow-moving hours when the magnitude of what I had done raised its head and stared at me, the dark shadow of myself. And I couldn't shift it, the enormity of what I had committed us to, and how we were going to cope with what lay ahead. But in the morning, Ros would never have guessed, waking next to me, smiling and whispering 'Today's the day'.

I drove them, of course, to Euston station with L plates, which Ros insisted on. Rain swirled along the wind-tunnel streets, everybody struggling with umbrellas, eyes looking downwards. We hardly spoke a word. We would be seeing each other again in a week. 'Won't be long, Ros,' I said.

'I'm sure you'll survive without me.'

'Let's hope you can without me.'

As Euston came into view she came out with a long list of reminders, last minute things that must on no account be overlooked. Each job had to be ticked off in a notebook.

At the ticket barrier I knelt down beside the twins, who were looking up at me from their buggy. It felt strange to be saying goodbye to them. Then I held Ros in a long embrace, staring into her hazel eyes, stroking her wild frizzy hair.

'I will miss you,' I whispered in her ear.

That night Jack and I ate at the bistro in Ladbroke Grove. We met up with a couple of friends, musicians who were forming a pop group, and spent the evening listening to them talking about chord riffs and great guitar solos with the same enthusiasm that Jack and I felt for our venture out into the wilds of Wales. It's funny how things that once absorbed you gradually wane, no longer hold your interest. London in the sixties, those summers of love, couples swaying dreamily at pop festivals, tripping out in a psychedelic world. All that 'love and peace, man' was wearing a bit thin. It was time to move on. That's how it struck me, sitting there, getting bored. These people were our friends, involved in our lives; now all this was passing away. I wondered who we would still be in touch with a year from now.

So the day came. We were leaving on the stroke of midnight, the moment the new decade arrived. We had survived the swinging sixties and a new life lay ahead. We had indulged in all the excesses, lying in flats in a purple haze listening to Hendrix, being cool; there was nothing more to discover.

Fireworks exploded around us, sky rockets bursting into an array of colours, cascading droplets of light. Everyone cheering, arms around each other. It was midnight, 31 December 1969. I looked at my brother. 'Happy New Year, Jack. Who knows what it will hold for us.'

I turned on the ignition, put the Traveller into first gear, flicked out the orange indicator: we were on our way. Jack opened the AA map; he was going to navigate. We crawled in first gear between the revellers crowding around us. They blew kisses at us while a girl pressed her wet lips against my window, a symbolic reminder of what we were leaving behind.

On Jack's lap I could see clearly marked in fluorescent yellow ink the route we were going to follow, snaking its way across the page. We had a portable tape player, and as we drove we sang along to the Stones' 'You Can't Always Get What You Want'.

We drove on through the night, heading out into the dark countryside. No street lights here, Jack pouring coffee from a thermos, changing tapes, making roll-ups of Golden Virginia that he lit and passed to me. We talked or hummed along to whatever we were listening to.

Out of the blue Jack asked me how I got on with Eryl, my mother-in-law. He had only met her once, at the wedding.

'What did you think of her?' I asked.

She had given him the impression of being full of her own importance. He described her as a force to be reckoned with.

'You're right there,' I told him.

She had been against the marriage, not wanting her daughter to marry an Englishman. I remember the morning Ros opened the letter expressing her extreme disappointment. She was an international golfer, and in an emotional plea said that if Ros didn't reconsider her decision, in other words dump me, she feared for the effect it would have on her game. That's when Ros told her she was pregnant, and not another word was said about it.

'It doesn't concern you that she doesn't like you?' Jack asked.

'Not really. Ros says she'll come round in her own time.'

We pulled into Ledbury, sleeping quietly in its timber-framed buildings. You wouldn't have known here in rural England that it was New Year's Day. The houses were dark and silent, only an occasional Christmas tree lighting a window, the pub where we parked draped in the orange glow of fairy lights flashing *Happy New Year*. We got out to stretch our legs, whispering to each other, as one does when surrounded by silence. We sniffed the air, taking in the smells of the night, tasting damp grass blowing in on the breeze from the darkened fields.

'Wood smoke,' said Jack, 'the sweet smell of wood smoke,' coming from the chimney of an old thatched cottage. However, our little trip into the olfactory delights of the night evaporated in an instant. Ahead of us the local police constable was shining a torch into the back of the Traveller, bending close to the window, looking at the contents with a suspicious eye. The one thing I feared was now happening; why hadn't I listened to Ros?

As we approached, I turned to Jack. 'Let me do the talking.'

'You had better be good at it.'

'Officer, a very happy New Year to you.'

A jovial response was not forthcoming. Instead he gave us the policeman's look: the up and down, or is it the once over?

'Where are we off to, at this time of night?'

'To North Wales,' I said.

He stepped back from the car, directing the torchlight onto the front and back tyres.

'Bit overweight, aren't we?'

'Do you think so?'

'I know so.' He nodded purposefully, walking round to the windscreen, checking the tax disc.

'To North Wales you say . . . and all this stuff in the back? Going camping, are you? A little late in the season,' letting a sardonic smile make the point that he was onto us and knew our game.

'No, no, we've bought a farm near Penygroes. What's in the back is just the basic essentials,' I said. Surely he could see the truth of that.

'The house we're moving into is unfurnished,' said Jack.

'New life, new beginning, New Year.' I could tell he enjoyed the way that tripped off his tongue. 'Tough life, farming,' he said, kicking a front tyre. I've never known why people do that.

'Who's the owner?'

'It's mine,' I said, 'given to me by my father-in-law.'

'Who's driving?'

'I am.'

'Hop in, will you. Turn on the lights . . . full beam . . . now dip them, please . . . left-hand indicator . . . right-hand indicator.' He walked to the back of the car. 'Put your foot on the brake pedal.'

Everything worked. I wondered what he was going to do next. I was waiting for him to take out his notebook, start writing down our personal details, ask to see my driving licence.

'You two don't look like farmers to me. You're too young. Where have you come from tonight?'

'London,' I said. 'Left at midnight. We just stopped here to stretch our legs.'

'You haven't got the build. There's not enough meat on you. You'll be lucky to make ends meet. It certainly wasn't for me; I got out of it and joined the force.'

'We'll do our best,' I said.

'Lonely, as well.'

Then he fixed a benevolent gaze upon us, a reflective look, maybe remembering himself as a younger man. He might have been in his late forties; it was hard to tell under the helmet.

'Go on then, boys. Good luck to you.'

I started up the car, wishing him again a happy New Year.

'You're overweight,' he said.

As we left Ledbury behind us, nerves dancing, I could feel my heart thumping against my ribs. Why hadn't he asked to see my licence, taken our names and addresses? I told Jack I couldn't go through that again. I would take my driving test as soon as we had settled in.

We calmed down singing along to Otis' 'A Change Is Gonna Come', together reclaiming our composure.

After we had passed through Betws-y-Coed the road narrowed; for the next half an hour I never got out of second gear. Around sharp bends stray sheep stood staring at us, their eyes illuminated, blinded by the headlights. A dishevelled motley crew, with tangled coats, loose wool hanging in great balls from their fleeces, these early morning stragglers were indifferent to any danger. I was constantly having to avoid them. I didn't know what the sheep population of Wales was, but I didn't want to reduce it through careless driving on my part.

For the first time on the journey my eyes blurred. Sleep floated up, until suddenly I heard Jack shouting my name. He said the car was veering across the road into a stone wall.

'Don't be so dramatic!'

We opened both windows, letting a vicious wind blast our faces; I was wide awake now. I kept telling Jack, 'It's okay, I'm awake.'

Ahead of us was a stretch of flat road, a chance to conserve fuel. Over the hills an aura of light broke along the ridges; on either side of us conifer plantations appeared out of the darkness. The countryside opened up. Dotted against the backcloth of this barren landscape, balancing on sheer rock, a few suicidal sheep stood staring down on us.

'Sheep have all the best views,' I said to Jack.

As the light increased we could see a ruff of small clouds skirting the peaks. Almost transparent, they vanished like a whim in the high breezes. I was filled with a sense of having crossed over from one country into another.

Then our journey came to an abrupt halt.

Ahead, a herd of cows swayed towards us. Following behind I could see the flat-capped figure of a farmer waving his stick, shouting into the wind. There were fifty of them at least, so we reversed some two hundred yards and sat waiting.

Then followed a sequence of events that whetted Jack's appetite, capturing the magical relationship between a man and his working dog. Suddenly a collie jumped on to the stone wall and raced along the jagged edges, perfectly balanced, overtaking the whole herd in a matter of seconds. Leaping down, lying in front of them ears pricked, swerving rapidly, running between their legs, never barking, holding them on course.

We got out of the Traveller, thinking we could be of some help, at least by waving our arms to steer them through an open gate into the field. But we weren't needed. We could hear the herdsman's short, sharp whistles and see the dog responding, nipping at their hocks, retreating, lying down, tongue flapping, then leaping up again to head after a cow who had taken a fancy to the open road. Moving swiftly, she brought her back to the herdsman and he closed the gate behind her.

He was a drab figure, wearing a hessian sack like a shawl over his shoulders, carrying his crook across his arm. She waited affectionately for his hand to stroke her face.

Jack shouted over to me, 'What did you think of that? Did you see it? The concentration, the swiftness of every movement. It was beautiful.'

'Balletic,' I said. And I meant it.

Jack was enthralled; I'd never seen that expression on my brother's face before.

'How old is she?' he asked the herdsman.

'She's three now . . . I had her mother before her,' he said, leaning on the gate, taking a tin of tobacco from his trouser pocket. Eyes a watery blue, words softly spoken, his weather-beaten face seemed to glow with a rusty hue. His deeply lined forehead gave the impression of a frown even when he smiled. Thumb and forefinger were missing from his right hand. He rolled a single-paper cigarette with dexterous fingers, using only his left hand. Even holding a box of Swans, taking a match and striking it, showed a skill that had been refined well beyond adapting to an impediment. As the match lit in his calloused hand, his palm curved elegantly around the flame, sheltering it from the wind, an art well practised.

'Her name is Jess,' he said, exhaling smoke from both nostrils and mouth. We recognised that he was a man at home in his world. On that quiet stretch of road we talked as dawn spread its light over boulder and stone and the silvery grass. We quite forgot about continuing our journey. He was open about himself and Jack, eager to know more about the dog, questioned him with a new enthusiasm.

'Discipline and praise is the secret to having a good dog,' he told us. 'Start them off at six months. Easy on them, mind you; no more than lying down till you call them. Remember, it's in their blood to work.' He clicked his fingers, and she was up at his side. 'You see, they never switch off. They listen to every word. Get away, Jess,' he whispered and she was gone in a flash, tearing up the asphalt. Bringing his hand to his mouth, he stopped her with a whistle.

'Remember, a whistle travels further than a voice in the wind.'

He turned and left her there, asked us where we were going, what we were doing out so early on a New Year's Day. We told him our plans. Listening to the naïve aspirations of two city boys, he gave not a clue as to what he was thinking, passed no judgement, said only that we were young men with plenty of time to fail or succeed.

'But you,' he said, looking at Jack, 'I see the shepherd in you.'

Then he whistled to bring Jess back to his side. 'Good luck to you,' he said walking away, dog at his heel. We watched them slowly disappear back into the landscape, our hands numbing in a stiff breeze.

It was nearly nine o'clock. On the deserted road with the morning still brightening we continued on the last leg of our journey. I thought of Ros and the children, stopping at a telephone box, ringing to wish them a happy New Year. But it was too early, and to get a disgruntled Eryl out of bed was not a good way to announce our arrival in her homeland.

'No more than five miles to go,' said Jack as the landscape changed from the barren wildness we had seen coming from Capel Curig into the Nantlle valley. Hills of slate spilled over from the Dorothea quarry encircling the terraced houses of Talysarn with an oppressive greyness. Now for the first time I recognised where we were. Talysarn had stuck in my mind when we had driven through it looking at smallholdings in the area. It weighed on me then just as it did now, surrounded by the waste of an industry that prevented any view to please the eye, a constant reminder to all who dwelt there of the lives given to labouring down a huge hole.

No sooner had we passed out of Talysarn than we came into Penygroes, the two villages separated by the secondary modern school whose stone buildings dwarfed the squat dwellings that flanked it. Penygroes was not a place of architectural interest, but a rather drab cluster of narrow streets whose faded front doors, once brightly painted, had the flaky look of a community down at heel. The main road ran through the middle, on its way to Porthmadog or Caernarfon.

We turned right and climbed the steep hill out of Penygroes. It was demanding on the Traveller, but she kept going, drinking the last dregs of fuel, until we arrived at the rusting metal gate, the faded sign *Dyffryn Farm* skewed at an angle, flapping in the wind. It was 9.50 a.m., and the whole journey had taken just under ten hours. There was no celebration, not even a sigh of relief, just silence as we sat there, my head slumped on the steering wheel.

We put together a couple of roll-ups and got out of the car, taking in everything around us. In the distance the calm Irish Sea mirrored the quietness of the morning. Cwm Silyn rose as a shadow, its peak sharply defined by the blue background of a cloudless sky. Above us the hills, the irregular shapes of sloping fields. Out of this landscape steel pylons towered, stretching their cables, buzzing with electricity over the grazing flocks. Squawking gulls floated overhead on the sea air breezing in, no doubt eyeing up the newcomers.

We drove down the stony track that cut between the fields of one of our neighbours, Hughie Catchpole, to the middle gate that opened onto the top acres of Dyffryn.

Facing us was a barn with corrugated roofing, surrounded by outbuildings, including a small milking parlour. The drive down to the house was lined on either side by larch trees. Adjoining the house stood another barn, and opposite it a hovel used by a shepherd during lambing, where the keys to the house were hanging on a nail behind the door.

Now that fatigue which follows the endurance of a long journey swept over us. Just to unload the car seemed like a mammoth task. We needed sleep, and although I wanted to speak to Ros to tell her we were here, the phone was dead. Even if I could drive to Penygroes to call her, I doubted I would make it back. It was all we could do to empty the car, unroll two mattresses and shake out our sleeping bags. We got into them fully clothed, for the house was damp and cold. I pushed the button on the cassette player and drifted off listening to Fats Domino's 'Blueberry Hill'.

I wondered what thrills lay ahead for us.

2

Moving In

I woke amongst a pile of clothes, tins of food, a stack of LPs, a few bottles of Mateus Rosé. I had no idea of the time, and felt as though I'd slept an incredibly deep dreamless sleep. What with the journey and the sea air, I lay in a semi-conscious state. Through the window grey-flecked clouds were passing at speed, the odd bird floating in the wind. All I could see of Jack was his head poking out of his sleeping bag. It was as if he were cocooned within it. I could hardly hear him breathing. Maybe some kind of metamorphosis was taking place.

I unzipped myself and got up knowing there was no electricity, but tried the light switch anyway; one always does out of hope rather than expectation. On the mantelpiece I saw an envelope, my name scratchily written by what seemed like an elderly hand. I opened it. The writing sloped across the page, words smudged by drops of ink from a leaking fountain pen.

> *Welcome to Dyffryn, the place that has been my home since I was a child. I know you have come with your own children and these hills, so long a part of my life, are now yours to farm. I wish you well and good luck making a living from this land.*
>
> *Daphne Musto*
>
> *P.S. Beware of your neighbours.*

I read it again. What did it mean, beware of your neighbours? Why was she warning us?

I left Jack sleeping and went outside. Those first deep breaths filling my lungs woke me up, invigorating and clean, so different from London's polluted air. I wanted to find some wood to make a fire; surely there'd be a few logs around the place. I walked up to the top buildings, empty but for some old mildewed bales of hay, half-doors blowing in the wind. I shivered. There was a ghostly feel to the farm. I stood in what once had been the milking parlour, its stone troughs covered with bird droppings. A bundle of baler twine swung from a beam; metal chains that once tethered cows hung from the walls. I could sense the history of the place passing through me.

I was kidding myself if I thought I was going to find a pile of logs. There were some fallen branches which I broke over my knee. I unearthed a wooden box that had once held apples to use as kindling, but the best find was a few lumps of coal in the hovel opposite the house.

I made a fire, Jack still sleeping in the same position as when I left him. Upstairs were four bedrooms that I had to lower my head to enter, all with stripped pine doors and those old, pre-war brass knobs. The master bedroom at the front of the house showed the view across to Cwm Silyn in one direction, the shoreline of Dinas Dinlle beach in the other. This was where I would be sleeping with Ros whenever that would be; weeks away no doubt.

I toasted a slice of bread over the fire.

'Jack,' I shouted. 'Come on, wake up.' He didn't stir. I held the toast an inch from his nose. 'Smell that.'

'Is it breakfast?'

'More like afternoon tea.'

'What time is it?'

'I've no idea.'

I heard the sound of a car pulling up, the blasting of a horn. It was Ros in Gwyn's VW Beetle with Sam and Lysta in the back. After all the hugs and kisses we sat with children on our laps in front of the fire. Ros had come with much-needed supplies, including boxes of candles and two folding chairs. There was a table strapped on to the roof rack.

'You'll find a sack of potatoes in the boot, and a saw to cut wood.'

Ros also brought a book of addresses and telephone numbers, including a plumber and an electrician. The telephone would be connected on the fifth of January, MANWEB would be here on the sixth. So a bit of hardship for a few days, we could cope with that. Ros lit a couple of candles.

'No television. What on earth will the two of you do?'

'Read my *Farmers Weekly*, or *War and Peace*, I haven't made up my mind.'

'Ma and Pa have invited you for supper tomorrow night. You'll need a good meal by then.'

As I got the sack of spuds from the boot, Ros told me to take the can of petrol. 'Pa said there won't be a garage open anywhere today.'

We carried the table into the sitting room, put a chair at either end.

'Look,' I said, 'we've moved in already.'

I asked Ros if she would leave her wristwatch.

The following day, after ten hours' sleep, I awoke in a fog. It had to be sea air, the fresh winds. Or was it withdrawal symptoms, no longer breathing in petrol fumes? It was a struggle to enter consciousness, let alone get up motivated. The night before I'd had only one thing on my mind: to wake early and cut as much wood as possible. It was twenty past ten already.

'Jack,' I shouted. 'Come on, let's get on with it.' No response whatsoever. So I shook him awake.

We drank tea, ate four slices of toast. Rain lashed against the windows, a wind whistled under the door. I could feel it on my ankles through my socks.

We apparently had two thousand larch trees, not only the ones down the avenue to the house, but a wood full of them bordering the lane that led to the lower fields.

We were dressed in loose-fitting boiler suits, bobble hats, and three-quarter length raincoats that came down just below our knees. We put on wellingtons and went out into a gale-force wind blowing in from the Irish Sea. With saw in hand I entered the wood to start cutting out those trunks that were spindly enough to get my hands around.

Jack had set himself the task of cleaning the holding tank. The stream that crossed the higher fields ran into it and became our water supply. It was the most primitive set-up, simply following the laws of gravity and flowing down through a metal pipe no more than five inches in diameter whose end was covered with a fine mesh. This is what we relied on to fill the tank that fed the house. That morning when we washed, the basin had filled with a muddy brown liquid the colour of oxtail soup.

I worked for three hours, my clothes completely waterlogged. I had long discarded my raincoat; I couldn't cut wood with it on, unable to get into a rhythm. My pullover had put on weight, absorbing every drop of rain that fell. Even my underpants were soggy, and water sloshed around in my wellingtons. I had reached saturation point, and the result of this hard labour: a pile of logs that wouldn't burn anyway.

I stood there, a dripping mess amongst the swaying trees, a howling wind in my ears, and had to laugh. I could see myself, but thank goodness Ros couldn't. I think she might have given up hope there and then. The first thing to learn about farming: dress appropriately and buy a chainsaw. 'Call it an initiation,' I said to myself.

When I got back to the house, Jack was bent over the kitchen tap throwing crystal clear water over his face.

'God, look at the sight of you,' he said.

We boiled a saucepan on the Calor gas stove, and had our first proper wash and shave for three days.

After lunch the wind dropped and the rainclouds drifted away over the sea. We worked under a blue sky, stacking logs in the hovel. We knew they wouldn't burn; they'd just spit when we laid them on the fire.

It was cold. Already on my soft hands a blister had appeared.

We were sitting on a stone wall outside the house smoking roll-ups when we saw him. A solitary figure walking down the drive, with his Border collie beside him. He approached with a heavy step in hobnailed boots, brass bands over the toecaps, wearing a threadbare serge coat held together with baler twine tied around the waist, and a well-worn flat cap with a split in the peak. He was pink-faced, myriad tiny blood vessels covering his cheeks in red patches. In his gnarled hand he carried a crook with a curved horn handle. His dog walked to heel. At a guess in his late fifties, he had the look of a life hard lived. He came with no handshake, just pushed his cap back above a deeply lined forehead.

'I'm Gethin Hughes, your neighbour. Came over to say hello,' he said without a fuss of words or wishing to elaborate further, or broaden the welcome with a smile. He had delivered the message and nothing else needed to be added. Uncomfortable as people are in silences, Jack and I were much more forthcoming. Through a light-hearted banter we extracted, rather than were given, some basic information about the man. He farmed eighty acres at Cae Uchaf, mostly sheep and fattening store cattle to beef. Married thirty-odd years to Ceinwen; no children. 'They didn't come along with us.' Jack walked over to the collie lying behind him, always happy to be in the company of a dog.

'Don's his name. Eight years old,' said Gethin. 'A good dog until there's a bitch on heat.'

He asked nothing of us, what our plans were at Dyffryn. Maybe displaying an interest would have put too much of him on show. Gwyn had told me that these hill farmers kept what they were thinking very much to themselves, the isolation of their lives resulting in not so much a problem with language as little practice in the art of conversation. Despite his reticence, he did not hold back in telling us the law of the land.

'You'll learn soon enough how life is lived up here,' he said. 'And remember, good boundary walls make good neighbours.' This was delivered as a commandment to be obeyed at all costs, accompanied by a severe look from hooded eyes, and spoken in a solemn tone. He had got it off his chest, for this was really what he had come to say.

Then, putting his signature on this little get-together, he pulled down his cap, tapped his dog with his crook, and walked away. No handshake, no goodbye.

'A few barriers to be broken down there,' said Jack.

'Was he being friendly?'

'With a double-edged sword.'

Late in the afternoon we walked the length of the stream that ran through our land. It needed to be dredged, the banks trampled down where cattle and sheep had crossed. Water overflowed into the fields in several places, causing boggy swamps. The stream, never more than two feet wide, was partially blocked with clumps of reeds and water grasses, reducing the flow to no more than a trickle. I wondered what our neighbour below us, Hughie Catchpole, thought about it. Surely it reduced his supply? Why had it been allowed to get into such a state of neglect?

Jack and I stood in front of the bathroom mirror putting the finishing touches to our appearance, wanting to create the right impression for Eryl. If there was one thing I knew about my mother-in-law, she liked people coming for supper properly dressed.

Our shirts were still creased from lying unpacked in a suitcase, so we covered them under V-neck pullovers, minus ties. I had found a pair of corduroy trousers. Jack, as he had done when we went to the solicitors, rubbed Brylcreem into his hair. It was the best we could do.

Eryl met us at the front door with a look of cold indifference. I thought she was going to tell us that the tradesmen's entrance was round at the back.

We all sat at the dining room table, watching Gwyn expertly carve the roast pork. Eryl made no eye contact with me, simply pushing the mustard and gravy in my direction when required, but Gwyn was relaxed and friendly and keen to hear about our first impressions of Dyffryn. He was well aware of the scale of our undertaking, and said he admired our sense of adventure. Eryl kept her conversation as much as she could with Ros, speaking in her mother tongue, but after Gwyn whispered something to her she switched to English, asking Jack if he had any farming experience, making the point that she knew I hadn't. She shook her head when Jack said absolutely none, murmuring under her breath, 'How are Ros and the children going to survive?'

Gwyn tried to lift the mood, making light of it, saying that the challenges ahead would excite any young man. The idea did nothing to put a smile on Eryl's face, and she turned her full attention to her grandchildren.

After we had eaten, Jack and I sat in the sitting room with Gwyn. 'Your enterprise is something I would have relished years ago,' he said. There was about him a self-assuredness gained through his own journey. It was good to know he would be close by.

I didn't mention our meeting with Gethin Hughes, or the letter that Daphne Musto had left. Both made me feel uneasy. Maybe Gethin was setting the tone, making it clear that in our future dealings with him it would be he who had the upper hand.

When we were leaving, Jack gave Eryl a kiss on the cheek and Ros whispered in my ear, 'I'll be glad when we're sleeping together again.' I saw in Eryl's eyes a disapproving look for the affection I was showing her daughter.

Three weeks later, with various designs of Laura Ashley wallpaper in every room, we brought in the last of the furniture. Ros and the twins were moving into the house at last. Happy as I was, I realised that I was going to have to make some adjustments. I'd slipped back into living as a single man. Old habits had resurfaced in areas that required self-discipline, such as personal cleanliness, shaving every day, changing my clothes, not being lazy. You don't have one more glass of wine, one more roll-up last thing at night, when your wife is there to remind you.

I was glad it was all over, that Jack and I had actually managed to get the wallpaper on the walls. From time to time the whole thing had become a slapstick comedy, but the house finally felt like a home.

Gwyn and Eryl carried the twins across the threshold, while Ros rode me piggy back into the sitting room. A log fire blazed in the hearth. Jack brought in a bottle of champagne, and we toasted 'a happy future'. It was the first time I had seen Eryl with a smile on her face; maybe she was beginning to believe in us.

The only major job left was the installation of the coal-fired Aga. Ros and the twins had gone to Harlech for the day, where Gwyn and Eryl had a house close to the golf course, overlooking the sea. Ros was uneasy about leaving me to oversee the operation; they were going to have to remove the kitchen door and some of the wall to get the thing on to a concrete platform that had been laid directly behind the fireplace in the sitting room. They had to get a flue through a two-foot thick wall and push it halfway up the chimney to get the necessary draw. I told her not to worry; I always did, being the habitual optimist.

The Aga Team, for that's what was printed on the back of their overalls, were actually four Liverpudlians, three of them obese, the fourth a diminutive chap known as the Think Tank. He had a high academic forehead and heavy black-rimmed National Health spectacles, and was as bald as a university intellectual. I could tell he was the mastermind of Aga installation. In a reassuringly soft voice he told me why a brain was needed as well as brawn for the successful fitting of these hernia-inducing monsters.

Think Tank, actually called Malcolm, was someone you could put your trust in. So Jack and I let them get on with it. We had bought a chicken coop out of *Exchange & Mart* and now had to go to Pant Glas to pick up six point-of-lay Rhode Island Red pullets.

'Do you think they know what they're doing?' I asked Jack, as I lowered the back seats of the Traveller, chucking in a wooden crate to carry the chicks.

'Yes, I'm sure. They're registered, aren't they?'

When we came back down the drive a couple of hours later, the team were in a huddle in front of the house. Not many things in the universe move more slowly than an Aga making its way along a low-loader, held tight by a steel cable. We watched this tedious unwinding inch by inch, the alignment critical, rolling across a series of scaffolding poles which had to be positioned precisely at the end of the sloping ramp. Finally they pushed the thing towards the kitchen by moving poles from stern to bow as it moved forward, eventually managing to dock the leviathan. It took nearly an hour. There was an eruption of cheers and backslapping followed by cans of beer and a well-earned fag break.

Malcolm maintained his aloofness, and rather like a priest leading a couple to the altar beckoned Jack and me to stand in front of him so he could read aloud to us from the instruction book as if it were the Bible, taking us painstakingly through the workings of the Aga, giving emphasis to the dos and don'ts in the way one could imagine Moses delivering the Ten Commandments. 'Thou shalt not use any other coal but anthracite.'

Later that evening, as the sun set over the Irish Sea, Malcolm with dustpan and brush tidied up behind them. He shook my hand, and off they went to begin a new job in Chester the next morning.

When Ros returned I told her there was no need to be concerned. The whole thing had been completed without a hitch.

Every day since Gethin's visit we had made time to walk the boundary walls, the size of the undertaking soon coming home to us. Every few yards there were gaps where stones had fallen. So began the work of rebuilding. Our hands were still soft and blistered easily; torn fingernails were patched with strips of Elastoplast. The biggest headache was finding the right stone to sit comfortably next to another. We carried on regardless of the weather, determined to see the job done. We were single-minded, and Hughie Catchpole, seeing us buffeted in a force eight gale, staggered across his fields shouting to us, 'You're fools. Pneumonia can take a man at any age.'

Hughie had, I'm sure, not a hair on his body. Certainly not on his head, and this was of his choosing, for he was clean shaven, his smooth face glowing not from Welsh summers but from harsh winds and sea air. He had a gold tooth and eyes the colour of walnuts. A once broken nose made an uneven ridge down the middle of his face. After years on the Old Holborn he spoke as if constantly needing to clear his throat, guttural and hoarse. He was tall, lean as a javelin, and married to a porcelain doll several inches shorter called Myfanwy. She compensated for her lack of height by wearing dresses with large floral patterns and lots of make-up. Wellington boots did not compliment her or raise her stature. But there was a glint in her eye; a strange sexiness oozed from her. She had a naughty look, and wore her hair in an old-fashioned style with curls that flicked back upon her shoulders. They were indeed a strange couple.

Once, when I was talking to Hughie, he told me one of his cows had just tested positive for brucellosis. 'You know, it's a big loss to bear. Cows don't grow on bloody trees.'

Midway through this sentence Myfanwy came over and handed him a chicken, and without giving it a second look he wrung its neck.

'I'm on a short fuse today. One down with mastitis too,' he said, passing the dead bird back to his wife. And in what seemed like a long embrace, she held it to her breast until its wings quietened down, its broken neck flopping over the crook of her elbow. She stayed with us, plucking the still warm body, feathers floating around her head. She seemed short of some of the vital ingredients, but Hughie showed affection towards her, picking feathers from her hair.

'I'll be in my pocket again, having to buy in another heifer. You never get ahead in this game.'

They had a son, Bryn, a dishevelled teenager who liked sitting in hay barns or leaning against gates, spitting into the wind and aiming his catapult at the arses of any livestock within range. He wasted his time grievously, targeting the geese and chickens in the yard. Jack and I watched him as we repaired the boundary walls. After asking us three times for a roll-up, which we refused, he stomped off, unaware that the catapult had dropped from his back pocket. We hid it in a stone wall, pleased that this small act would prevent some pain in the animal world.

Of the many people who turned up at the door in those early days, all claiming to have skills we needed, Harry Thomas proved to be our man. In his late twenties, he had a muscular build. Under a denim jacket he wore only a T-shirt even in midwinter. He had thick dark hair undulating from a high wave that fell to the back of his head. It was neatly combed, and I imagined some time was spent on it, especially first thing in the morning before he made a public appearance. He had the looks of an American pop singer, showing himself off by removing his jacket to reveal a tattooed forearm: *He who dares wins.* Jack and I liked him; he was easy-going, and seemed left over from the 1950s. He could have been Tony Curtis; somehow his Welsh accent didn't go with his American looks or tight jeans with six-inch turn-ups. He had the light, agile step of a ballet dancer or featherweight boxer.

'On the cheap and for cash' was his motto. 'Of course, I can give a written estimate if that's what you prefer.' He dismissed the competition by simply saying, 'To be fair to the man, he's not really an electrician' – or plumber, or mechanic – 'but to be fair to the man he only does it part time,' and decent as they were, he would not recommend them. That's how he convinced us, by diminishing those who had come before. 'Oh, him,' he would say, 'but to be fair to the man, he's not got the accreditation.' But Harry was, as he put it, an all-rounder. After we asked him what exactly an all-rounder was, he gave us a long list of trades he had mastered, including tractor driving, roofing, carpentry and plumbing, and assured us that he was a 'bloody good sparky' and a butcher as well. 'Also, I breed sheepdogs in my spare time.'

Having biked up from the village, he replaced his cycle clips, dragged a comb once more through his hair, leant over the drop handlebars of his multi-geared racer, raised his arse out of the saddle and with the flashiness of a good-looking cyclist riding in the Tour de France disappeared up the drive and out of sight.

'What did you think of him?' I asked Jack.

'Well, to be fair to the man, let's give him a chance to prove he's as good as he says he is.'

Gradually, at the end of each day, jobs were being completed and Ros would announce, usually at the supper table, that the house was now nearly finished. Yet she always found something that still needed to be done, bagging Harry as he dismounted at eight in the morning, before he had even removed his bicycle clips, and cornering him with a list.

'Just want him for a few finishing touches,' is how she put it.

I thought she meant no more than putting on a final coat of paint here and there, but one of the 'finishing touches' led to a row between us. No matter how much she asserted that we had discussed it, I could not recall any conversation about opening up the fireplace in the sitting room. As far as I was concerned it was a unilateral decision. It took Harry three days to chip away the plaster and reveal the old stone hearth, big enough to roast a pig in. It was almost a room in itself, a huge gaping hole, but Ros wanted log fires to warm the long winter nights. We had to get a steel lintel to bear the weight of stone. Then Harry was off to Groeslon, to the blacksmith, to order a dog grate, and none of this was cheap. Ros and I argued. 'We've got five thousand pounds in the bank. That's to start a farm,' I barked at her. After a week I slipped Harry a hundred pounds in cash. He told me Ros wanted draught excluders fitted to the doors, and the flagstones in the kitchen to be pointed.

We thinned out the larch trees, stacking a pile of logs in the hovel opposite the house. We disinfected all the outbuildings, and Harry, having at last finished all the work Ros wanted done, now began hanging doors, replacing tiles on the barn roof, and putting glass into the empty frame of a steel building where I hoped to house sows and rear piglets. Meanwhile we took delivery of fencing posts that would protect the vegetable garden behind the house. Armed with a crowbar which we speared into the topsoil, we hammered in our posts to a depth of nine inches. We had tossed a coin, for the law of averages dictates the inevitability of the odd mis-hit, that the one on the receiving end of the sledgehammer would not be able to avoid the excruciating pain as a pool of blood slowly congealed like black ink under a fingernail. The hit was followed by damning, cursing, and running round in circles after the brain had sent out its agonising message. I am sure our yells carried on the wind to Gethin Hughes, telling him those English brothers were at it again. It was only after Harry came over and threw us a pair of protective gloves that we realised some of the pain could have been prevented.

Each night, as the blood pulsed in our swollen fists, we sank our hands into a basin of cold water and Dettol. But the real inconvenience of these self-inflicted injuries was the difficulty in rolling a cigarette. We had worn away our fingerprints and so had to resort to a rolling machine, something we hadn't done since we first started smoking.

However, the job was only half done. Now we had to staple on yards of rabbit-proof fencing, below a single strand of barbed wire. Harry started us off, reassuring us we'd soon be experts.

'Duw, boys, after you've done it once, you'll have the knack.'

Jack and I watched him as a cold rain swept in across the fields. In a matter of moments he had secured wire mesh to the first post, using staples he held in his mouth, banging them in rhythmically, a hard hit at first, then a second to see each one home. Rapid, neat movements expending a minimum of energy.

'There,' he said, unrolling the whole length of the mesh and holding it against the posts. 'Three staples to each post working from the top down. It's child's play.'

So Jack filled his mouth with staples, I knelt beside him, pushing the mesh against each stake and off we went, at a snail's pace to begin with, but moving up a gear when we found it easier handing each other staples rather than having a mouth full of metal. By lunchtime we were bent double, walking into the house as if heavily constipated, our backs completely seized. After we had eaten we massaged each other with Deep Heat, which loosened us up enough to believe we should at least try to finish the job.

It took us five days to fence round the vegetable garden. Gwyn gave us the once over, deciding that torn muscles and exposure to the cold wind had done the damage. He thought we should each wear a corset, to add strength to the lower back. Jack and I agreed to this in the strictest confidence; we both thought it wasn't quite the right image for two young men to be wearing undergarments associated with middle-aged women.

Yet another job was added to the list: to put flues in the chimneys on each end of the house. Whenever there was heavy rain, water would run down into the fire, causing the logs to spit and hiss. If someone opened the door, creating a through draught, a huge cloud of smoke and steam engulfed us, as if we had suddenly become a family of Norwegians sitting in a sauna. We seemed to be on a treadmill of running repairs. This was the price you paid for living up here, exposed to the elements.

We either learned from experience or got Harry to sort things out, but we were reluctant to do the latter too often. One reason was money, but also what the hell were we doing here if we couldn't take charge of such matters? We were half asleep by eight in the evening, flopped in chairs like a couple of puppets. Every night I asked Ros to massage the small of my back. Must be some genetic weakness.

'This farming is a hard lark,' I told her.

'Yes,' she replied, 'and you haven't even got any livestock yet, apart from the chickens.'

Gethin Hughes came over one morning, 'A quiet word in your ears, boys.' I wondered what problem he had uncovered. He put me on edge; every time his name cropped up I thought of Daphne Musto's note. I was ready for the veiled warning, the barbed comment. But no, I was wrong. He'd come to give advice, telling us to take advantage of an opportunity that had arisen.

'You boys,' as he liked to call us, 'will be wanting to acquire a tractor soon.'

Jack and I looked at each other. 'Will we?'

'Well, of course. You're here to farm the place, aren't you?'

We looked at each other again, nodding convincingly. I think.

'He over at Llwyndu Canol has one for sale,' he said, 'one that would suit you two.'

Apparently Hughie was wanting to sell his Massey Ferguson 127 and replace it with a Fordson Major, a much larger beast that could do the work in half the time, but Gethin said there were tactics involved, which he suspected we had no idea about. 'What are these tactics?' I said.

'Tactics so you will come out of the deal right.'

He spoke as a godfather might, telling us the right way to approach Hughie, not to show too much keenness, open with a low bid and learn to shrug our shoulders. 'You boys, you've never done a deal up here. Turn your face away when he asks for more.' Also we had to keep our hands in our pockets, look at the ground when he spoke. 'Show him your back as if you are about to walk away.'

'How much is the tractor worth?' Jack asked eventually.

'He'll ask a hundred and fifty,' said Gethin.

Jack and I agreed that we would be needing a tractor, so why not this one? At least if anything went wrong Hughie could be called upon; surely having sold the thing to his neighbours he would want to fix it. Gethin seemed pleased with our decision; maybe he was taking a backhander on the deal, and we were being set up. He told us to stroll over to Hughie's the next day and have a chat, but not to bring up the subject of the tractor, to let him mention it first. All this bluff and double bluff over a simple transaction mystified us.

'Why on earth can't we just go to Hughie and say how much do you want for that Massey Ferguson?' I said to Jack.

'And he'll say a hundred and fifty quid, and we'll say will you take a hundred and forty. Simple enough.'

The more I thought about it, the more likely it seemed that Gethin was involved in the deal. He had an air of aloofness, of someone who liked to control things, coming over as a man with a finger in many pies. But Jack and I didn't care; if we could get the tractor for £140 we would be happy.

For at least a week everyone who walked past the Traveller told me I needed to replace the front tyres. Even Harry said they were getting as bald as a parson's head. So I left Jack reading *The Working Dog* and drove down to Penygroes to change them and get a spare as well.

In the Paragon garage I parked behind an old Land Rover, its torn canvas roof partially repaired with strips of tape. Looking out from the back was a grey and white Border collie, pacing restlessly from side to side. I sat in the Traveller for a minute and watched the mechanic slide out the rusting exhaust.

'Been meaning to come and say hello.' The speaker surprised me; I hadn't seen him approaching. He seemed to ghost up to my window. 'Arfon Williams is my name. I'm a neighbour, got the land above you. The field with that bloody great pylon in it.'

He was a slight figure of a man, skinny, with a thin neck, a bulging Adam's apple. He didn't wear his clothes, they seemed to envelop him. Worn, bony knuckles clenched around the crook he leant into, shifting from one leg to another, looking past me, like Gethin, not offering me his hand. His hollow expression gave him a haunted look. A greyness, as if he were overcast in cloud. He had clearly brought himself forward for no other reason than to say hello as quickly as possible and be done with it.

What a struggle it must have been for him to farm. The physical demands. How did he get through the working day? I knew nothing of him except that he had a flock of Welsh ewes. But he could drive, and no doubt, fired by the fierce independence of the hill farmer, survived by living on his wits. For it was a way of life. What else could one do having been born into it?

After supper that night, Ros made a list of seeds she said we needed to order from an organic supplier. Nearly forty quid's worth. I couldn't believe the cost.

'Why can't we just buy a few packets from Unwin's?' I asked.

But she wanted to build up her own stock of organic seed, and there was no compromise. She had hired a Rotovator and thought that if Jack and I could start tomorrow we would have the initial work done in two days. If not, she suggested we pay Harry, who had said he could do the job in an afternoon.

'Bloody cheek,' I said. 'We're not that slow.'

'Look how long it took you to fence it.'

So in the morning, rather than go to Hughie and look at the Massey, we got on with ploughing up the vegetable garden. The Rotovator was a crude bone-shaking machine, noisy and slow, cutting out every time we hit a stone. You gripped hold of it, both arms vibrating so violently that after half an hour all your muscles went into spasm and continued to twitch long after you'd turned the machine off. We carried on vibrating through the whole of lunch, as did our knives and forks as we tried to eat. It was hopeless trying to hold a cup of tea. I couldn't close my fingers round the handle. At least Sam and Lysta thought we were very funny. We should have hardened up to all these physical demands by now, but no, here we were again walking around like Bill and Ben, determined Harry would not be called upon to finish what we had so rashly started.

We worked on through the afternoon, clearing the field of stones that could be used to fill gaps in walls, and by the time the sun went down the job was done. Heavy-legged, with our wellingtons clogged with mud, we sat either end of an upturned water trough smoking roll-ups, picking out in the fading light the orange beaks of blackbirds hopping around us looking for worms. We welcomed the evening breeze wafting over our faces, which were glowing with the heat from our physical exertions. The satisfaction of seeing what had been achieved always brought with it a reflective mood. It was how we enjoyed the end of the day, when the slog was over, sitting quietly, full of our own thoughts. It was an interlude before we went into the house to join Ros and the children.

Coming from the bathroom clean and refreshed, the day scrubbed out from under my fingernails, I realised Sam and Lysta were becoming two little people. Gradually I was connecting with them more, although getting them to eat their food always seemed to be a serious challenge.

When in their high chairs they seemed to think it hilarious to throw their food across the room. Ros did not approve of my finding this sort of behaviour humorous, and told me in a raised voice that it had to stop.

'You're not with them all day. Don't encourage them.'

On Saturday morning we made our way over to Llwyndu Canol to have a look at Hughie's Massey Ferguson. Despite Gethin's insistence on the tactics needed to come out right on the deal, Jack and I hadn't rehearsed a single line. It was early April, and although spring might have appeared in the south of England there were no signs of it here. Admittedly, there were lambs running around in the fields, but nothing in the hedgerows had popped up green yet. Gwyn told me we were usually two or three weeks behind the rest of the country. The chill in the wind from the Irish Sea made my eyes weep. I had my collar up and my thermal underwear on, the most unattractive articles of clothing I possessed. When I got dressed in the morning, Ros would roll over in bed and ask me where my arse had gone. 'Old man's clothes,' she would say, a huge turn-off to anyone desiring a successful love life. But they were effective so I stuck with them, despite Ros's ridicule.

Jack and I walked down the narrow track towards Llwyndu Canol. I could see the surly figure of Bryn, no longer armed with a catapult, throwing a sheath knife into a railway sleeper. As we approached he took a long deep drag on a roll-up, then threw the butt down in front of us, exhaling a blue cloud of smoke that cleared into the cold daylight. He kept his belligerent face turned away from us as he retrieved the knife. From his trouser pocket he took out a handkerchief and cleaned the blade, touching the tip with his finger.

'Pa's down below bringing sheep back,' was all he said.

We could see Hughie in the distance, far below us. He was working his dog, Jobber, shepherding ewes and lambs towards an enclosure. Already Jack could see the dog was too close to the sheep. 'He should be further back. There's trouble coming,' he said.

Myfanwy stood as if frozen to the spot, holding open the wooden pen gate, Hughie shouting orders as the dog moved frantically from left to right. Ewes bleated anxiously as they became separated from their lambs, turning in all directions to search for them. We could see the disintegration, the loss of shape in the flock, as increasing panic dispersed them. Myfanwy's high-pitched screams stung the air with mounting hysteria as Hughie stood over Jobber beating him with his crook. The dog would have none of it and leapt over the wall, disappearing towards Penygroes, terrified by his master's violence. I looked at Jack. 'Not the dog's fault,' was all he said.

Myfanwy was so angry she was throwing a series of punches into Hughie's chest. One did not need to translate from the Welsh to guess what she was saying.

'I don't think this is a good day to be doing a deal with Hughie,' I said to Jack, still watching the scene unfold. Calmness did return and lambs found their mothers again, but without a dog what could Hughie do now? On our way back to Dyffryn I remarked to Jack that the wonderful relationship between a man and his dog is as vulnerable to breakdown as marriage or friendship. But Jack wasn't listening. The scene we had witnessed had affected him much more than me. 'It was all too frantic, too fierce, too hurried,' he said.

Two days later we did finally talk to Hughie. He told us he had been waiting for over a week because, as he put it, Gethin had mentioned in passing that we might be interested. I became uneasy about being set up, fearing that Jack and I might be played for fools in someone else's game. But once Hughie had fired up the tractor with a starter handle and revved it up by pushing his hand down on the accelerator, causing plumes of smoke to billow out from its vertical exhaust, I thought it would suit us. Jack took it on a test drive up the steep track on to the Carmel road. When he eventually reappeared I drove it back to Hughie to shake hands on the deal.

'A hundred and fifty cash,' he said.

Gethin's tactics kicked in, and although Jack and I hadn't discussed doing the deal we turned our heads away in unison. It happened just like that. Hughie remained silent as we stuck our hands into our trouser pockets, casting dubious looks to the ground.

'Duw, boys, come on, what's with this?' he said.

'We were thinking a hundred and twenty,' I said.

He looked disgusted at this derisory offer and, turning, began to walk away. Over his shoulder he shouted back at us, 'You insult me.'

I couldn't remember what came next in this charade. Then Jack called after him to ask if he would throw the rear-end loader into the deal. Smart move, I thought. What made him come up with that? 'You won't be needing that on the back of a Fordson Major,' he added.

'No, that's true,' said Hughie, coming back to join us.

So I jumped in, offered £130 cash with the rear-end loader.

Hughie threw his arms in the air and removed his cap, his baldness glowing in the sunlight, his mouth open as if mortally wounded. A silence floated up between us and I thought us all actors in a play. Who should speak the next line?

'Put five more pounds on it and we're home,' he said.

'The rear-end loader and the Fergie for a hundred and thirty-five,' I said.

'It's yours,' he said, putting out his hand. So we shook on it, me and Hughie and then Jack. The ordeal, because that's what it felt like, was over, at last.

Back at Dyffryn, Ros thought the two of us had smug looks on our faces. I did feel we had come out of the deal on the right side. I asked Jack what made him suddenly throw in the rear-end loader. 'I just saw it lying there, thought we would need one some time.'

'I think it will always be like that,' I said.

'Like what?'

'Having to do deals.'

'Yes, you're probably right,' he agreed.

'Why don't you put one together? Let's listen to some music.'

I dug out a Beatles track, 'Strawberry Fields Forever'. I said to Jack, 'Living might well be easy with eyes closed, but we're not going to survive here misunderstanding all we see.'

3

The Dummy Run

Summer at Dyffryn, a sweet warm breeze blowing through the hay fields. Swallows skimming the grass, Jack's store lambs grazing the land in front of the house. Harry had sold them to us after doing a deal with some distant cousin who was bedridden and could no longer farm.

'To be fair to the man, his body should have given up years ago.'

Jack walked amongst them every day. If we ever needed to gather them, Harry brought up his old dog Axel, a cunning collie whose working days were behind him. He had a black patch around one of his eyes. When Harry sent him out to bring back the sheep, he ambled out towards them rather than put too much effort into it.

We never seemed to be in the house. Everything happened outside. Already we were eating new potatoes, lettuces, radishes and shallots from Ros's flourishing vegetable garden. Sometimes she made a picnic supper, which we ate sprawled out on a tartan rug, watching a fat sun dimming over an expanse of empty sea. We soaked up these occasions, because there was another reality to living on a farm that brought an anxiety far removed from the peace of the long summer evenings.

It was the bull calves. We had bought twenty Friesians from a dealer in Devon and lost six in the first two weeks from scouring. We were feeding them powdered milk and all had healthy appetites, but we noticed that in the mornings some of them looked unsteady on their legs. They suffered from rapid weight loss and dropped so quickly. We thought they had no resistance to the bacteria in their new surroundings; added to the stress of the long journey so soon after weaning, this was a fatal combination for some of them. We realised it was a mistake to have bought them from an advert in a farming magazine. It was a hard lesson learned, and we vowed from then on only ever to buy locally. We had rung the dealer, but he was unsympathetic and didn't want to listen to our tale of woe. 'They were fine when they left here,' was all he said. The remainder grew in strength, and following a two-week period of no further losses we were through it. Soon they would be eating calf pellets, and it wouldn't be long before we could turn them out, watch them graze with the sun on their backs.

But first we had to cut our hay and Harry, who was spending most of his time at Dyffryn these days, had assumed the position of chief decision maker, a role he played naturally and with flair. In some ways he had become a blood brother, after we swore him to secrecy concerning our greenhouse project, hidden away in a clearing amongst the larch trees. Jack and I came up short on self-assembly skills. It is something you're born with: you either have it or you don't. We certainly didn't. But because it had to be top secret, we agreed to give the greenhouse a go, and had promised not to curse and swear at each other or storm off saying, 'You bloody well finish it then!' We began the undertaking quietly enough, speaking politely to each other, studying the neat instruction diagrams carefully, but our equanimity began to fade when after an hour nothing seemed to quite line up.

We weren't out by far, just a sixteenth of an inch or so, but it was far enough to make us begin to lose our patience. And who was the clever dick who came up with the idea of the Allen key? Somcone called Allen, no doubt, Jack said. To have the arrogance to get a worldwide patent on a minuscule gadget you couldn't open a tin of sardines with! When we stood back and looked at the thing, it leaned so far to the left that the gentlest of breezes would have blown it over.

'A complete waste of time,' said Jack.

So we got the right man on the job. Harry, of course.

When we told him what we wished to grow in the greenhouse, we should have known what his reaction was going to be. 'Oh, I do love a bit of dope. To be fair to the two of you, it's a brilliant idea, what with street prices on the up. You know, I have to go all the way to Bangor to score a nice bit of hash.'

Harry put the greenhouse together in a morning. We were going to pay him twenty quid, but decided to settle up when we harvested the crop. We already had seedlings growing in pots hidden away in a bed of compost down in the lower fields, surrounded by a rectangular border of red bricks, over the top of which we had laid an old car windscreen. Not pretty to look at, but effective, tucked away out of sight behind large gorse bushes.

Although Ros knew what we were up to, she wasn't keen on the idea. She did smoke the odd joint at parties, or relaxing sometimes with friends, but Jack and I wanted a regular supply. We carried twelve seedlings up to the greenhouse, where we watered them twice a day. Now we just had to wait for them to reach maturity.

Meanwhile we had been making friends with Rose Tobias, a well-to-do American who owned the cottage above Dyffryn at the highest point on the Carmel road. She enjoyed panoramic views sweeping in every direction, taking in the mountain of Cwm Silyn and stretching as far as the Menai Strait in the north. If one ignored the pylons you would not have known you were living in the twentieth century.

Only in Wales from May until September, she would put an easel in her garden and paint the cloud formations, the ever changing shades of light, as the day passed between dawn and dusk. She was more than happy to talk about her work, which consisted of a vast collection of sunsets and distant horizons. There wasn't a single person in any of the canvases she showed us.

'Where are all the people?' I asked.

'Gee, I can't paint people. Far too complicated, and anyway what do they add to a glorious sunset?'

Like many Americans, she was confident, direct, and didn't take herself too seriously; traits that always gave our conversations an easy-going friendliness. She had a sparkling eye for Jack, at least twenty years her junior, and teased him with suggestive innuendo. She was attractive, washed by the Californian sun, her flirtatious nature belying her maturing years. Heavily lipsticked, she smoked Peter Stuyvesant cigarettes, which she held between fingertips varnished the same colour as her lips.

Whenever we passed she would be out in the garden at her easel, waving her paint brush.

'Why don't you come in, boys? My door's always open,' she would say, but we knew if we did, we would be there for at least an hour, time we didn't have to spare.

However, Jack did spend the odd evening up there. Maybe it was to give Ros and me some time alone together. We didn't talk about it; the only hint was when Rose would say, 'Hey, did you enjoy your supper and all the rest last night?'

No matter if she was playing games, she was serious about a proposition she put to us. She had eleven acres of good grazing land and offered it to us rent free, if we would look after the cottage when she returned to California.

'Perhaps Jack could stay up here in the winter months,' she suggested. 'It would stop the place becoming damp.'

It was generous, but her real concern was leaving the cottage empty for so long, especially as some Welsh activists had been putting petrol bombs through the letter boxes of holiday homes.

'What do you say to that, Jack? A good offer, is it not?' she said. 'You could help me plant a few trees out back. It could be our little project.'

Gethin Hughes had given Jack the nod on a nice little collie bitch, so we drove over to Waen Fawr to take a look at her. Every time we went out in the Traveller now we kept our fingers crossed; bits of her were disappearing down farm tracks and I had lost count of how many times we had to push her out of potholes hidden in puddles. Only one windscreen wiper worked, we had lost the rear number plate and only two hubcaps remained intact. Fungi grew on the wooden framework, and when the wind was up, the back doors would suddenly burst open.

The old farmer who swayed towards us on a pair of gammy legs introduced himself as Hank. Housed in an old chicken shed on a bed of straw, four puppies were rolling around amongst chicken feathers. He scooped a large hand under one of them and held it high in the air.

'Take a good look at it,' he said, shoving the puppy into Jack's chest. 'Here, take it. It will be ready in two weeks for fifty pounds cash.'

'Do we have a choice?' asked Jack.

'No. That's the last one available, take it or leave it.' With that said, he rolled away, poking the shed door shut with his crook, leaving us to make up our minds. Jack and I looked at each other; what did I know? This was Jack's decision not mine. 'What do you think?' I said. 'How do you know if it's going to make a good dog at this age?'

'I don't, but Gethin said the mother won a county cup at the Caernarfon sheep dog trials.' Impressive, no doubt. Maybe Gethin was in on the deal again, getting a tenner out of it.

'If the breeding is that good, why is it only fifty pounds?' I asked.

'I don't bloody know!' Jack said, running his hand through her coat.

'Is it the runt?'

'No, it's the same size as the other three.'

'It's up to you, brother.'

'Let me think. Why don't you go and have a roll-up?'

So I left him to it; this was a big decision for Jack. If he took her he would keep her for the rest of her life, beyond her working days. But after half an hour, when he hadn't appeared and Hank, whose surname turned out to be Jones, had told me more than I needed to hear about his father's death when a tractor had rolled over him, I went searching for him. As soon as I opened the shed door he turned and said, 'I've made up my mind. I'm taking her.'

Unlike the long drawn out charade with Hughie, Hank got straight to the point. 'I don't haggle, so don't even think about it. Give me ten pounds now, the rest when I deliver her in two weeks.'

It was a relief to have done the deal there and then. Hank and Jack shook on it. On the drive back to Dyffryn, as the old Traveller groaned and squeaked on its failing suspension, little passed between us, Jack staring silently out of the window, me worrying about money. We were running out of it.

As we drove past the Dorothea quarry into a greying sunlight, for the day had become overcast with darkening clouds sweeping low over the piles of slate, Jack said, 'I'm going to call her Meg.' Climbing up the hill out of Penygroes at a steady twenty m.p.h. as the skies opened and a torrential downpour created rivers of water down the gullies, we lost the remaining windscreen wiper, which had been flapping like an insect in its death throes for some time. I couldn't see a thing, so for five minutes we sat outside the gate of Dyffryn waiting for the rain to ease.

'Jack, the old girl's giving up on us.'

When we eventually walked into the house, Ros handed me an official-looking letter in a brown windowed envelope. I had a date for my driving test, 28 June; it was about time. I needed to pass that test, get legal. Also we needed two cars, or rather one Land Rover and a runaround for Ros, who was forever on her way to Gwyn and Eryl, or out to tea with friends scattered between Penygroes and Bangor. It had never dawned on me that she would have such a busy social life, but then of course why not? She was born and brought up here, educated here. She was Welsh, amongst her own. I just hadn't thought about it, being completely wrapped up in the plans we were making for the farm. Then Ros gave me the good news that Eryl was buying a new car, and offering us her Hillman Imp.

Harry was putting a corrugated iron roof on a stone outhouse, which would hold six pens for the first gilts (young female pigs who have never had piglets). I'd taken the advice of a successful pig farmer called Josh Hummel, who had a state-of-the-art set-up over in Bethesda. He was a man with modern ideas far removed from my own, certainly knew his stuff, and was more than happy to pass on his knowledge to this long-haired rookie.

He had built up an intensive factory farm. All his breeding sows were hemmed in metal farrowing crates under one huge roof, lying on slatted floors. He was extremely proud of his automatic systems, which were operated by the touch of a button. He had a giant squeegee that pushed all the slurry along the length of the building, out into a holding tank, and a contract with local farmers who took it away to spread on their fields as fertiliser. He sold breeding stock and was in no doubt that I should purchase Large White Landrace cross gilts to get my enterprise up and running.

Josh was an Englishman from Shropshire who had married a Welsh girl, and because property was so much cheaper here had moved to North Wales. In his office, which was full of wall charts and coloured drawing pins denoting where every single pig was in its breeding cycle, he spoke as a man obsessed with systems. But every time he worked up his enthusiasm to explain them to me, I clouded over and stopped listening. He employed two people to run this 300-sow unit and had a reputation for ground-breaking ideas and making money.

Much more interesting at this time was my correspondence with Deirdre Wainwright. We met through the personal ads in the back of *Pig Farmers Monthly*, a magazine aimed at the whole industry, including those who had smallholdings and just a few pigs. Deirdre had organic farming forced on her, rather than following a philosophy. She simply did not have the financial means to use chemicals or fertilisers on her eight acres near Skelmersdale. She had five Tamworth sows living rough in a pig ark, who foraged around ploughing up the scrubby land. Very efficient and natural, and although she did supplement their food with small amounts of concentrates, most of it came from the dustbins of a hotel and two village pubs. Swill, as it's called.

She sent me a photograph of herself, a woman of unattractive contours; she looked like a Russian shot-putter. On the back of the photo she had written *You can see why the men stay away.* She was wearing a knee-length skirt and a pair of wellingtons.

She was at the other end of the spectrum from Josh Hummel. Yet within her farming methods was a wisdom, a naturalness that was of benefit to an animal's way of life and kind to the earth. It couldn't have been simpler. She moved the sows around her smallholding to break up the sods, and planted vegetables that fed both her and her beloved pigs. The surplus she sold from a market stall to the local community. She grew swedes and turnips that she boiled up to add to the swill. Who was the richer, I asked myself, Josh or Deirdre? We had a lot in common. Then I told her I was married and she backed off.

I had never had a single driving lesson in my life, so the day before my actual test I had agreed with Ros to go on a dummy run with a local driving instructor. I was, after all, self-taught and Ros was concerned that I did not have the correct technique, as she called it. It was a calm summer's day. I'd put on a decent pair of trousers and a tie and shaved, and Ros said if I looked like that every day instead of dressing like a hillbilly she could fancy me again.

I wasn't apprehensive; the only slight doubt I had was that I was taking it in the Hillman Imp, a car I had only driven a few times to Penygroes. I tied the L plates to the front and rear bumpers, cleaned the windscreen and sprayed the dashboard with air freshener. I was ready, firmly focused on what I had to do. The thought of failure never entered my head.

I shook hands with the instructor, Dafydd Rowlands, who graced the world with an immaculate neatness. Everything about him was well trimmed: his moustache, his eyebrows, no doubt his nasal hair. There was the air of an ex-military man about him as he walked around inspecting the car. On his tie were little pictures of people playing golf. He had obviously spit-and-polished the front of his shoes, but I did notice a spot of dandruff on his navy blue jacket. He held a clipboard in his right hand and had four biros in his breast pocket, seemingly lined up ready for inspection.

'Now, I understand you wish this lesson to be a mock driving test, Mr Perry.'

'That's right.'

'Fine. Let me explain a few things before we proceed.'

He told me that the test consisted of two parts. The first would be driving in traffic around Penygroes, and then we would go into the country to carry out particular manoeuvres.

'Do you understand, Mr Perry?'

'I do.'

As he sat down beside me, I adjusted the rear-view mirror, something I knew examiners noticed, and slid my seat forward an inch or two. Turning to me, he said, 'Don't I know this car?'

I was nonplussed, concerned that he had found fault with something.

'It belongs to my wife. Is there a problem?'

'It used to belong to Mrs Gwyn Griffith, my golfing partner,' he said.

'That's my mother-in-law,' I said.

'Well, well, what a coincidence. I was speaking to her just last night. We are playing over in Harlech this weekend.'

I didn't want to say isn't it a small world, so instead told him I'd heard Eryl was a wonderful player and how much she adored her grandchildren. He laughed and said, 'Of course, you are married to Ros. Remember me to her.' And at last, after looking at his watch, he said, 'We're running ten minutes late.'

We set off through the streets of Penygroes, he with his clipboard on his lap making notes, me changing gear as smoothly as possible, keeping the correct distance from the car in front, staying under thirty m.p.h.

I stopped in plenty of time to let a lollipop lady usher schoolchildren across the zebra crossing. He didn't acknowledge the girl with pigtails shouting to him 'Uncle Dafydd', pointedly ignored a chap who stood to attention and saluted him as we went past. We eventually turned into Tram Road, a quiet backstreet, where he asked me to pull over to carry out a three-point turn. This I did without too much difficulty. He gave me a red tick in a little box.

'Now I want you to reverse in here, park between the blue Volvo and the Rover please.'

That seemed to go OK. I glanced over at his clipboard. I now had three ticks.

He told me to turn right into the high street, and immediately we were confronted by a tractor and trailer stacked high with hay, its load leaning precariously to the right. It stopped the traffic as people stood staring up at it. We were stuck in a side road next to the post office for several minutes. I made no attempt to converse, well aware that my every move was being scrutinised. Then eventually we drove around the broken bales, through the hay being blown down the high street and headed up the hill towards Carmel. He spoke only when giving instructions, but occasionally smiled to himself and shook his head gently from side to side.

Some five hundred yards after passing the track into Dyffryn, I pulled into a lay-by and turned off the engine as instructed. It had suddenly got very windy, which was often the case up here, even though the day was bright and sunny.

'In your own time, Mr Perry, I require you to carry out the statutory hill start. Do you understand?'

'Yes I do.'

This, I suspected from the emphasis he had put upon it, was when most people failed their test. We were on an extremely steep incline, making me somewhat nervous, as he stared straight ahead with the wind whistling through the car windows.

'In your own time, Mr Perry.'

So I turned on the ignition, put her into first and, increasing the revs, slowly released the clutch and then the handbrake, and pulled away without a stutter.

'Bravo,' he said. 'That's where they come a cropper, up here, you know. Some plead with the examiner to have another go. But he has to stand firm. He can't show favour.'

As we climbed on up the hill I noticed a lamb with its head stuck in the fence on the other side of the road, bleating in distress, frantically turning and twisting in the wire mesh. It was one of our store lambs; I recognised the blue dye on its rump. We were about half a mile from the land we rented from Rose Tobias.

'Dafydd – do you mind if I call you Dafydd?'

'Well, test etiquette would require you to address me as Mr Rowlands, but, you know, because of who your mother-in-law is . . .'

'Dafydd,' I said, 'you see that lamb over there?'

'Well, there're a lot of them.'

'It's one of mine, the one that's strangling itself to death. I'm sorry, but I've got to rescue the poor blighter.' I didn't wait for his reply. I got out and started running against the wind.

'Mr Perry,' he shouted after me. 'This is most improper, you're meant to be behaving as though you were taking your driving test!' But I lost his words in the gale howling in my ears. I could guess what he was saying. If I would fail the test, so be it. I reached the poor thing and began to turn its head this way and that, trying to release it. How on earth did it get itself stuck so tightly? Its head seemed too big to have got through the wire in the first place. I climbed over the fence into the field and put my hand over its face, pushing it gently, trying to reverse it through the square mesh. I called over to Dafydd.

'Can you get hold of it from behind?'

'This is completely out of order. I'm a civil servant.'

'Please grab a handful of wool on its neck and ease it towards you.'

Eventually we managed to manoeuvre the lamb free and I carried it over to the Hillman. I could feel its heart throbbing against my chest. I opened the door, pushed the seat forward and put it in the back. There was a wet patch on the front of my shirt. Well, the poor thing was terrified. What would you expect?

I sat down in the driver's seat, Dafydd was next to me running a comb through his hair, brushing grass from his jacket, checking his appearance in the mirror.

'Sorry about that. Now where were we?' I said.

'Well, we can't possibly continue the lesson, not with a bloody sheep in the car. It contravenes all the Ministry of Transport regulations.'

'Surely we can? No one knows about it. There are no witnesses. It was an act of human kindness; we have rescued an animal in distress.'

'This has never happened to me before, not once in twenty years.' The lamb, behind me on the back seat, started nibbling my earlobe. It managed to find a hidden erogenous zone of which I'd been completely unaware, and I found it quite a pleasant sensation. However, I was trying to save a situation that was getting completely out of hand. That's when I appealed to Dafydd's better nature.

'Can we just drive on for half a mile so I can put it back in the field?'

I held my breath. Dafydd was clearly the type of man who did everything by the book. I could see he was wrestling with his conscience, and then his face gradually softened.

'Well, I'll turn a blind eye this time. But not a word to a soul.'

I did another perfect hill start, which went completely unnoticed.

'I'm doing this for Eryl, you know that.'

Distracted by events, I was somewhat surprised when Dafydd told me the next requirement for the test was the emergency stop. He suddenly hit the dashboard with the palm of his hand and I slammed on everything, pulling up the handbrake. The lamb somersaulted into the front of the car, landing between the two of us.

'Oh dear,' I said. 'It's not having a very good day.'

'It's not the only one,' said Dafydd.

I drove as fast as I could, keeping my eye on the speedometer.

Pulling up outside Rose's cottage, I let the lamb back into the field. It was over. I told Dafyyd I would be eternally grateful.

The lesson was completed without further incident. We returned to Penygroes and Dafydd turned to me with a look of resignation.

'Well, to be honest with you there was nothing wrong with your driving, in fact you seemed to drive like a man with vast experience. But in reality the whole thing was a farce, and any examiner would have failed you. There is no provision in the Ministry of Transport regulations that allows for livestock to be in a vehicle during a driving test.'

'I appreciate that, Mr Rowlands, but an animal's welfare comes first.'

'I would also respectfully ask you not to mention the trauma you have put me through today. I do not wish to become associated with what some would see as a comical incident.'

'Not a word,' I promised.

Later, when I caught up with Jack and Ros, I told them everything and swore them to secrecy. We agreed that it would have been a terrible embarrassment for Dafydd if word ever got out. He might even have lost his job, so the secret stayed between the three of us.

That night we listened to The Band, drinking whisky; we were all celebrating in some way. Jack was sitting with Meg on his lap, Hank Jones having brought her over from Waen Fawr that afternoon. She was mostly grey, with white circles around her eyes. Now my brother had what he wanted I wondered what changes we'd see in him.

At nine thirty the phone rang. It was Harry, saying we should fatten up some turkeys for Christmas.

'There's money in fresh turkeys,' he said. When I reminded him it was only June he replied, 'Forward planning, to be fair to you, you've got to have them in by August.'

He went on about free range prices, building a run. He would slaughter and pluck them. But I didn't have a conversation in me. I kept seeing that lamb somersaulting into the front of the Imp.

'Tomorrow, Harry,' I said, and left it at that, while everyone around me was singing 'The Night They Drove Old Dixie Down'.

4

Gilts, Vindaloo
and Dave

We finished haymaking at Dyffryn in the traditional way, propped up against the last remaining bales in the heat of a big bright July sun. Dehydrated, shirtless, our arms and shoulders scratched from lifting hay bales onto the trailer to be driven away and stacked in the barn.

Ros joined us, bringing cold beers and lemonade, sandwiches and cakes. The twins toddled around throwing grass at everyone, while Myfanwy produced sweets with a sleight of hand that left them mystified. Even Hughie entertained them with strange noises, I'm sure helped by loose-fitting dentures, sounding like a drum roll, quietly at first, then reaching a climax. Jobber barked incessantly until Hughie had completed his party piece, which he finished by sticking his tongue out and licking the end of his nose.

Gethin had cut the hay on our Massey, hiring us his baler. We owed him £120. We had rented Hughie's trailer for two days, which squared the deal with him, as Jack and I had done at least that much to help him over at Llwyndu Canol. There was a friendly atmosphere, and for the first time I felt relaxed with our neighbours. It made me even more curious about why Daphne Musto had left that note. Today, with the work done, they engaged in long conversations with Ros, broken by swathes of laughter. Jack and I hadn't a clue what was being discussed, but Ros translated snippets about the men's childhoods, haymaking with their fathers before the machine age, the working horses, men stacking the hay with pitchforks. Even now, the hay on the steep slopes where you couldn't take a tractor was scythed. Suddenly their conversation dropped in tone as they swigged down more beers, becoming serious.

'What are you all talking about?' I asked Ros.

'Arfon, how distant he is since his wife died.'

It was Ros they wanted to talk to, so Jack and I swung the children over our shoulders and walked with Meg to the far gate, where Jack was going to show us the progress she was making. After he told her to stay, she lay down obediently, watching us walk away. With ears pricked, not moving a muscle, she waited as the distance grew; surely at any moment she would rush forward to join us. But not until Jack called did she scramble to her feet and break into a lolloping stride. Then, on the command 'Lie down', she stopped instantly.

'God, Jack,' I said, 'that's impressive. And she's only six months old.'

We left her there and walked on, not looking back until we were out of sight. Then Jack summoned her and again she came rushing to his side.

In the morning, Dewi Hughes, the 'flying postman of Penygroes', one of the sarcastic nicknames bestowed upon this likeable man, pulled up outside the house, sounding his horn to announce his arrival. His post office van was caked in dry mud and in the dirt across the back doors someone had written *Speedy Gonzalez*, for Dewi was not noted for punctuality and it was impossible to predict when the post would be delivered. Also known as the 'singing monk', he had a heartiness about him, an abundance of good humour. He had a bald pate, fringed with a fine band of white, floaty hair, like the hem of a frayed curtain. His voice seemed to roll out of him, coming from the deep. It was not hard to imagine him in a habit, singing psalms in a monastery. He reminded me of Friar Tuck. His eyesight was poor, but he didn't wear glasses, holding the envelopes close to his eyes and scanning them slowly before putting them in your hand. He was a member of the eisteddfod committee, dedicated to the preservation of the Welsh language. The postman's alter ego kept a few Welsh blacks on the undulating slopes above Llanllyfni. Unable to make hay, he liked to buy off the field as early as possible and pay in cash. He drove a hard bargain, backed up with a wad of notes: 'Instant bliss!'

He could smell our hay on the wind, said we should talk about my selling him a couple of tons. I shrugged my shoulders to show my indifference, a mannerism that now came naturally.

'I'll be back to take this up with you again, my boy,' he said, passing me a hand-written letter and an official-looking envelope: my driving licence – thankfully I'd passed the test in Caernarfon a week ago. 'And besides, I've put in a good word for you to join the FUW [Farmers' Union of Wales] on preferential rates. We don't allow just anybody in, you know. You'll owe me favours, you know, all these doors I open for you.'

That said, he was off, with only one thought in his mind: he was softening me up to get the best price he could. Dewi was a staunch Plaid Cymru man, a party activist who passed among the community putting over his point of view not only on politics, but on the arts as well. He held forth sitting in the kitchens on his round, drinking tea and eating cakes, hence the size of his girth and irregularity of the post.

Jack, who was never without Meg at heel, told me he had seen an advert in the newsagent's offering a Land Rover for sale, £750 o.n.o., over in Nebo. We needed one urgently, for the Traveller had come to its final resting place, wedged between a lean-to and the old milking parlour. Harry said it still had some value, that we should get a few quid for spare parts.

'Put it in *Exchange & Mart*, see who bites.'

I had always thought it a woman's car; in all our time in Wales I had never seen one on the roads being driven by a man. So we paid for a couple of inserts. 'There's always someone out there wanting something,' was Harry's optimistic take on things.

He had persuaded us to rear two dozen turkeys for the Christmas market, certain there was good money to be made from free range and fresh.

'Good God, man, your father-in-law could sell them all to his friends.'

I hadn't thought of Gwyn as a turkey salesman.

'Use your assets, man.'

It didn't take me long to realise that all Harry's new ideas required capital expenditure. We needed to build a run, which involved buying in rolls of fox-proof wire and eight-foot posts that would have to be creosoted, all up front. The birds would also need to be housed, so Harry was on the look-out for a second-hand shed. We were spending more money than we were making.

I found in my pocket the letter Dewi had delivered earlier as we drove over to Nebo to meet Tom Felce, who was selling the Land Rover.

'Open it, Jack.'

It was from Rob Marshall, a friend of ours we hadn't heard from in over two years. He was one of those who, following the life-changing experiences of LSD, had gone east to India. I had known a few who'd gone that way, who'd travelled the spiritual highway, opened Huxley's *Doors of Perception*, been influenced by Alan Watts and Herman Hesse, and changed their lives. To help Rob get the money together, I had bought the contents of his single room in Shepherd's Bush.

'I won't be needing any of this where I'm going.'

I gave him fifty quid for the lot. After raising a couple of hundred from his family, he was off. I hadn't thought we would see him again.

'What's he up to?' I asked as we pulled into a driveway populated by gnomes peeping out through the Leylandii. Others were holding fishing rods around a garden pond.

'He wants to come and see us.'

A little woman made her way from the bungalow holding a rolling pin covered in flour, wearing a plastic apron with a picture of Bambi splayed out on ice.

'You'll be wanting to see Tom. He's expecting you – he's around the back, smoking,' she said.

Behind the house was a black-timbered shed surrounded by rows of herring, hanging from coat hooks on aluminium rails. Smoke billowed from the chimney, spiralling upwards to merge with the low cloud that drifted over the hills. We knocked on the door and eventually a figure appeared. It could have been Count Dracula walking out of a pea-souper fog. He was completely dressed in black: black raincoat, black bobble hat and a black roll-neck pullover, finished off with black plastic gloves and black wellingtons. Smoke engulfed us as he introduced himself.

'I'm Tom,' he announced. He was English, but I couldn't determine the accent. He smelled of kippers, which wasn't surprising, and wood. He was very woody, and nearby in what used to be an old railway wagon were piles of wood shavings. Tom proved to be an interesting man: self-employed, having taken over his father's enterprise. Every Wednesday he drove to Birmingham fish market in his Land Rover, leaving at two in the morning and bringing back his 'catch', which he'd bid for amongst a crowd of fishmongers. On Thursday he gutted and filleted it, and on Friday sold what he didn't keep back for smoking to the restaurants and hotels around Llandudno. He was doing well, so had bought a Transit van and decked it out with shelves to give it the look of a professional business.

'The heater doesn't work,' he said, handing us the keys to the Land Rover, 'but she's steady and reliable.'

Jack put Meg in the back and we set off for a run down to Dinas Dinlle beach. The steering was heavy as I crunched through the gears, having to push the clutch to the floor. She took up the width of the narrow lanes and when we met a tractor head on it took several attempts before I could get her into reverse.

At Dinas I put her into low ratio and slowly drove over the stones and pebbles along the beach. I could feel her sinking into the loose shingle, but she kept going, not stalling once.

'Hey, Jack, now we really are a couple of farmers,' I said, as Meg stood with her front legs on the tailboard, having her first sight of the sea. 'Have a go.' I stopped a few yards from where the waves rolled in over a thick band of seaweed. Meg was off before we even noticed she was gone, chasing after a pair of cormorants. With the noise of the crashing sea and the wind, Jack couldn't bring her back. Not until he put two fingers to his mouth and whistled, a piercing note that would have shattered a wine glass.

'Wow.' I was astonished. 'How did you learn to do that?'

'With a little help from Gethin and a lot of practice.'

'Show me,' I said.

'It's simple, once you know how. You just roll your tongue back till it touches the top of your mouth, then put these two fingers either side and blow.'

But I couldn't. All I managed was a hissing sound like a kettle boiling. I remembered how I used to mock Jack's attempts to emulate the shepherds on *One Man and His Dog* and felt slightly guilty, but fortunately Jack was more interested in reprimanding Meg than in raking over old grievances.

'No . . . do you hear me? No,' as Meg sat looking up at him.

'She knows,' I said. 'Those eyes are asking to be forgiven.'

After Jack's ten minutes at the wheel, I opened the throttle and sped along the beach road, my foot flat to the boards, managing to reach fifty m.p.h., but that was her limit.

'What do you think?' I asked. 'Shall we buy it?'

'Seven hundred and fifty's a bit steep . . . let's knock him down a hundred.' It was now ingrained in us never to offer the asking price.

Tom stood his ground on seven hundred. Jack and I stuck our hands in our pockets, casting dubious glances. We turned to walk away, Jack saying, 'We can't meet you on that.'

We'd only taken a few steps when Tom said, 'Are you paying cash?'

Jack and I looked at each other. 'Yes, we can do cash, but hold on a minute. You've got to allow us something on the heater not working.'

So we got her for £625. Not a bad deal, and Tom, having already splashed out on his Transit, had recouped some of his outlay. We got on well with Tom, and as he searched for the log book we were joined by his mother in the bungalow. She it was who collected the gnomes that were dotted around the house, sitting on either side of the fireplace, perching on windowsills, some acting as door stops.

'It's my hobby,' she said. 'Once you start collecting you can't stop. I'll do anything for a gnome.' I asked her what attracted her to them in the first place. 'Oh, I think the likeness to my husband.' That I couldn't believe: the things were eighteen inches high and made of concrete.

As Tom showed us the paperwork we talked about the deals we could do; swapping eggs and vegetables for fish seemed like a good idea. There was no fishmonger in Penygroes, and the Co-op only sold frozen cod. So we agreed that on Fridays he would call in on his way back from Llandudno, bringing what was left in his van in exchange for our home-grown fresh vegetables. The idea of bartering goods always appealed to me. There was more character to it than handing over money. Ros was delighted that she could add fresh fish to our diet.

'We need to find a bee-keeper next.'

'That's it, all done,' announced Harry, having completed the last of the farrowing pens.

We were ready to take the six gilts from Josh Hummel. We had decided to house them together for a month in one building that had a large exercise area, to let them acclimatise. Then, as they came on heat, we'd take them to the boar, and during pregnancy move them to wooden pig arks in the lower fields. Most of the land down there was rough scrub, boggy with a lot of gorse, ideal for pigs. Meanwhile, Josh had selected a young boar with an outstanding pedigree. I didn't doubt him; why should I? He was the man with the reputation to lose. He recommended Crosfields as a supplier of concentrates and asked the local rep to get in touch to set me up as an account customer. At last, we were there. The pigs were coming.

'Hey! Isn't that Rob?' I shouted to Jack.

'Where?'

'Opening the gate.'

'Are you sure?'

He was carrying a rucksack on his back, looking as if he had walked from India.

'Why don't the Welsh pick up hitchhikers?' he said, throwing his arms around us.

'You look like a tramp,' I said.

'More like a beggar, all tattered and torn.'

'Hey! I never thought we'd see you again!'

'Well I'm back. What a journey. Things were fine leaving London – two lifts got me to Capel Curig. Nothing after that, just farmers in pickups and tractors. Sheep on the road slowed us down. Then the chap who gave me a lift from Betws-y-Coed kept stopping and talking to everyone we passed. The only thing I overtook was the guy pulling a freezer down your farm track.'

And sure enough, as we spoke, a lone figure struggled through the gate, pushing a two-wheeled trolley and bumping along the drive with the freezer Ros had ordered.

'Duw, boys, I hope I haven't buggered it up. The motors on these things are bloody sensitive. They gave me a seven-tonner. It doesn't have the lock to turn down your track,' he wheezed, dabbing his forehead with a handkerchief. 'Any chance of a cup of tea? I turned fifty last week.'

As we sat in the kitchen he poured out the woeful story of his life (a failed business, a collapsed lung, a painful divorce); meanwhile Rob rummaged through his rucksack and handed round beedis, little Indian cigarettes wrapped in a leaf.

'Can you get stoned on it? I'm Cledwyn Ap Jones, by the way.'

'It's herbal,' said Rob.

It was an unsatisfying smoke. It burned down to your lips in one drag. It didn't seem to have a nicotine hit, the only thing that makes smoking worthwhile.

'Thanks, Rob, but I think I'll stick to Golden Virginia.'

Ros walked into the kitchen, her hands thick with earth, holding a tray of seedlings, her hair wild under a loose scarf.

'Rob! Oh, how wonderful to see you. Sorry I can't put my arms round you, but give me a kiss. Let me go and get cleaned up. I want to hear everything. I'll be back; wait for me.'

'Anyway, as I was saying . . .' Cledwyn would have continued on his lamentable monologue, but then from his rucksack Rob produced a collection of miniature brass figures engaged in Kama Sutra gymnastics, which immediately distracted him. 'That's not possible,' he said, examining one of the trinkets from every angle. 'No, that's not possible. For a start, the chap's got three legs. It is a leg, isn't it?'

But before this mystery could be untangled, an orange Marina pulled up. Meg jumped onto the windowsill, barking, letting us know a stranger had arrived.

Cledwyn told Rob he could sell his figures in the pub. 'How many have you got?'

'I'm not interested. They're gifts for friends.'

A man appeared at the door wearing a trilby hat, and a Gannex raincoat of the type made famous by Harold Wilson. He introduced himself with a floppy handshake and a smile that showed a missing tooth.

'I'm Evan Evans.'

'Good heavens, it's Evan Evans,' I said.

'Don't think I haven't heard that before.'

'I'm sorry . . . who are you?'

'I'm the rep from Crosfields. Josh Hummel asked me to pay you a visit.'

So Evan Evans joined our little soirée. As he removed his hat and coat he looked at me suspiciously, his nose twitching like a rabbit. 'What's that smell?'

'A blend of Indian herbs,' said Rob.

'Not hashish? You see, if it was, I couldn't take your business, being a Calvinistic Methodist. We take every sin very seriously, you understand.'

'No, no, Mr Evans,' I reassured him.

'Call me Evan, please. If it's not convenient, I can come back some other time.'

Cledwyn, realising he had overstayed his welcome, handed me the delivery note for one freezer received in good condition, and turning to Rob said, 'How much will you sell me one of those for?'

'If they mean that much to you, take one.'

'Why, thank you. A most interesting time I've had, very educational in some respects.'

I left Jack and Rob in the house and walked around the buildings with Evan Evans, telling him our plans. As all reps do, he ingratiated himself, complimenting me on what I had achieved. In reality he was securing a new account in a fiercely competitive market, especially here in North Wales, among the sceptical hard-up hill farmers. The nationwide feed suppliers, such as Spillers, BOCM Silcocks and Crosfields, employed every tactic they could think of to steal business from one another.

I gave the business to Evan Evans because of Josh Hummel. He assured me he would come by once a week and handed me his business card, with his home telephone number written on the back. 'I'm on twenty-four hour call.' I told him it was highly unlikely I'd need to ring him out of office hours. He patted my arm, saying softly, 'For your own peace of mind.'

That evening Rob cooked us all an Indian supper. Dressed in a white linen shirt and baggy trousers, with shoulder-length hair and a bushy beard, he looked like the Maharishi. Lapis lazuli beads hung round his neck. We listened to Ravi Shankar as he told us stories of his travels around India.

As the room filled with exotic aromas, Ros, taken over by the atmosphere, performed a belly dance. Sam and Lysta were not impressed by their mother's behaviour, and once Rob added the chilli they were evacuated to their bedroom.

The phone rang. It was Harry's habit to make impromptu calls that seemed to coincide with his third pint down in the Quarryman's. He always opened with the same line: 'I've been thinking about things.' We hadn't even finished building the turkey run yet and he was already making plans for the next money-making enterprise.

'Sausages,' he said.

'What about them?'

'Do you know how many sausages were eaten last year? More to the point, pork sausages. Do you understand where I'm coming from?'

'Yes. Millions.'

'Exactly, and by a stroke of luck I know where I can lay my hands on a sausage-making machine.'

'Harry, can we talk about it in the morning? We're eating Indian food and belly dancing.'

'It'll never catch on. The Welsh aren't ready for it.'

'See you in the morning.'

So we sat around the table, Rob serving up a taste of India, a selection of small dishes with rich spicy sauces.

'This one will burn your tonsils,' he said, pointing to a vindaloo. 'Help yourselves to chapattis.'

Today Josh Hummel was bringing the six gilts. I was up early walking around the farm clearing my lungs, breathing in the sea air, which over Dyffryn mixed with the mountain breezes. At this time of day there was a pleasing solitude, dew glistening in the grass. The remnants of a soft veil dissipated as the sun rose, mists floating skywards, like ghosts getting dressed. Often I was captured like this in the summer months when out alone. But never for long; my name being called, I made my way back to the house. Meg bounded towards me with an enthusiastic greeting. She hadn't seen me since last night, a long time in a dog's life.

Jack told me Josh Hummel would be with us in ten minutes. So we fetched the straw bales from the barn, broke them up and scattered the bedding through the building we had prepared for the gilts' reception.

Josh brought them in a horse box towed by his Land Rover, reversing it to the gate. The cleanest pigs you'd ever see made their way down the ramp, sniffing the strange smells, snouts to the ground. I could hear them saying to themselves, 'What the hell is this stuff ?' 'It's earth,' I told them silently, 'you're smelling the earth.'

Yes, they would walk on a concrete floor, but they would have plenty of space to run around in. They could see the sky, feel the rain. They could lie on their backs at night and stargaze if they wanted to.

I watched Josh make his first assessment of the place. I could tell he wasn't impressed by what he saw. I hadn't expected him to be. He couldn't hide that look; he didn't need to say anything. This ramshackle set-up fell way short of his own standards.

'It isn't what I was expecting. Certainly different from anything else I've seen.'

I began to explain the layout to him, but he wasn't interested. I could feel his disappointment.

'I'd better be on my way.'

'OK, Josh, but you're welcome to a cup of tea, or breakfast if you like.'

'No, things to do. I've got an article to write for the Pig Association. I'd better get on with it.'

Why did I feel a sense of regret? I'd never pretended to be Mr Modern Pig Farmer with air-conditioned buildings. I had no ground-breaking ideas; far from it. If anything, my thinking was regressive, wanting to get back to the land. But now we had our breeding stock and were only a month away from putting them to the boar.

Harry skidded his bike to a stop next to me, wearing a T-shirt embossed with the image of a sizzling sausage. Underneath it said I am a great British banger.

'That's me, you know,' pointing at his T-shirt. 'That's what the girls around the village call me.'

'Oh, I thought you were advertising the sausage-making idea,' I said.

The pigs seemed at home immediately, turning over the loose straw, having fun, suddenly breaking into an excited run, enjoying the space.

Jack held Meg, showing her our new arrivals. Her eyes darted from one to the other; these were the first pigs she had seen. She followed every move they made. Whenever one came near and she heard them grunting, she growled.

'Good God, what's that?' Harry gasped, clutching my shoulder, nearly losing his balance.

It was Rob walking up the drive. Dishevelled would be an understatement: he was smoking a beedi, while his baggy white linen suit, inflated by the breeze, seemed to puff out his figure. Wearing Jesus sandals, as they were called, he had the look of a holy man not out of place in India, but I suspected the ultra-conservative people round here would feel threatened by such a strange intruder. This was the land of chapel-goers, Methodists with hard-held religious beliefs. I could imagine the dropped jaws in the Co-op when Rob queued to pay for his shopping. Harry did hesitantly shake his hand, but the expression on his face said it all. *What on earth am I looking at?*

Of course as soon as Dewi saw him, word of the second coming, and the news that Jesus resided at Dyffryn would be around in no time. We really did need to have a word with Rob about his appearance. What's more, the previous night we had talked about his plans and he'd made it plain he would love to stay a while, working on the farm, for no more than his keep and tobacco. He was a friend, like-minded, and thought the possibility of becoming self-sufficient wasn't a wild dream, but an idea to be pursued with enthusiasm. We had added one to our number.

It was unusual to see Harry so ruffled. He always took everything in his stride, being the playboy of Penygroes, but the arrival of Rob unnerved him. For Harry had slipped comfortably into his role at Dyffryn, offering advice, always having the final say on how we approached most of our projects. I reassured him that there was no need to feel threatened; everything would continue just as it had been. Thankfully it all settled down when Rob emerged two days later clean shaven and sporting a crew cut, a complete change in appearance from one extreme to the other. Sensitive Rob had taken a walk down to Penygroes and seen the looks of disbelief as the dour folk of the village watched this alien passing amongst them.

I had been thinking for some time that we needed a house cow. It irked me that Ros's regular shopping list included four bottles of milk from the Co-op. We could be making butter too, or cheese, although I couldn't see us set up for that just yet. But in amongst my stack of booklets was one on butter making. As far as I could tell it required no more than a wooden churn, a strong arm and the patience to stand there and while away the time as the butterfat congealed into a bright yellow slab. Then it just needed patting into shape. 'Surely we can do that,' I said to Ros, adding, 'How much time do you have on your hands?', a remark that didn't go down too well. But I was keen on the idea. It was another step on the road to becoming self-sufficient. Ros thought we could never achieve it completely, since we would always need to buy things such as razor blades, tobacco, tea and coffee, which was true, but we could reduce our purchases to the bare minimum. She suggested we should have a budget of no more than ten pounds a week.

I'd already had a word in several ears about a house cow that would suit us. I wanted something docile and friendly, that the children could get involved with. A cow that would have to grow accustomed to several different hands grabbing her udder, which I am sure is a very personal thing for a cow. Jack thought he should be excluded from the milking rota, because he was becoming a full-time shepherd and could not be relied upon to be available for domestic duties. Ros, Rob and I were more than happy to milk, we agreed, and the following Tuesday Rob and I would go to Bryncir market and see if we could buy a cow.

It was September, when dramatic sunsets filled the sky. Flocks of migrating birds spread across the evening, squadrons of winged shadows. All of them had gathered somewhere, synchronising their leaving to make the long journey; the wide open spaces were theirs now. Almost overnight the swallows had gone, once there was a hint of autumn in the air. The log fire was lit again and before supper we would walk in the last glow of day, when the horizon was on fire and the sea reflected the dying light. The bull calves were now being given hay. I would wander out to see them grazing quietly in the field. Then I'd shine a torch on the gilts, who slept in one pile of flesh, as if folded into each other, snoring loudly. And finally, my last job of the day, in those quiet moments when I was always alone, I watered the marijuana plants in the greenhouse, all of them strong and healthy. Just the smell of them now was almost enough to get me stoned. In a week we could harvest them, a crop that would last us several months. This was what it was all about: self-sufficiency in all our needs.

The freezer was now full of vegetables and there was a stack of logs in the hovel. The turkeys, which Rob locked up every night, were putting on weight, the chickens were still laying about three eggs a day. They too were part of my nightly routine of doing the rounds, making sure everything was secure. We had a fox prowling around, and in five minutes he could massacre the lot.

Back in the house after we had eaten I would spend some time upstairs with Sam and Lysta, letting my imagination run riot telling them stories I hoped wouldn't disturb their sleep. Then, with the children settled and the day done, we would talk about our plans, listen to music, sometimes get stoned.

Another landmark day was approaching. Josh Hummel was bringing over our Large White boar, Rattlerow King David the Fifty-seventh. And Rose Tobias, after an emotional goodbye to Jack, was flying back to the Californian sun for the winter. Jack would move in and act as caretaker.

We had bought a young ram and soon the tupping season would be on us. Jack wanted lambs to be born in February, so from the beginning of October we would run the ram out with the flock, hoping he would do the business.

Every morning the calves gathered by the gate, a white mist rising from their nostrils into the crisp air. They bellowed impatiently, waiting for me to appear carrying a bale of hay on my back. They always knew the time of day, head-butting one another, following me across the field. They were a band of ruffians at feeding time, with their own pecking order. I scattered the hay in a long line to give them all a chance to get their fair share.

The pigs too knew I was up and about, and whined as if some traumatic event had befallen them. They rattled the steel-sheeted gate of their pen, putting their snouts under it and trying to lift it from its hinges, while the turkeys, not to be outdone, gobbled like an insane mob pursuing their leader, who was in fact Rob with a bucket of feed, attacking each other spitefully until he had filled the trough. It certainly was every turkey for himself.

Even Jack, with a sack of concentrates over his shoulder, did not escape an onslaught at feeding time. The ewes encircled him, bleating, and trapped him amongst them while he shook out the pellets. Meg lay some distance away, waiting for any command, always keen to play her part. But Jack never called her on these occasions and continued to wade through his charges dropping a trail of feed until they were all eating quietly, the melée over. This had become the morning routine before we grabbed breakfast ourselves.

It would have been fitting to mark the occasion with a crescendo of crashing drums, so grand was the arrival of Rattlerow King David the Fifty-seventh as he stepped down from Josh Hummel's trailer with all the swank and confidence of a well-endowed male, sniffing the tantalising pheromones in the breeze. As if listening to the sound of his own fanfare, he was well aware he was in the spotlight. He was, after all, entering his harem. Certainly the gilts whining in the building nearby knew of his arrival.

Coming from a long line of potent beasts, he boasted a royal pedigree that had produced champions across the British Isles.

Jack said he was overqualified; all we needed was a randy bugger who had an appetite for shagging. But as I watched him I knew we had a young boar who would stamp his bloodline on the pig herd at Dyffryn. He had that thing called 'presence', the look of a winner who wasn't going to take no for an answer. I'm not overstating the impression he made on me. This was a day I had long awaited. We had been here nearly ten months, but for me the entrance of Rattlerow King David the Fifty-seventh marked the beginning of my own adventure.

He was in no hurry to enter his pen, and when Josh slapped his arse he turned sharply, giving out a series of short sharp snorts, as if to say, 'I'll do things in my own time.'

He was perfectly proportioned, walked like an athlete. His bollocks, well rounded and pink, but high up, not hanging between his legs, swayed gently. His flanks and shoulders were muscular, his trotters neat and clean. He raised his snout high in the air, catching another waft of the gilts' female scent. This boar was my prize possession. I couldn't wait to get to know him, his quirks, his habits.

'So what are we going to call him? Surely not Rattlerow King David the Fifty-seventh?' asked Rob.

'Bit long-winded,' added Jack.

'What about King David?'

'David?'

'Let's call him Dave,' I suggested.

So Dave it was, a mate's name if you like.

Again Josh Hummel refused to come to the house and join us for a cup of tea. After I handed over the cheque for £250 he gave me the documents concerning Dave's family tree and left without any further conversation. How I had fallen in this man's estimation. I'm sure he saw us as a group of young hippies playing games in a world he took so seriously.

That night I went up to Dave's pen to make sure he was settling in. I'd given him a good bed of straw; when I shone the torchlight on him he was up in a flash. I'd brought some carrots, which I hand fed him, scratching behind his huge floppy ears, talking to him gently. It occurred to me that he might be homesick, like a boy on his first night at boarding school. Everybody who knew anything about pigs told me I was going to have to ring his snout like a bull, for there was no way to move him except to pull him on a rope. I didn't like the idea, and believed I could train him to walk on a lead, become one man and his boar, rather than one man and his dog like Jack. After all, this was my new mate Dave.

It was a cold night as I walked back to the house, a sickle moon coming and going between passing clouds. I could hear the stream pouring into the holding tank. The smell of the farm was in the breeze as I made my way down the drive and I lingered for a while, thinking about what our lives had become. All of us here farming in Wales, believing in what we were doing, making plans for things we hoped we could achieve. I wanted us to grow an acre of wheat, bake our own bread, make butter, cure bacon, and, as Harry had suggested, make sausages. All this I was determined to see happen soon. But we still hadn't found a house cow. We had eaten far into our capital, and although we had reduced our shopping bills we still had no income. It came home to me then, as Ros called me from the garden, that I should pay a visit to our bank manager. I shivered at the thought of it, that this way of life was impossible to achieve unless we could survive in the material world. I had to face up to the economic truth: we were running out of money.

I walked into the house to Bob Dylan singing 'Like A Rolling Stone'.

I wondered how long it would be before we were scrounging our next meal.

5

Radiohead

Ros was convinced, but Jack and I weren't so sure, while Dewi, struggling with a parcel, remarked it was certainly different. Harry said it had altered the face of the landscape. Rob was of the opinion that it would mellow, blend back in with the surroundings. We stood in a huddle as if in a gallery looking at a work of art.

'What colour did you say it was?' asked Dewi.

'Tuscan red,' replied Ros, adding that we shouldn't judge it now, before the paint had dried and the weather had got into it. But no matter what, the façade of our house glowed like a bright tomato. Hughie turned up, putting in his tuppence-worth.

'Duw, Duw,' he muttered, rubbing his hairless chin, 'have you all been taking those transcendental drugs?' Hughie, believing the youth of London were all on LSD having non-stop sex, from time to time dropped these misplaced observations, never quite hitting the mark. Dewi got into his van, suggesting we should photograph the house, get it on the front cover of one of those trendy magazines. In the weeks that followed, whoever called by was clearly taken aback. But Ros was pleased, saying it had warmth; and sure enough its garish overpowering redness did begin to fade.

That morning Jack, Rob and Harry joined me in the greenhouse. It was the day of our private little harvest of the marijuana crop. There was an air of nervous expectation as we cut the stems, twelve in all, with their sticky rich green leaves. They had grown to a height of at least five feet. The most potent smoke would come from the highest shoots, lots of little clusters of them. We all leant towards them and breathed in that heavenly aroma. But for now we would have to resist the temptation; they needed to be hung and dried in the milking parlour. Harry suggested we could speed this up by putting in a blow dryer.

'Come on, to be fair to us all, why prolong the agony?' So we blasted them with Ros's hair dryer with the heat turned up to its highest level. At eight o'clock that evening we rolled our first home-produced joint, and were soon crying with laughter at every trivial word anybody uttered. We began every sentence with 'Well to be fair to the man', and it went downhill from there until we all got hungry and raided the kitchen for bread and honey.

Winter was upon us. The prevailing winds, gathering strength, whistled under doors and rattled windows; storms brought down trees, leaving us without power from time to time. Luckily we always had the Aga, so we could cook and were never without hot water.

I'd secured an overdraft facility with the National Provincial bank. The manager, Geoffrey Nicholls, was yet another acquaintance of Gwyn's. Following the care of his son, who had suffered life-threatening complications after a bout of glandular fever, his admiration for my father-in-law was sincere and heartfelt. Gwyn told me he was a Freemason and wanted him to join this inner sanctum of the favoured few, a small circle of Caernarfon businessmen who lined one another's pockets. Gwyn declined, being a Quaker, but they still pestered him, refusing to take no for an answer. When Geoffrey Nicholls agreed to a £3,000 buffer, as he called it, to help our cash flow, I hoped it was just an arrangement between me and the bank, and that he would not approach Gwyn again on the strength of it.

Our Sunday lunches at Trefanai (Gwyn and Eryl's house in Caernarfon) were tricky affairs. I could never relax or be myself, always aware that Eryl would not accept me, and not just because I was English. She didn't understand how I could be farming without having been to agricultural college. She thought Ros could have done better for herself, and rather than try to get to know me she said as little as possible to me. Ros assured me that all I had to do was give her time, but I knew I would never come up to her high standards. Our eyes never met, her niceties amounting to no more than asking me if I would like more gravy on my roast. The subject was never touched upon, yet it was obvious to all that she tolerated me because of her grandchildren, whom she fussed over incessantly.

Yet between Gwyn and me a warm friendship had developed. We sat in his library before those lunches discussing all manner of things, including the struggles modern man was facing. His bookshelves were full of the great philosophers; midway through sentences he would go and pull out a volume and read to me a relevant passage to emphasise the point he was making.

'These books are for you too,' he said. 'Take and read them at your leisure, for here are the riches we all need.'

And so I did, because I was hungry for knowledge. He introduced me to Carl Jung, and last thing at night, tired out by the physical demands of the day, I would fall asleep with a heavy volume in my hands.

Christmas was nearly upon us and Dinah, my mother, was coming to stay. Sam and Lysta lay by the log fire in the evenings looking at the pile of Christmas presents under the tree with all the attention Meg gave the pigs. They couldn't take their eyes off them.

'They're not going to move,' we told them, 'and the big day is still a week away.'

Evan Evans came by and asked if I'd ever tried Boarmate. I told him I didn't think I'd reached that stage in my life yet.

'Duw, boy, that's not what I meant. Simply spray the stuff on to the pinky bits of the sows. It will bring them into season quickly enough.'

I'd never heard of it. But Evan had some and suggested I should use it. He thought the gilts should be in litter by now, and wondered if I had missed their coming into season. So I sprayed on little bursts of the stuff, but it also occurred to me they might be stimulated by Dave paying them a visit. Jack and Rob thought he would run amok, unable to control his male instincts, so all three of us were there the day I put a leather belt round his neck, fastened a rope lead to the buckle and walked him like a dog into their run. It took all my strength to restrain him as the gilts gathered around him, getting excited, shoving their snouts into his underbelly. In an amazing exhibition of what can only be described as role reversal, they rode Dave from behind. I held on to his lead and shouted to Jack and Rob, who were trying not to laugh, to open the gate and get me out of there. It was too soon; we should have waited. It was my mistake. Evan Evans' comments had reminded me that these animals were being fed every day, eating into my profits, my margins. God, I was beginning to think like Josh Hummel. I regretted the experiment now, hoping I hadn't psychologically damaged the blameless Dave.

That night, under the great sparkling sky, with temperatures dropping below zero, I spent some time with him. I took apples in my pockets. I'd done him no favours, probably injured his pride. As he scoffed down his treats I scratched his back and had a word with him, personal stuff, man to pig, so to speak. Then I took myself off across the fields. The night was clear and still; not a leaf trembled. I could hear only the frosted grass crunching underfoot. There was an unearthly silence about the place. I leant against a boundary wall smoking a roll-up, looking back at the lights of the house some hundred yards away. This need for solitude was becoming a habit, my mood dipping like the falling degrees of the night. Self-doubt began to rise. There was so much I didn't know, but I was in too deep now. Everything I had set in motion would have to run its course.

In the morning Harry turned up as we were all eating breakfast.

'It's colder than a quarryman's arse out there,' he said. 'But today's the day, and the sooner we get started the better.' He was as enthusiastic about death as he was about life. We were going to slaughter the turkeys, something he had done for years, but for us it was the first time and I was not looking forward to it.

He had bundles of baler twine hung like a lasso over his shoulder. The turkeys were locked up in the shed and Rob and I were sent in to catch them. Easier said than done; they all rushed into one corner, then scattered, flying into us, that infernal gobbling noise bouncing off the walls. We dived in, grabbing them by the leg, their claws digging into our wrists. We put our arms around their wings to stop them flapping, holding the birds against our chests. Harry had already screwed butcher's hooks into the beams of the old feed store and there, as they hung from the twine, he cut their throats. Buckets were placed below to catch the blood. As the life drained out of them they quietened down, and became still. It took no more than a minute for each one to give up the struggle, Harry saying, as he sharpened his knife, that they didn't feel a thing. We slaughtered all two dozen in a couple of hours. Harry began plucking them while they were still warm, sitting on an old wooden stool with the bird lying across his lap. Their feathers fell into a cardboard box, which he emptied into a hessian sack.

We could have sold far more: Harry was right when he told us there was always a strong demand for fresh free-range turkeys. Nearly all of them went to friends of Eryl, and Harry took the rest. We kept one for our own Christmas dinner. But I found the whole thing unpleasant and made up my mind that we wouldn't be doing it next year. Harry said we'd made good money, though how much I wasn't sure.

Finished with the turkeys, walking to the house to wash the sticky blood from my hands, I suddenly heard Rob shouting for me. It sounded as though there was something wrong and I ran, full of fear of what was about to confront me.

'She's on heat!' pointing to one of the gilts. 'Look at her vulva, how swollen it is.'

There was no doubt about it. The others were showing an interest in her too. So we separated her out, coming between them holding two plywood boards, and steered her off towards Dave's pen.

Whatever the sensation a pig feels coming into season, it takes over her whole behaviour. She charged ahead of us, her snout to the ground, pushing aside loose stones, tugging at clumps of grass.

'Rob, get in front of her. We've got to turn her.'

I picked up a length of 3x2 timber and whacked her on

the rump. Then Harry arrived, looking as if he was wearing a feathered dress, and took the board from me. I ran towards Dave, who was now pacing up and down, producing a thick lather as if he'd covered his face in shaving foam. A long, slippery pink lipstick was showing beneath his flanks. I don't know who was more excited, him or me. I opened the gate and she joined him. Neither was interested in foreplay. We all three watched, keeping our distance, not wanting to embarrass them. They were both virgins, after all. Then Harry said in a bland, almost indifferent voice, 'You know, you're going to have to get in there with them. To steer him in.'

And sure enough, as she now stood quite still, offering herself, Dave's long thin penis, with the twirly bit on the end, repeatedly missed its target. So what else could I do? I rolled up my sleeves and entered the pen. Suddenly it had become a threesome.

'Go on, grab it,' said Harry, while Rob, who had remained silent up to this point, started to shout, 'Higher. No, lower. A bit to the right. Now straight ahead.'

I still held him as at last he hit the bull's-eye. I got out of there as quickly as I could. A strange expression came over Dave's face as he thrust away, staring skywards. It was more than a look of utter pleasure, it was almost divine. He was doing it. Then, as he dismounted, I swear he winked at me. It was a milestone for all of us. It was without doubt the most satisfying day since we had come to Dyffryn. They both stood there, I suppose in a shared afterglow. Dave, now a spent force, wasn't interested in her any more than she was in him.

'Let's hope he's got a high sperm count,' was Harry's only comment.

It was lunchtime; what a morning. We wouldn't know whether she was pregnant for a month, until her teats became distended. But it was a day to be entered in my notebook, where I was to record when each pig came on heat and when she had been served. After nearly a year, our first gilt could be four months away from farrowing our first litter.

Why does everything take so long, require so much patience? Cycles in the farming world move at varying speeds, but all are slow, and some are slower than others. Then there are those that are monotonously slow. I'm talking about livestock, of course. For arable farmers life is simpler: you have four seasons in which to sow your seed, spray your chemicals, wait for the crop to grow, and harvest.

Dave, having sown his seed, now flopped over in his pen, taking a well-earned siesta in the December sun, dreaming no doubt that he was in Torremolinos. The underlip beneath his snout quivered as he slept with a smirk on his face, while his trotters flicked to and fro as if he were running. I imagined him wearing sunglasses lying by a pool, his picture on the front cover of *Pig Farmers Monthly*. I was very fond of him. He had personality; he was an individual, more expressive than any sheep could ever be. I'd told Jack that's why we counted them, we fall asleep because they're all the same.

During our lunch of lobscouse, a dish that Ros made at the beginning of the week then left on the warm plate at the back of the Aga, adding vegetables as the days went by, I sat mulling things over.

'What are you thinking about?' Rob asked.

'It's not easy, is it?'

'What isn't?'

'Farming. I mean all the sort of thing we went through this morning.'

'Would you rather work in an office with a collar and tie on?'

'No! Of course not.'

'So what's the worry?' asked Jack.

'I just realised what my worst nightmare would be.'

'And?'

'That Dave fired blanks.'

When I put the phone down to Vida Koeffman I thought at last we might have found the cow we were looking for. Vida sounded elderly: not ancient, but going in that direction. There was a gentleness in her voice that purred on the end of each word. Her soft German accent had a delicate rhythm, dying away like musical notes. She hesitated as she completed her sentences as if the meaning were hidden in the silence. Because of arthritis she could no longer milk her cow, but wanted no money for her, just a good home. Through a friend of a friend she had heard that we were looking for a house cow.

This did not surprise me. The most effective way to advertise any need in a remote community is by word of mouth; let Dewi know, and within twenty-four hours the details would spread like wildfire through the villages and farms. I arranged to go later in the week and take a look at this cow. Her name was Frieda and she was six years old.

For once, Jack agreed to come with me. He was spending more time at Cae Uchaf than at Dyffryn these days, helping Gethin Hughes douse his sheep for liver fluke. All good experience for Meg, whom Gethin allowed to gather up his flock. She now impressed our neighbours, but Jack, I knew, wanted more than that. He wanted her to be entered in the local trials, to be recognised as a working dog.

Up-ending ewes, checking for foot rot, clipping and tidying up their feet, is backbreaking work. Gethin was lucky to have my brother at his beck and call, but when I heard he was not paying Jack a penny I was upset that a neighbour should take such advantage of him. I confronted Jack about it, told him he should be paid for the work. We needed an income; every week there was still more going out than coming in. Jack's defence that we were gaining in the long run, that the goodwill was benefiting us at Dyffryn, did not convince me. That wasn't how I saw it. Gethin was using my brother as free labour. Jack was reluctant, but I made him promise to talk to our neighbour about a daily rate.

My suspicions were growing about Gethin. Some days he seemed friendly and helpful, but there was something going on with the man. It was his motives that I didn't trust. Why couldn't

Daphne Musto have spelled out what she meant in plain English?

After a cup of tea in the kitchen of Vida's stone-built house in Penmaenmawr we went out to meet Frieda. She came as soon as she was called. I could tell straight away she would be at home with us, happy to let me run my hands over her. I'd no idea what sort of cross she was, but there might have been a bit of Jersey and Charolais in the mix. Her breeding was not important to me. I wanted her to be part of the family; I wanted Ros and the children to be close to her. Vida told me she was being milked by the local butcher, whom she tolerated, but she was used to being made a fuss of.

'I know your father-in-law. I want you to take her.' And I did. It was an easy decision; we had found our house cow.

Hughie rented us his trailer for a fiver, and Rob and I went the next day to bring her back to Dyffryn. We put her in the field opposite the house, but as soon as we left her she stood with her head over the gate bellowing.

'She's homesick,' I told Sam and Lysta. 'We need to give her a lot of attention to make her feel at home.'

She bawled all night; in the moonlight through the bedroom window I could see her at the gate. At two o'clock in the morning we were wide awake and Ros was pushing me out of bed, so I got dressed and went out to her. I knew full well that there was nothing I could do to ease her unhappiness. It'll just take a day or two, I said to myself. She was quiet whilst I was with her, but as soon as I was back in bed she started up again. Ros and I slept with pillows over our heads. When I woke and looked out she was still at the gate.

After Rob and I had done the feeding I brought her in from the field. She followed me to the parlour where I was going to try to milk her. I didn't tether her, and when I put the bucket under her udder she seemed unconcerned by the new hands beneath her. But not a drop did I get for five minutes. Was it me or her, I wondered? Then Harry, the man always there when I needed him, pulled up on his bicycle.

'Like this, man, like this,' and out it squirted. So Harry squeezed two teats on one side and I squeezed the two on the other.

'Four or five pints, I reckon,' he said. She had not taken a single step. It was done, and as I carried our first bucket of milk down to Ros, Frieda followed me back to the field.

I picked my mother up on Christmas Eve at Bangor, our nearest mainline railway station, a forty-five minute car journey. The station at Caernarfon had been closed down by the Beeching cuts. When we got to Dyffryn she was met by Sam and Lysta, who although not yet two years old were in a state of pre-Christmas excitement. Under a twinkling tree, decorated with an assortment of chocolate reindeer and what were no doubt intended to look like three wise men, she placed a pile of presents. The twins spent an hour before supper rearranging the parcels, pretending they could read the names.

Every evening since Ros put up the tree they had sat beneath it, mesmerised, and every night the paper angel I had made fell off and got stuck in the branches. In the end I sellotaped the thing to the ceiling and stuck a twig up it.

After my mother had got them to bed and we thought they were at last asleep, they reappeared. All the noise from downstairs and the waiting for Father Christmas was too much for them. It wasn't until two a.m. that Ros and I crept in and filled their stockings. We fell back to bed and they woke us at six, emptying out everything Santa had brought them. Meg was barking, for Jack had failed to make it up to Rose Tobias's cottage for the night. My mother appeared in our bedroom; practically the whole house was awake. Rob came in with cups of tea and by seven we were out of the house doing the early morning feed. Jack, as always, slept through it all.

A wet snow was falling as we fed and mucked out the pigs. The bullocks were sheltering under the larch trees and the wind was strengthening, sweeping large flakes across the fields. Dawn lacked the brightness to break through the heavy gloom; only a faint rim of light on the horizon showed the sun was rising. We scattered hay for the bullocks, while through the darkness I could see the lights of Gethin's house glowing in the distance. Jack appeared with a bale over his back to feed the sheep in the top fields.

The snow did not settle on Christmas morning, so the singing of 'White Christmas' over lunch was abandoned. The day had cleared, the skies brightening and becoming cloudless and still. We all jumped into the Land Rover and drove to Dinas Dinlle beach. Down here as always we walked into a strong headwind, heads bowed, arms linked, all words lost to the roar of the sea. We charged like front-row forwards, pushing against an invisible scrum. Seagulls with outstretched wings were carried sideways, no more than white flecks blown like scraps of paper, before disappearing high above the beach. Over Cwm Silyn clouds poured in great rolling shapes like stampeding rhinoceroses, while waves broke upon the shore and soaked our shoes. But no one cared, all of us in our own way exhilarated, shoved together, laughing, shouting silently to each other. Then, when we turned and the wind was at our backs, we ran, stumbling over the shingle, slipping on the seaweed, clothes flapping, ears burning with the cold.

All this we shared on an elemental Christmas morning, as our turkey roasted in the Aga. The table was laid with crackers, and two expensive bottles of wine brought by my mother that Rob had decanted. With our own logs burning on the fire, we tucked into a home-raised bird surrounded by vegetables grown at Dyffryn. There is, without doubt, great satisfaction in having produced what sits before you on the table.

That evening Sam and Lysta suffered post-Christmas syndrome, their deflated little souls unable to take any more, falling asleep like two crumpled parcels amongst the gift wrapping. Ros and I carried them upstairs and as I closed the curtains I glimpsed Dave strolling past the house in the light from the downstairs windows. No sooner was I in the kitchen than I was out of the door, grabbing a torch, shouting to Rob and Jack as I ran into the night. Meg immediately sensed the excitement and rushed past me as I got into my wellingtons, taking a sharp left turn and disappearing towards the sheep grazing in the higher fields. Dave was heading in the opposite direction. How on earth had he got out of his pen? I was annoyed with him. Why didn't he appreciate it was Christmas?

Jack went after Meg, Rob and I after our wandering boar. We turned down the winding lane that led to the lower fields, but when we got to the closed gate there was no sign of him.

'Bugger me, where is he?'

We called for him, listened to hear him grunting. Nothing. He had disappeared.

As we made our way back to the house, I saw that the small gate that led to an overgrown garden of old blackcurrant and gooseberry bushes, an untended area that one day we would tidy up but which now lay neglected, was standing open. And there we found him, happily turning sods over, getting hold of the roots, smelling the decaying leaf mould, having his own private Christmas party. He did not like being disturbed; having come upon this treasure he now laid claim to it. Pigs have a vicious bite. I had not experienced one, but Hughie had told me he had once been bitten by a sow, who locked her jaw round his thigh and wouldn't let go. It was agony, he said; her teeth sank so deep the wound had to be stitched, and he still bore the scars to this day. Not that I'd seen them. All this went through my mind as I approached Dave, calling him gently. He was aware of me, but was more interested in uprooting a blackcurrant bush. Rob stood below the open gate, holding a corrugated roofing sheet to stop him turning to the right and heading down the track.

As yet I had not seen a nasty side to Dave, so I got behind him and gave him a couple of pats on his back. 'Go on, Dave,' I kept saying as he walked slowly towards the gate, sniffing the smells that stirred his curiosity. No wonder those French truffle hunters use pigs to unearth that highly prized fungus, for Dave was certainly on the scent of something that lay hidden beneath the soil.

Jack appeared with a bucket of pig nuts. And that was all it took to move the unmovable; just rattle a bucket, sprinkle two or three nuts in front of his great bulk and he will follow wherever you want to go. So on Christmas night we got Dave back into his pen, but we never did discover how he'd made his escape.

On Boxing Day my mother and I walked to the village of Carmel. We had one of those long talks that begins in the past, going over the changes one has been through until it arrives at the present, hatching plans for the future. She was only fifty, living alone in a flat in West Hampstead, working in Leicester Square for Spotlight, the acting agency. 'Too many years in the same routine' was how she put it. Then we stopped on the road, as people do when deep in conversation and a significant point is about to be made. She told me how much she had enjoyed the last few days, that she had felt a sense of freedom. 'Maybe it's the landscape, the mountains and the sea; life is so unrestricted. And my two boys are here, and Ros and the grandchildren.' She asked how I would feel if she were to move here and join us. 'I can buy a little house nearby.'

'I would be more than happy,' I told her, 'and everybody else would be too.'

When we got to Carmel I showed her the village school, the kindergarten that Sam and Lysta would go to, the bakery where Ros bought our bread, the newsagent's. These villages, I told her, didn't have a lot to offer, just the basics, something I reminded her she should bear in mind if she was going to be living here.

She couldn't drive, and Caernarfon, the nearest town to Penygroes, was seven miles away. She would have to rely on the bus service. It made me think about the practicalities of her decision. But Ros had a much better idea of these things than I did.

'Tonight,' I said, for she was leaving in a couple of days, 'you should have a talk with Ros about it all.'

With Dave having proved his potency and our gilts now all in pig, I ordered another five from Josh Hummel. The plan, allowing for the vagaries of Mother Nature, was to have a continuous flow of porkers to go once a month to the abattoir in Caernarfon. Our first farrowing was due within a week, and now the gilt looked close. I squeezed her distended teats each morning, to see if she had that pre-milk oozing from her. She seemed uncomfortable, and even though she lay on her side she could not settle. Last thing at night after I'd done the rounds I would go and check on her. There were so many things that could go wrong, especially with a first litter. I started to leave the infrared light on in her pen just in case she farrowed early. It was not uncommon for a sow to stand up and tidy her bedding after giving birth, only to lie down on a piglet unawares and suffocate it. The infrared light was to attract the piglets away from the mother to where they could lie in warmth behind diagonal planks that they could crawl under but the sow could not. Also, piglets can stagger around, disoriented, until they collapse in some dark corner of the pen and die before they're discovered. Sometimes, the worst thing of all, a gilt would eat her litter. All these things I needed to keep an eye on. Even if you have done everything to reduce the risks, the farrowing pen is still fraught with danger; and in the winter, with our set-up, the cold weather was another threat.

I had another sleepless night and at three a.m. got out of bed, found a torch and went up to look in on her. The light shone in the corner of the pen, but she was up chewing the wooden boards that separated her from the piglet area. She began turning in circles, trying to catch her rear end, obviously uncomfortable. I gave her a scoop of pig nuts and she scoffed them down, but then she resumed her pacing. I didn't enter, she was too agitated, so I leant over the pen door and spoke to her softly, but I couldn't comfort her. Time crept by, and after an hour there was still no sign of her lying down and giving birth.

I went back to bed, managing not to wake Ros, and lay in the darkness unable to sleep. At seven a.m. I was back in the farrowing shed and when Rob joined me for the early morning feed I told him of the night I'd been through. He thought we should ring Barry Evans, our vet. All sorts of things were going through my head: maybe a piglet lying in the breech position, or the litter dead inside her. Hughie was of the opinion that you only called the vet out as a last resort. Hill farmers were tight with their money, thought that you paid through the nose for vets to come out in their expensive cars to stick a syringe full of drugs into the suffering beast. 'They talk arrogant and don't know the animal.' I decided to wait; she wasn't due for another three days. Her appetite was normal. As she ate I squeezed a teat again, and a yellowy milk dripped from her.

It was a Saturday morning, and after I'd milked Frieda Ros and I drove down to do the weekly shop at the Co-op. She bought the ingredients to make bara brith, a kind of Welsh fruit cake that she and the twins were going to bake in the afternoon. We shopped only for the necessities, never exceeding our ten-pound budget. In the Paragon garage, as I filled up the Land Rover, Tom Felce came over and gave me six mackerel. 'That'll put me in credit,' he said. 'I'll come by next week to square up with vegetables.'

After lunch I wanted to listen to the rugby match from Cardiff Arms Park. Wales were playing England, and I decided to sit with the expectant gilt rather than watch the game with Rob on TV. It was a cold, clear February afternoon. She was up and about again, restless, snorting heavily. I put in fresh bedding to occupy her. She continually pushed the straw into heaps, tossing it all over the place, eventually making a bed that resembled a large bird's nest.

I put my transistor radio on top of the breeze block wall and sat in the pen with her. Not the most comfortable way to listen to the game, but the pig came first. I opened a thermos of tea and ate a Kit Kat. Wales were hot favourites to win, and took an early lead through a penalty.

For a minute or two she seemed to have settled down, but then she was up again, walking around the pen. Whether it was the noise of the crowd or the singing that annoyed her I don't know, but in one frightful moment she leapt forward and closed her teeth tightly round the radio. All that remained visible was the leather strap. I could still hear the commentary, the sound coming in waves as she paced about. Then I noticed the tip of the aerial protruding between the loose flabby skin of her mouth and managed with two fingers to extend it, picking up a much clearer signal. By this time England had scored and converted the try. At last, twenty minutes later, she lay down. I knelt close to her, listening to the match. Then it began. She pushed, she gasped, she groaned, and she opened her mouth, allowing me to grab the radio. What a relief when the first piglet arrived.

Rob appeared at half time and asked what I thought of the game so far.

'If I told you, you wouldn't believe me,' I said, wiping the radio with my handkerchief, trying to straighten the aerial.

'Don't tell me you lost reception!'

'No. Even inside her mouth the match came through loud and clear.'

'Inside her mouth!'

'Yes, she grabbed the thing in the tenth minute. Look at the state of it. What will Ros say tomorrow morning when she listens to her beloved Archers?'

'Thank goodness she didn't swallow it.'

By six o'clock that evening she had ten piglets lined up along her, all feeding vigorously. Wales had beaten England 22-6, but we still had something to celebrate after what had been a long and eventful day.

We all went to the Quarryman's Arms in Llanllyfni, the first time we'd eaten out. Harry was playing darts with the barmaid and, strangely for him, didn't come over, acknowledging us only with a wink as he raised his glass of beer. In the corner two old timers were arm wrestling, surrounded by a crowd of rowdy locals. The money was down and both were soaked in sweat, their faces looking as if they were about to explode. We ate steak and kidney pie with a bowl of chips, trying to have a conversation, but I couldn't hear a word Ros was saying.

'Tomorrow is a dry day. That's why they're going at it hammer and tongs tonight,' she shouted across at me.

Dewi came in, dressed in shirt and tie, with an elderly lady on his arm.

'This is me ma,' he yelled. 'We come in here for our Saturday night rave-up. She puts her long life down to a pint of Mackeson and a pickled egg, don't you, Ma?'

She couldn't hear a word he was saying. They sat down at a table obviously reserved for them, the lure of Mackeson and a pickled egg too much to resist even amongst the hullaballoo.

I put my mouth close to Ros's ear. 'Is there any point in staying any longer?' She shook her head. Sam and Lysta seemed not the slightest bit bothered by the din. Then all suddenly went quiet as the lights were switched on and off. Coming from behind the bar, the landlord had a special announcement to make.

'Ladies and gentlemen, may I have your attention please. First of all, I'd like to say I know of no other person in Llanllyfni who has ever reached the staggering age of seventy-five. It is quite remarkable, the longevity one can achieve after forty years on the Mackeson and a pickled egg. Or is it, I ask myself, a clean mind, because I hate to think what her insides are like. Ladies and gentlemen, please stand and raise your glasses for Glynnis, and let us sing to the most beautiful lady in the village *Penblwydd hapus i chi . . .*' (Happy birthday to you).

When we got back to Dyffryn, I went to check on the piglets. They had found their way under the warm infrared light and were sleeping, a little contented heap of them. In the sitting room Rob and Jack were bemoaning the fact that there was a sad lack of good-looking women in Penygroes. Ros said they would have to cruise the nightlife of Caernarfon, or better still go to Bangor; at least that was a university town. 'You don't come to these parts looking for a girl,' she told them.

'It's not that I'm getting desperate, but I'm beginning to find sheep attractive,' said Rob.

'Me too,' replied Jack. 'Maybe I'll ask one home for the night.'

'Shampoo its fleece, put on some lipstick. There must be some accommodating ewe out there in the field who wouldn't say no to a one-night stand,' Rob carried on.

'There is one, actually. Very friendly, called Nibbles.'

'Yes, I've come across her. A bit like mutton dressed as lamb, though.'

Their expressions said it all, and I wondered how long they would tolerate a life of forced celibacy.

Then we did what we always did: rolled a joint, put on some Pink Floyd and watched the fire burn and fade. Jack and Rob were certainly hanging on in quiet desperation.

6

The Great Escape

Every couple of weeks Jack, Rob and I would go to Bryncir market, five miles away, to keep up with what was going on. Everything passed through there: fat cattle, stores, barren cows, lambs to be sold on for fattening, ewes at the end of their breeding life and bought by the butchers for mutton, even old sows, whose meat would fill pork pies for Roberts of Port Dinorwic. All had a hammer price that showed the level of demand for livestock in Caernarfonshire.

In plumes of smoke the bedraggled hill farmers gathered together in a huddle of flat caps and torn coats, downcast as the weather. The auctioneer's voice gabbled faster than the repeated rhythm of a train over the tracks, 'Who'll give me forty, forty, forty-five, forty-five, do I hear fifty, fifty, fifty-five.' Or so we guessed in this world of theatre, always fascinated by these weekly rituals acted out in such a strange atmosphere. Choreographed by whom, I asked myself, for all were playing their part, shuffling from leg to leg. A word of English rarely rose from this great sea of wagging tongues in toothless mouths. The unknown language buffeted our ears like waves breaking over rocks, animated with fingers and fists and growling faces. Here all the deals, the buying and selling, were sealed with no more than the raising of an eyebrow. It was a mystery, grotesque yet balletic, a dance of its own making amongst the nodding and shaking of heads. Swollen knuckles, dirty scarred hands clasping crooks, men leaning towards each other, swaying to and fro, haggling, offering a spat-upon palm to show a price had been agreed. No more than bystanders, never acknowledged, we moved through them without a sign of recognition, although they knew who we were all right. We were ignored as outsiders within the crowd.

Gethin Hughes cast glances our way but turned his back, never greeting us or introducing us to anyone. Hughie too showed no friendship, despite all the weeks we had come to Bryncir. We were not part of them, excluded not only because we didn't speak Welsh, but because we were English. Or maybe they saw us as no more than fools playing at farming. Gethin's response to my suggestion of bartering had been a tut tut, a look of disdain and just one sentence: 'I deal only in hard cash, my boy.' I almost said 'Well, why don't you pay my brother with some of it?' but thought better of it, fearing the consequences of falling out with a neighbour. Mrs Musto's words were never far from my thoughts, a constant reminder that a step too far would leave us ostracised in a community that despite Ros's family connections had never embraced us. Anti-English feeling was running high at this time, hitting the headlines; the buying up of Welsh properties as second homes was bitterly resented.

As the lots were sold, the farmers wandered across the road to the County Inn to down pints and meat pies and feed the flames of local gossip. Then, with beer heavy on their breaths, they drove off in tractors, lorries and vans. Gradually the car park emptied, the pens were hosed down and the place became deserted.

Usually, following these visits to Bryncir, we would drive to Dinas and give Meg a run. We'd sit in the Beach Café, eating a bacon sandwich, squirting ketchup from a plastic tomato, drinking tea and smoking, talking about what we had seen at the market. The bay window would visibly vibrate, while outside the advertising boards spun chaotically before they toppled over in the high wind. Why Gwyneth Thomas kept the place open out of season, I had no idea. She busied herself behind the counter, the tea urn letting off so much steam that the windows misted over with condensation. She allowed Meg inside no matter how irritated she must have felt when the dog shook out her coat on the clean floor. She was a kind woman and brought Meg titbits from the fridge. In the winter months we never saw anyone else in there and we always left a generous tip, which she would sometimes gather up and slip back into our pockets.

With Ros and the children speaking Welsh around the house, it seemed only right to try to learn the language, but it was a hopeless undertaking. Most of the words rolled out over a curled tongue, requiring the same mechanisms from the back of the throat as bringing up phlegm and spitting. After a lot of effort I acquired individual phrases such as 'Sut dach chi heddiw?' (How are you today?), 'Dim parcio yn Stryd y Castell' (No parking in Castle Street), 'Nos dawch' (Good night) and 'Diolch yn fawr iawn' (Thank you very much). Not enough to carry on a conversation, just a little string of polite words I could use in the Co-op or at the chemist.

Rob did no better, but Jack knew all the commands for a working dog in Welsh: 'Dos!' (Get away), 'Cymbei!' (Come by), and 'Gorfadd!' (Lie down). Rob thought the only Welsh he required was 'Hello, my darling' and 'What are you doing tonight?' He hadn't had any luck in finding a girl, and no one had taken his eye.

Meanwhile, Sam and Lysta were well on their way to becoming bilingual. Their favourite book was *Dick and Dora*, and Ros read it to them in Welsh. It would be their first language when they went to the village school in Carmel. Every day she introduced new words to help broaden their vocabulary, thinking they had a better chance of being accepted, less noticed for their Englishness the more Welsh they spoke. She told me that's how it was around here, and we had to prepare them for life beyond the farm. Children who lived in the village already knew one another. It was harder for those coming from the remote hill farms, some of whom had difficulties mixing with others, who had formed their friendships in the village playground and running into one another's houses. It was a struggle for anyone from a farming family, harder still without a sibling by your side. Those first days at school can be a painful initiation, when newcomers stand alone at break time.

With the lambing season now upon us Jack rarely had a night's uninterrupted sleep. We had fifty ewes at Dyffryn in the top acres. The barn was full of pens made from wooden hurdles where Jack kept the ewes needing special attention, the lambs who had had complicated births, and the orphan lambs needing to be bottle fed. Jack was running the show; every night he watched the ewes with Meg. Welsh sheep are hardy creatures, spending most of their time up in the hills, but they can still need a helping hand when it comes to giving birth.

In that month Jack never got near a razor blade. A thick black beard covered his face. He wore rubber overalls to protect himself from the rain. He looked haggard, not like my brother at all, more like Rob when he first arrived. He grabbed what sleep he could, lying fully clothed on the sofa, Meg beside him. Sometimes we would pass him in the mornings snoring, still wearing his wellington boots. He looked like some homeless figure who had wandered in during the night. I saw very little of him and we hardly said a word to each other. He was out in the fields during the day, and at night walked amongst the sheep with a torch, or sometimes bottle fed lambs in the barn. He had asked Ros to keep as much of Frieda's milk as possible, and it was she who carried the warm bottles up to the barn and saw most of him. He came into the house only to stuff food into his pockets, or collect a thermos of soup.

The last of the gilts from our first batch had farrowed, and we were rearing forty-eight piglets. Usually two or three days after their birth, Rob and I carried out the most bestial of acts upon the male piglets. Castrating them was cruel but necessary, Josh assured us, because uncastrated porkers produce what is called tainted meat. So Rob would hold them with their back legs apart and I, armed with a scalpel, cut them, squeezed out their bollocks and sliced them off. As if that wasn't bad enough, we then sprayed on an antiseptic which stung the poor little blighters, and they ran around the pen squealing in pain. We hated it. Out of all the chores, there was none worse. It affected me so much that I asked everyone from vets to butchers to the Fatstock Marketing Corporation, who owned the abattoir, if it really needed to be done. And, of course, back came the predictable response. 'You don't have to, but it will mean you lose your premium price.' In other words, I would make a loss on every male pig I raised. So I continued doing it, hating myself for it. But like everything that happened on the farm, you became hardened to it.

Another five gilts arrived from Josh; now we were in a cycle that later in the year would see porkers being finished off at 140-lb live weight and ready to be slaughtered every month.

Word was getting out about what we were doing at Dyffryn. Although I had never considered who might become interested in what we were trying to achieve, more and more people were seeking an alternative to a materialistic world. We received a letter from a group of ex-hippies living in wigwams in the Brecon Beacons who thought it would be a 'cool idea' to come and join us, 'spreading the word, man'. The very thought of it filled me with horror. The last thing I wanted was a band of drop-outs invading the place, playing flutes and penny whistles and dancing round their tents at night.

If someone had asked me 'So exactly what is the plan?' I would have said it was no more than a continuous push towards self-sufficiency, so that we could live off the land as naturally as possible. The exchanging of goods, bartering, brings an added richness that cash doesn't provide. Of course, there has to be a comparable value to what is being offered in the transaction; a jar of honey is worth a dozen eggs, for example. For now we had only Tom Felce, happy to swap fish for vegetables, but once we had enough produce I planned to open a farm shop, and if the customers preferred to barter rather than pay cash, that would be fine by me. I was sure this would appeal to people. It wasn't going to replace the hard currency of everyday dealings, but I did wonder what the Inland Revenue would think about it. Maybe they would allow me to pay my tax with a bag of turnips and half a pig.

During one of my enlightening chats with Vida Koeffman, who liked my bartering idea, she told me she knew several people who would be keen to give it a go. That very day I got a phone call from Jim Best, a retired naval officer who lived in the hamlet of Nasareth. A friend of Vida's, he had six beehives he could no longer look after. His hips had gone, ground down through the years, and now his knees were following. 'Brain still works, though. Gosh, I wish I was thirty years younger.'

I was immediately excited at the thought of having beehives at Dyffryn. I visualised them down in the lower fields, amongst the gorse and heather. Honey from wild Wales: I could already see the label on the jar. But what did I know about bee-keeping? Absolutely nothing. I had once read Maeterlinck's *Life of the Bee*, a beautifully written book, explaining life within the hive in the most poetic language. A collective intelligence, full of self-sacrifice for the benefit of the greater whole.

Jim couldn't wait to pass on the art of apiary. Despite his arthritic hips, he took me to his garden shed, which was full of wartime radios, receivers and strange-shaped aerials. On a desk a pair of headphones lay beneath a microphone. 'I keep in touch with the remaining few.' He meant radio hams dotted around the world. He put on a pair of white overalls and a straw bonnet, flicking away the black veil, and stepped into a pair of wellingtons. I followed him as we trudged through the bog of a rutted field almost in slow motion, as if walking on the moon. Ten minutes later we came upon his colony of hives, set out in a wide circle under lichen-covered apple trees in an old orchard. Although it was late March there was still a nip in the air and no more than a handful of bees were in flight. Jim walked towards the hives and lifted out one of the vertical frames, full of golden honey.

'This treasure has been gathered by the most highly evolved community on the planet,' he said.

Without hesitation, although a complete novice, I agreed to take the hives on the understanding that Jim would be my mentor, visit us once a month to get me into the swing of it. I could see it being a profitable sideline. Jim walked the lower fields of Dyffryn, deciding where the bees would best thrive, and we moved them in amongst the flowering gorse in mid-April.

In exchange for the colony he accepted a fattened lamb for his freezer and a retainer of six jars of honey per year. This was bartering at its best, with both parties happy.

I could never get to grips with our financial situation. The only thing I knew was how much money we had in the bank, which was dwindling. Surely things must improve soon. After all, we had bullocks fattening up, lambs putting on weight, piglets being born, porkers soon going to the abattoir. This is what I kept telling myself, but I was always anxious. We'd been at Dyffryn for over two years, so I made an appointment to go and see Winford Hook in Porthmadog, an accountant recommended by Dewi, who warned me he was a realist who spoke with a cruel tongue.

One of the peculiarities of living amongst the North Walians was that I had never been addressed by my Christian name. Nor had I ever heard, within the dysfunctional farming community, any other man called by his either. They referred to one another by the place they farmed. 'Better speak to him over at Llwyndu Canol,' Gethin Hughes would say, meaning I should talk to Hughie. Likewise Hughie, when referring to Gethin, 'That neighbour of yours at Cae Uchaf.' It intrigued me that they could not speak each other's name. It was as if the place was neutral, and these men could not bring themselves to show any personal feeling. Indifference has no emotion attached to it.

Such was the case when I walked into Winford Hook's office in Porthmadog for the first time and saw a dim shape struggling to rise from the mahogany chair behind his desk in the gloom. I reached for his hand, saving him considerable effort. Then as he sat back behind towers of accounts and folders, my vision of him was largely obscured by the paperwork. It occurred to me that he looked like King Kong, peering at me through the skyscrapers of New York. He did indeed resemble a gorilla. Thick eyebrows, puffy cheeks, hair swept back, a broad neck that bulged against a tight-fitting collar.

'Perry,' he said, indicating an embroidered chair. There was a cat asleep in a disused fireplace. 'Sit yourself down.'

There were books in glass cases around the walls, all containing the word tax in the title. A frail woman appeared at the door, her curled hair neatly styled, as if the rollers had just been removed.

'Tea, Perry?' said Hook, giving me a long look, his eyes following me until I sat down.

'Yes, please . . . is there something wrong? I have come at the right time?'

'I was expecting somebody older.'

After he had leafed through my invoices, suggesting I should use a bookkeeper to present my year-end accounts, the delicate lady returned and began a slow journey across the room, holding two cups with spoons clinking in the saucers. As she put them down on the desk, I noticed that the cups stood in moats of brown tea. Who she was I did not know; we had not been introduced. Maybe Hook's assistant, or receptionist; she could have been his wife, or perhaps all three. She appeared to be suffering from some nervous disorder. I made a special point of thanking her, while Hook ignored her. We sat in silence, he with his head resting on his hand, nothing more than a sigh coming from his lips. He eventually looked up and said bluntly, 'This is a bit of a mess.' Then he delivered the hammer blow. 'You would have been better off staying in bed for the past year.'

This damning remark quite winded me. It was like a punch in the stomach. I had to put my tea down, my hands shaking. In the moments that followed I could offer no response. It felt as if all our efforts had been worthless, and to Winford Hook, who dealt only in the financial reality of profit and loss, that is exactly what they were. That afternoon in his office, my life had been reduced to a pointless exercise, the dabbling of an idiot pursuing a naïve dream.

'Well at least the tax man won't be coming after you.'

Winford Hook began a monologue that I timed at nearly twenty minutes on the sad decline of hill farming in North Wales. Propped up by subsidies, families working together, tied to a harsh way of life with a meagre profit to show for their labours; sons no longer wanting to endure long hard winters merely to earn a pittance, as their fathers and grandfathers did. Sons who could see factories being built where a man could work a forty-hour week for a living wage.

'I know of over a hundred hill farms where the boys have left the land. Most of them work down at the Firestone factory in Caernarfon.' He summed it up by telling me of a forklift truck driver working the night shift who brought home more than his father farming fifty acres over in Nebo. 'And he drives a Rover to boot! So what are you going to do, Perry? Invent some new way of farming?'

'I have some ideas,' I said.

'Well they'd better be good. You made a loss of eight thousand pounds.'

I didn't drive straight back to Dyffryn. I needed to be alone, to straighten myself out. It was as though every hope had been crushed. I drove to Dorothea and walked around the abandoned slate quarry, ghostly as it was, submerged in cloud, with rusting cranes and other machinery drowning in the rising waters. It felt as if I were staring at a manifestation of the psychological state I found myself in. It offered a strange comfort, the derelict buildings roofless, trees growing through the rafters. Waterlogged sheep took one look at me and turned away, indifferent to my presence. The old engine house with its cogged wheels, the handless clock face dripping its monotonous raindrops. The eeriness seeped into my soul as I walked around the piles of slate. There was a constant whispering in the damp air, as if those who once worked here haunted the place. I read the graffiti on the walls, the bits that were in English, mostly by lovers, hearts pierced with arrows proclaiming undying devotion. I cursed Winford Hook for his brutal honesty, while the survivor in me was determined to prove him wrong. But I had to admit that perhaps it was foolishness that had initiated this whole idea in the first place. Regardless of the outcome, I decided that what had been said at our meeting would remain my secret. For Ros, Jack and Rob it had been no more than a discussion about the accounts: we were doing OK but still needed to reduce our overheads. What else could I say? What good would it have done to have come back defeated?

Driving up from Penygroes, slowing to a crawl on the tight bend outside the cemetery, I met Arfon coming down from Carmel. As I squeezed past his Land Rover he wound down his window and said, 'If you can be bothered to catch them, they're yours for the taking.'

'What are?'

'The chickens in the yard. I don't want them. It was she who liked eggs not me.'

'Are they laying?'

'I don't know. Probably somewhere in the hay barn. Come by if you want them.'

Then he was gone. Every conversation with Arfon was like that, always in passing. I'd see him out and about from time to time, and wonder what he was up to, where he was going. He seemed on the wane, a man withdrawing, caring less and less, as if he was giving up the fight. Was it he or his wife who had pinned the little enamel horseshoe onto the front of his cap? Probably her, hoping to bring him some good luck.

My mother had been paying flying visits, Ros driving her around looking at properties in the area, making arrangements to meet estate agents. In June Dinah finally settled on a stone cottage, Hendy, at the end of Tram Road in Penygroes. She could walk easily into the village from there and was no more than five minutes from the bus to Caernarfon. She paid £9,000 for the property. It had been the home of a batty old spinster, a retired librarian who was now being hived off into a bungalow nearer her family in Bangor. It stood in a quiet position without close neighbours, bordered on one side by a dairy farm where Gareth Hughes kept a herd of Friesians. I didn't know him; apparently he had a glass eye after being horned by a bull.

My mother had failed her driving test at least a dozen times, finally giving up hope when she reversed the car into a telephone box. Now she was flirting with the idea of buying a moped so that she could get up to Dyffryn. She wanted to be independent, hating the thought of being reliant on us to come and pick her up. It worried me that in the winter she would be faced with wet slippery roads, ice and snow. She had no affinity with machines. After she bought her moped she did little trial runs up Tram Road, wearing a large red helmet like a glacé cherry. She wobbled a lot, over-revved, had difficulty changing gear, sounding as if she was riding an angry mosquito. Eventually she mastered the basics, especially the crucial skill of balance and the importance of slowing down to take corners.

Dinah was a good-looking woman, bringing a touch of glamour to Penygroes as she zipped around the streets at a heady twenty m.p.h. She still dressed fashionably, and turned a few heads amongst the men who, completely out of character, would bashfully introduce themselves, offering their services if she were in need of a handyman, or someone to mow the lawn and look after the garden. Cards were pushed through her letterbox and Ted Williams, the womanising window cleaner, couldn't wait to get his chamois leather out.

And these were the dour, insular menfolk of the village, who had never once come forth to shake my hand. What a difference a pretty woman made. I imagined nervous wives behind net curtains feeling threatened by the blonde bombshell on the moped. But my mother thought it all jolly good fun and was determined to play an active role in village life. She organised Welsh lessons from the chemist Owen Bethel, a widower of some years, who out of hours was seen walking a sad-eyed bloodhound up and down the high street. A man of unbroken routines, he would sit in the snug in the Vic, downing a pint at eight each evening, leaving promptly twenty minutes later. It was rumoured he had a stash of cash hidden away, and he was the only person in the village who had been on an aeroplane. Every year, the first week in July he flew to the Costa del Sol. In his early sixties, he was a man of some standing in the community. I knew he would make a play for my mother and I told her so. 'I'm old enough to look after myself,' was all she said.

One of the old Welsh superstitions is that you do not eat pork unless there is an R in the month. In August the price of pork was at its lowest, but probably because everybody was on holiday, reducing the demand for it. However, I had a batch ready for FMC and booked in for Friday, and rather than worry about the price I was going to get, decided to go ahead and take them to the abattoir. Harry offered to lend me his Austin A60 van, not wanting me to have to pay Gitto, the local haulier from Groeslon, who would turn up late and clobber me for twenty quid in cash there and then.

'The wipers are buggered, but it has got a tax disc,' Harry said. 'It will carry the pigs no problem.'

So Rob and I loaded eight whining porkers into the back of Harry's van. It was a warm, beautiful summer's morning, with not a cloud to be seen. Jack was being a guinea pig for Rose Tobias who was attempting her first portrait painting, and Ros and the children were over in Harlech, enjoying themselves on the beach with Gwyn and Eryl. Harry was going to investigate why the water levels had dropped so low in the stream, and I was giving Rob a lift into Penygroes. He was going to put a card in the newsagent's window saying *Caravan wanted. Must be in good condition.* He'd felt for some time that he shouldn't be sharing the house with us any longer. It was our family home and he wanted somewhere private, so we agreed a caravan should be parked below the house. We would run an electric cable to it and then he could have his own space, put in a TV if he wanted to, listen to his own music.

He was also going to have a chat with Tom ''Tatoes' (pronounced Tatters), the greengrocer, who drove twice a week to Liverpool and came back with a lorry-load of vegetables to sell in his wife's shop in Union Street. Rob could smell a business opportunity, thinking that if Tom was driving all the way to Liverpool every week, he would save a lot by selling locally produced vegetables instead. Harry was convinced he would be interested. Rob volunteered to discuss the idea with him for two reasons. One, because he thought we should grow more potatoes in the top fields. And two, because Tom 'Tatoes had an attractive daughter, the only girl in Penygroes who interested him.

So, after dropping Rob off, I drove to Caernarfon with a van full of pigs. I was wearing only a T-shirt over a pair of jeans, but with the heat coming from the porkers the windscreen steamed up and I lowered my window.

I was in a particularly good mood. I don't know why, but stuck in my head was Shirley Bassey's 'Big Spender'. I'd always sung my own version; the children loved it. *'The minute you walked in the room, you could see I was a man in suspenders, great big suspenders, good looking, so refined, honey, honey, won't you tell me what's going on in your mind?'*

Approaching Caernarfon high street, the traffic came to a standstill. After a few minutes horns began to sound and people were leaving their cars to find out the reason for the hold-up. Apparently a lorry had broken down, so I turned off the engine and sat in the sweltering heat, hearing the pigs behind me getting increasingly agitated. The van was becoming like an oven, so I opened the passenger-side window in an effort to circulate some air. That was my big mistake. With no grille separating the back of the van from the front, in a split second one of the pigs had jumped over my shoulder, out through the open window, and run off down the high street, scattering pedestrians in all directions. It disappeared into the crowd of shoppers, moving at such speed that I lost sight of it. It didn't help matters that some of the motorists who had seen what had happened leant on their horns, and cheered as the farce unfolded. I had to think fast, and winding up the windows I leapt out of the van and chased after the blighter. We were in the middle of the tourist season; families ambling with their children sucking lollipops prevented me from getting up any speed. The whole atmosphere in the street was one of a fiesta. By the time I had zigzagged through the nearest group I had no idea where the porker had gone.

'If you're looking for a pig it's in WH Smith's,' shouted an elderly lady.

'It's probably gone to pick up the *Radio Times*,' I heard some joker with a Brummie accent quip.

I charged into the shop to find the fugitive tearing a book by Enid Blyton to shreds. On the floor lay the half-chewed remains of a box of crayons.

'Don't worry,' I said to the customers cowering in a corner. 'Stay calm, it's only a pig.'

Some chap was approaching holding a broom, thrusting it out like a lance.

'Leave it to me,' I said. Grabbing the escapee's back legs and lifting its arse high in the air, I forced it to walk forward on its front trotters. Step by step we made our way to the door, past a shop assistant holding a mop and bucket. Somehow I tiptoed the porker through the astonished crowd, inching our way up the street. I displayed an exaggerated nonchalance, smiling politely as if it was no more than an everyday occurrence.

It's always best to downplay these things. The public don't know the damage pigs can do, and bloody quickly! This one would have destroyed most of the shop in half an hour. Now all everyone could see in front of them was a pig being manhandled, screaming and squealing as if in extreme pain. Nothing could have been further from the truth. Pigs like to ham it up.

The traffic was now on the move, although at a standstill behind the van. Despite no offers of help, I managed to get the pig to the back doors. Some of the onlookers had now taken out their cameras and were photographing the debacle.

'Please,' I shouted, 'can someone open the door!' and at last a policeman came forward, and between us we lifted the porker back into the van.

Out of breath and sweating like a pig myself, I realised the ordeal did not end there. The police officer insisted on questioning me about the incident.

'You say the pig was in WH Smith's,' he said, finding it hard to keep a straight face.

Then Branwen Pryce, the shop manager, appeared, asking what I intended to do about the damage. I gave her my name and address, telling her I would settle up when I returned from the abattoir.

'I will of course have to report the incident to head office.'

'So it really was in WH Smith's,' said the disbelieving policeman.

Within hours the whole incident was common knowledge. That night the telephone rang several times, one of the calls coming from a reporter on the *Caernarfon Gazette*. I could see the headline already: 'Pig causes mayhem in WH Smith'. Everywhere I went for the next two weeks people wanted to hear about it. My mother told me I was the talk of the village, that she had received lots of invitations to afternoon teas. 'Got yourself written into Welsh folklore,' was how Dewi described it. 'Something I've been trying to do for years, and you managed it with a pig that decided to go shopping.' When Ros and I took the children up to the Carmel school to be introduced to Bob Parry, the headmaster, he too had to mention it. And so it went on until gradually it faded away, and I was left in peace.

Over in Pant Glas Rob found the caravan he wanted. Stuck away in the corner of a field, it had been rented out to tourists in the summer months. It had all mod cons: a Calor gas stove, a little kitchen area, electric lights, an Elsan loo. The only problem was getting it out; our Massey Ferguson wasn't up to the job. The owner wanted £150 but we had to take it away. So Harry got hold of a mate, Boomer Harris, manager of Talysarn Celts, the local football team, a tractor driver on the Glynllifon estate. He would tow it to Dyffryn for £25. We levelled the ground below the house and Harry ran out a length of cable.

So Rob had electricity, but water was not so easy. From time to time through the summer we had run short, the holding tank not filling up, the stream no more than a trickle. Harry had his own ideas about this: he thought that Gethin Hughes upstream was diverting the flow to irrigate his crops, 'pinching water', as he called it. But we had no proof, and if we were going short, why had Hughie never come to find out what was going on? So I went and talked to him about it. He said he was on the mains, couldn't care less what the water level was. 'Animals piss in it, your pigs roll in it. I would never take water from that stream. Water and walls,' he said, 'the two main reasons men fall out. So what are you going to do about it?'

I didn't answer him, but asked why he was on the mains and Dyffryn wasn't.

'Distance,' he said. 'They only had to run an underground pipe fifty yards from the road down to Llwyndu Canol. You're half a mile away; that would cost at least a couple of thousand. The Mustos couldn't afford that. There's only one thing to do. Go and have it out with him over at Cae Uchaf.'

So I was going to have to face up to a situation I had been turning a blind eye to. All the alarm bells of Mrs Musto's letter started to ring out, but now I had no alternative.

It was less than a ten-minute walk to Cae Uchaf. I climbed the slate stile over the boundary wall, following the stream that ran across Gethin's fields. The water level was low but flowing clear, the well-maintained banks thick with grass and reeds, wild flowers growing in little clusters. I could pick out the sheep track snaking away ahead of me, disappearing through a gap in the wall where a gate had once hung. Above me I could see the farmhouse with its walls of stone under a slate roof. There were a few sheep penned in the yard, which Gethin was funnelling through a weighing machine. His wife, whom I had never met, was leaning over them, dabbing their rumps with red dye. Gethin saw me approaching and she scurried off into the house.

Don came running towards me barking, jumping up, pushing me with his front paws. He could smell Meg and stayed with me, sniffing, until I reached Gethin.

His greeting was friendly enough. 'What brings you here today?' Rather than take the long route through the pleasantries, I went straight to the heart of the matter, expressing my concerns about the water.

'What makes you think I've got anything to do with it?'

'I didn't,' I said, and asked him again if he knew what could be causing it.

'Well, see for yourself how it flows.'

I knew already trouble was coming. I could tell he resented my being there; it was the tone in his voice. So I asked him how much water was coming down from the hills.

'How do I know? It's underground.'

'But it runs as a stream through the fields before it reaches your house,' I said.

Then he turned nasty. 'Are you accusing me of diverting the water, boy?'

'No.' I asked him if he recalled our first meeting, how he had come to Dyffryn, telling me good walls make good neighbours. At this point I noticed his wife framed in the window staring at us unmoving, like someone hidden away in another world.

'You'd better be off,' he said, 'before I say something I might regret.'

I warned him that I wouldn't let the matter rest. What lay behind this man's mean-spirited attitude, someone who had no son to follow him, who was quick enough to exploit Jack's good nature? So I told him that I would take it up with the union, get them to investigate who was diverting the water. As I walked away he shouted after me, 'Don't set foot on my land again.'

Harry was the next person I saw. He knew immediately by the look on my face that things had gone badly. I was short-tempered with him. 'I don't need you to say anything about it. I want no poisoned opinion. It will do no good.'

'Don't take it out on me. It's not me pinching your water.'

When I got back to the house I rang Gwyn and told him what had happened. I needed some calm rational thinking. I was furious, and wanted to vent my anger. He listened to every word, and at the end of my diatribe said that ignorance is a heavy boulder to roll away from a closed mind.

Rob thought calling in the union was the right thing to do, while Jack said we should keep a door open with Gethin. 'You keep it bloody open then,' I snapped. Ros, apart from saying how disappointing it all was, seemed undisturbed, sleeping well that night. I couldn't get the thing out of my head.

Tom 'Tatoes rang, and asked me down for a drink in the Vic. Rob had filled me in, following their chat about our plan to grow potatoes at Dyffryn. As I walked into the pub, it came back to me why I stayed away from the place. I felt like a stranger coming to town, walking into a saloon in the Wild West, where the piano player gradually stops playing, heads slowly turn, glasses are lowered to the table. Lined up along the bar, a row of grim unshaven faces were staring into the mirror, watching my every move. Any one of them could have swivelled round, pulled out a Colt 45 and plugged me full of holes. That's how it felt.

But they didn't, and I asked for a packet of crisps and half a pint of light ale. I hate the stuff, but could sip it slowly while I sat waiting for Tom beneath the propeller-blade fans that whirled above me. The brightly patterned carpet was marked by cigarette burns and the wallpaper, embossed with curlicues, was covered with the patina of tobacco smoke. At the next table an old timer with a Jack Russell lit a Capstan Full Strength. Sitting opposite, his wife, no doubt of many years, was staring past him, lost in her own thoughts. Each time she took a drink from her sherry glass, with her head tilted back he quickly slipped a crisp into the dog's mouth. On the jukebox Ricky Nelson was singing 'Travelin' Man', a melancholy song about someone who was always moving on, unlike the drinkers in the Vic, who stayed put, bound to their habits; you could see it in the look of them. This was a man's place, women didn't come in here on their own. On Sundays the men would stay sober, clean shaven in their suits, walk with their wives to the chapel to pray for the mitigating circumstances of their lives to be taken into consideration. A way of thinking can spread like an infection through a small community; it can get into the bloodstream, nobody having the antidote. It leads to fixed opinions and hardened attitudes. There are no new ideas here, I said to myself.

'Sorry I'm late,' apologised Tom 'Tatoes pulling up a chair, putting down on the table a pint and two packets of peanuts. 'I saw you had a drink.'

Tom, at a guess in his mid-forties, exuded a positive energy. I warmed to him and his wife, the way they ran the shop, always welcoming. We talked about his business and I told him what I wanted to do at Dyffryn. He was keen, thinking of the future and his daughter Angharad who would take over the business, knowing that changes had to come.

'I'm not sure about all this organic stuff. Maybe down south, but here I don't think so, not in my lifetime.' It wasn't long before an hour had passed. He was on his third pint, me still sipping on my half. 'You drink as though you're having a cup of tea,' he said.

Tom was the first man in the village I felt a kinship with. We agreed to meet again and that Angharad would come along. 'And bring your friend Rob. He seems to have a lot to say on the matter.'

We were now making monthly runs to the abattoir, and rather than repeat the experience of the WH Smith fiasco we hired Gitto for cash up front and no invoice. He was good mates with Harry and they doubled up in the Quarryman's darts team. He had the look of a man who fell out of bed each morning, his thick curly hair matted with insect life; he was obviously without a woman. A wren could easily have been nesting in his untidy beard, and his ruddy complexion reminded me of Jethro Tull. From the evidence of his bumper and smashed wing mirrors, he was not a skilful driver. Every time he reversed through the gate at Dyffryn, removing more paintwork, his reaction was, 'I'm much better when I'm going forward.'

Our system for loading porkers was now almost foolproof. When Gitto eventually lined the lorry up with the holding pen, we placed barriers of corrugated sheeting either side and ran them straight up the ramp and into the back. Ninety-five per cent of our pigs graded A; they looked lean and healthy. Rob and I worked well together. We knew the routine; always after a batch left the place there was the inner satisfaction of a job well done.

Jack was now a full-time working shepherd. We only saw him in the evenings when he came by for a drink and a smoke. We talked about our day, and then he'd be off up to Rose Tobias's cottage, while Rob enjoyed cooking his own meals and would disappear into his caravan. Ros and I would get the children to bed and then eat together, the house quiet and calm, just the two of us. She was keen to push ahead with selling vegetables and to get Harry to butcher our pork, which I could sell door to door in the neighbouring villages. She knew we weren't making any money, but she didn't know how much we were losing. No one would ever know, unless they asked to see the accounts.

'We'll get it right soon, then we could think about having another child,' she said.

At which point I turned on the record player and pulled from the shelf one of my favourite Van Morrison tracks, and my brown-eyed girl and I went a-laughing and a-running upstairs to bed.

7

Just a-Walking the Pig

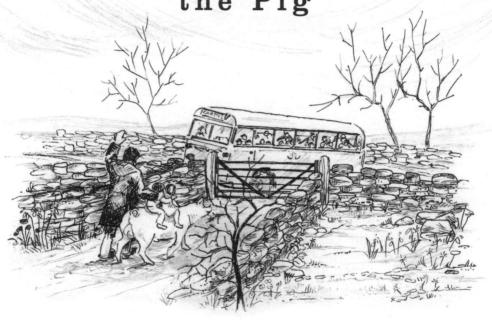

Within us all, to varying degrees, there is the need to take risks. I had taken us to the edge, stood on the financial cliff and stared into the abyss. I decided we had to take a giant step forward if we were going to become viable. In other words start making some money. I was going to have a cold store built in the barn adjoining the house. It would cost £1,000. We had pork, lamb and now at last beef coming through, and to exploit this fully we would butcher our own meat and sell direct to the end user, where the profit was to be made. Everyone agreed. I didn't feel alone, just nervous.

It was now the spring of '74, and all our food came from the farm. We had grown half an acre of wheat which we'd cut by hand using sickles and scythes; after gathering the sheaves, we threshed the grain into metal drums which we emptied into sacks. We had stored it over winter, and now Ros and I drove to Anglesey, where it was to be stone-milled into a fine flour. We decided to disappear for the day; I'd never explored Anglesey. After dropping off our sacks of wheat we drove to Plas Newydd and wandered along the Menai Strait. Looking across at Snowdonia on a spring day when the sun is high one can see the grass greening, advancing up the hills. The blueness of a clear sky accentuating the silvery waterfalls, a gentler face comes upon the solemn grandeur of the mountain ranges.

And so we walked, and had lunch in ancient Beaumaris with its castle, looking down on a beach that stretched for ever. Where sea birds floated between the yachts, Ros recalled her days here as a child when holidaymakers were few and only the locals dared to swim, for not even in the height of summer did the water warm. Late in the afternoon this little interlude in our lives came to an end and we made our way back to Newborough to pick up our flour from a Belgian farmer called Boinders who had farmed here since the war. Weighed down, we drove back to Dyffryn, Ros with her hand on my knee. All day she had felt like my girl friend, as though we were back in the past.

We reached another milestone when Ros carried our first loaf from the Aga. Although we should have let the yeast settle for forty-eight hours we couldn't wait that long. We sat around the table eating warm, buttered slices of freshly baked wholemeal, savouring the taste of each mouthful. Give us this day our daily bread. Sam and Lysta spread honey on theirs, Rob Marmite. Between us we ate the whole loaf. It was a meal in itself, our efforts rewarded, with wheat that we had grown no more than fifty yards from the table. Good for body and soul.

Every building was now full of pigs; we had forty sows and two hundred porkers fattening up. We'd planted three acres of spuds which Tom 'Tatoes was selling in his shop in Penygroes and wholesaling to the smart hotels in Llandudno. It would tell us whether we had a market for organic produce, apart from those individuals who cared about how vegetables were grown. We weren't selling to the middle classes in Tunbridge Wells. In that part of the world health food shops were springing up. There people had larger incomes than the rural population of North Wales. On one of our walks, Gwyn told me it was the right idea but too soon; he thought there would not be much interest from a community that of necessity believed in thrift. But people were getting to know about us. Through Vida Koeffman, Jim Best and Rose Tobias a network of people was building up who were prepared to pay a premium price. My mother, too, had joined various groups and was propagating the idea that Dyffryn's organic foods couldn't be beaten for taste.

Ros put together boxes of vegetables fresh from the soil. Earthy, with nothing topped or tailed, leaves and roots attached; at three pounds a box we were making money.

Harry came up on Thursdays and jointed the meat. We weighed and bagged it, stuck a price tag on. On Friday mornings I loaded the van, a Morris 1000 that my mother had lent us the money to buy, and began my weekly deliveries through the villages of Caernarfonshire. I was able to undercut the local butchers, which I knew might lead to conflict, even a price war, as I built up the sales. Feuds here lasted for years; Gethin Hughes hadn't spoken to me for fifteen months. Even the union man, who had received no reply to his letters, had been turned away at the gate. Following a solicitor's letter and the threat of court proceedings the water finally flowed again, clean and uninterrupted, but there had been no reconciliation, and once when we met at the Paragon garage, he gave me a threatening glare, spitting at the ground in front of me.

'There's bad blood in the man,' is what Hughie said. 'But it will die out with him.' At least with Hughie we had achieved a polite level of mutual toleration. He had his own troubles with Bryn, Dewi having told us the boy had problems holding his alcohol on a Friday night.

Rob's hopes of having a fling with Tom 'Tatoes' daughter Angharad were short lived. They did get together for a time, had a drink in the Vic, played darts, climbed Cwm Silyn. But it went no further than that. She was the only attractive girl in Penygroes and, what's more, she was switched on to new ideas. Who knows why it didn't work between them. Maybe because Rob was a traveller. He'd grown up in the metropolis, walked around India, pursued and lived a spiritual life. I couldn't see him staying much longer at Dyffryn. One day he'd roll out a map of a foreign land and hit the road again. He was still searching, whereas my brother had found a way of life that completely suited him. Jack was planning for us to rent another fifty acres of grazing, up at Cesarea above Carmel. A wild, remote place where the wind was fierce. I'd been there with him to take a look. We could only hear each other if we stood shoulder to shoulder, and were both hoarse after ten minutes. Meg's fur stood on end, the wind buffeting her like a toy. The whole place was exposed, with only the odd tree bending away from the prevailing winds. In winter the snow would fall heavy and deep. I gave him my opinion that we could only keep sheep here for six months of the year.

'Do you think I'm a fool? Of course I know that.' Then he told me the rent: 'Two hundred pounds a year, that's cheap. We could fatten lambs up here in the summer.'

We decided to take it, and when he told me an Englishman living in Shrewsbury owned it I said, 'Can't we do a deal with him? Let's offer him some meat for his freezer, if not for all of it, at least for part.'

'Not everyone is receptive to bartering,' he said.

'Try him; offer him a hundred quid and a pig for the freezer.'

Jack just laughed. 'You really are a wheeler dealer, aren't you?'

'One of us has to be,' I said.

'You're becoming just like them,' he said, shaking his head.

'No I'm not. I'm learning how to survive, that's all.'

On Friday, with a van full of meat and boxes of vegetables, I drove to Llanllyfni to knock on the doors in the high street. I had dressed for the part, wearing a white coat and a Panama hat. It was easier than I thought to tempt the householders to the back of the van, offering a ten per cent introductory discount. My sales pitch was 'local produce, farm fresh, brought straight to the door at prices cheaper than the shops'. I had sold out by lunchtime, hadn't even got all the way down the high street. I'd taken over one hundred and eighty pounds; a much larger profit, three times in fact, than if we had sold to FMC.

I was back at Dyffryn by half past one, when I saw Rob chasing a sow out of the potato field.

'We've sold out already,' I shouted.

'Help me get this bugger back.'

In my white coat and Panama hat I joined Rob as she zigzagged ahead of us. I knew this sow, a regular escapee. She enjoyed the fun of the chase. She'd let us get close, then be off again. Wearing leather shoes with no grip, I wasn't up to the task, but she ran into a dead end where we thought we had her cornered. Even then she wasn't finished but squeezed past us and made her escape down the drive past the house towards the lower fields.

These breakouts had become almost a daily occurrence. If a pig can work something loose it's like a child who keeps wobbling a tooth until it comes out. The bolts slotted into the wall were never a tight fit, so the sows played with them constantly. Eventually gaining unexpected freedom, they roamed at large, causing havoc. I put it down to boredom. I was always telling Jack that the way to tell pigs are much more intelligent than sheep is that they get bored. I told Harry we should change the name of the farm to Colditz.

If it happened during the night they could be a danger to themselves. One morning we found a gilt lying stone dead in the stream, her four trotters stuck up in the air. We lifted her out and she was unusually heavy. Always loath to call the vet, we carried out our own autopsy. With a scalpel I cut open her stomach, and saw it was full of a partly congealed grey powder, some of which had hardened into concrete balls. A mystery, until we discovered that after her escape she had broken down the door of the shed where we kept building materials, found a bag of cement powder and scoffed the lot. Naturally, after that she had needed a drink and made her way to the stream to quench her thirst. I cut enough cement out of her to make half a breeze block. It was no laughing matter, just another item for the loss column.

I had to get out of those clothes. On my way to the house I was met by Sam and Lysta who were involved in their own little drama. Both carrying bamboo canes, they looked most concerned about something.

'Dad, quick, come and see.'

'What is it?'

'There's a snake in the loo and it's alive.'

They dragged me towards the lavatory.

'Where's Mum?' I said.

'In the vegetable garden with Granny. Dad, it's a huge snake.'

'Why have you got those sticks?'

'We've been trying to get it out.'

I leaned over the loo bowl. It was grey, curled up, looking at us with a serpent's face.

'It's not a snake,' I said, 'it's an eel.'

'What's an eel?'

'It's like a snake, but it lives in water.'

'Shall we kill it, Dad?'

'No!'

It had obviously come down the stream and into the holding tank, slid along the pipe feeding the house, and ended up in the loo. It was a repulsive sight, and I supposed we would have to flush the thing away to meet its doom in the cesspit. But during these gruesome deliberations Ros and my mother joined us.

'What are you all doing in here?' Ros asked.

'Take a look for yourself.'

'Oh, how frightful,' said my mother. 'It's an anaconda.'

'No, it's just an eel. I was about to flush it away.'

'No, don't be so horrible. Get me my Marigolds,' said Ros.

She grabbed the eel behind its head and put it into a plastic shopping bag. We carried it out to the stream, released it below the holding tank and watched it slip away to continue its journey downstream, none the worse for its experience.

Sam and Lysta were straight on the phone telling the whole story in Welsh to their grandparents.

They wouldn't settle that night when we got them to bed, asking if it could happen again. 'Could one come down the bath tap?' Lysta wanted to know. 'I'm frightened of sitting on the loo.'

Such had been the distractions since my return from a highly successful morning in Llanllyfni that it was only at supper, when Jack and Rob had joined us, that we talked of the exciting possibilities that lay ahead. There was no false optimism in our discussion of what I truly believed was a turning point in our dire financial situation. Ros suggested we print business cards to put in letter boxes, asking people to telephone if they would like us to call. And what a response we got! I never knew there were so many people with freezers, most of the calls coming from customers wanting a price for half an animal. Our margins weren't as good when people bought in bulk, but it was still better than selling to FMC. The money rolled in, mostly cash from door-to-door sales. We banked it every Monday, Geoffrey Nicholls warming to me as the loan diminished.

One Monday he saw me standing at the counter depositing another £300 and he signalled to me to come and join him in his office. I had always felt his friendliness towards me was exaggerated, because of his relationship with Gwyn. But today his expression showed a self-satisfied smugness. I sat with him as he examined his fingernails, softening me up with superficial flattery such as 'You must be feeling very proud of yourself'.

'Just pleased to be paying off the overdraft,' I said.

He changed tack then. 'What an extraordinary man your father-in-law is. He's been telling me about the new paediatric ward that's opening soon. We're all helping to raise the money, each of us doing our bit.' But, finally he got to the point.

'A baler.'

'A baler?' I repeated.

Had I thought about buying a baler, rather than bringing in a contractor?

No, I hadn't.

'I could extend the loan. Perhaps you should consider it.'

Maybe I would, but rather than giving him an answer I suggested he should support my enterprise and buy half a pig for his freezer. It startled him somewhat. I said, 'You do, of course, have a freezer?'

'Yes, in the garage, next to the golf clubs.'

'Well,' I said, 'have a word with your wife. I shall look forward to your order.' I shook his hand and left the office.

Geoffrey Nicholls had seen another side to me that day. I'd come to realise that banks are sellers, just like any other business. Psychologically, we go to them cap in hand, our heads bowed, pleading with them to agree an idea's viable. But Geoffrey Nicholls' business was lending money, so why shouldn't he become my customer just as much as I was his. Maybe Jack was right when he said that I was becoming like them. But I hadn't pushed my luck too far, for the very next day his wife Gwenda rang, ordering not half a pig but a whole lamb to be delivered to their house in Bontnewydd.

It had crossed my mind that every day Dave wasn't shagging he fell into a state of boredom, pacing his pen and chewing the metal bars of his prison. It had always been my plan to run him down in the lower fields. But this was not possible for he needed to be near the sows after their piglets had been weaned. His presence stimulated their cycle, helping to bring them into season. Not a good idea to remove him from his kingdom and keep him far away, even if it meant he was living a more interesting life. So, just as one walks the dog, I walked the pig. Or rather the pig walked me. Dave never knew his own strength, and although he ambled along in what you could describe as a pedestrian fashion he was unaware that he was pulling the ball out of my shoulder socket. As Lysta watched me struggling to hold him she told me I'd soon have one arm longer than the other. This remark brought tears of laughter, as Sam imagined me having to wear a pullover with an extra-long sleeve.

When the children began at Carmel school I decided Dave should accompany us on the walk to wait for the bus that crawled up the hill from Penygroes. His lead was a double-linked chain attached to a metal ring on a studded leather collar. Very diamond Del Monte. We could see the single-decker bus some way off, labouring around the tight bends. It would appear then disappear, a thin exhaust cloud floating across the fields like a blue halo carried on the breeze. When we spotted the bus passing the cemetery gates we knew that it would arrive in three and a half minutes and in that time, every morning, we started to train Dave as one would a dog. We all had a go at trying to make him sit, but to begin with it was a complete waste of time. Sam lifted up his great floppy ears and shouted 'Sit', but it had not the slightest effect. However, in the animal as well as the human world, treats are a big incentive. Bribes serve a purpose, and Dave's taste buds succumbed to a broad spectrum of delights. So on these morning walks to the farm gate we filled our pockets with whatever we could lay our hands on. Toast crusts with Marmite were a particular favourite, and banana skins. It took a week, but eventually we got him to sit, not exactly like a dog because that would have flattened his balls, but slightly to one side in a rather elegant pose, his head always tilted upwards, fitting for a king from a long line of masculine success. Dave did indeed have a regal presence.

And more was to emerge from this pig with a developing personality. One morning Sam and Lysta were in the doldrums and were too grumpy to do anything, lagging behind, grumbling, dragging their heels. I shouted to them, 'Come on, Dave will give you a lift to the bus.' And to my surprise he readily accepted them, allowing them to ride him like two little jockeys. Sam and Lysta told their classmates how they arrived to wait for the bus, but no one believed them, so the next day when the bus pulled up there they sat astride Dave, holding their satchels. A busload of faces pressed to the windows. It became a daily occurrence if the weather allowed it, until Sam brought home a letter from the headmaster.

Ros read it to me over supper after the children had gone to bed.

Dear Mr and Mrs Perry

It has been brought to my notice that your children ride on the back of a pig to meet the school bus. Although this does not contravene any of the school rules, they unfortunately bring the smell of the animal with them into the classroom. The unpleasant aroma lingers, and some of the children sitting close by have been seen holding their noses.

This of course is a distraction to the teacher, who has informed me she does not have the class's full attention. If you could please resort to a more orthodox mode of transport, namely walking to meet the bus, this would be greatly appreciated by all members of staff.

Yours sincerely,

Bob Parry.

Rob now covered for me on the farm on Fridays and Saturday mornings. Leaning over the gate into Frieda's field one evening, watching an autumn sunset glowing over a phosphorescent sea, we discussed his being paid a wage. I would be lost without him. As we passed a joint between us, I said how about thirty-five quid a week. 'Cash, of course, on top of full board and lodging, I think they call it.'

It took him by surprise, and he told me it was far too much. 'Give me twenty,' he said, so we settled on twenty-five, the first time I'd had to bargain in reverse.

He did ask for some perks to be thrown in. He wanted the Land Rover on Sundays to get away from the place, go further afield than Penygroes. Who could blame him? 'Fine,' I said, realising that would be the end to any over-indulgences on a Saturday night. It was the only time Ros and I went to town with each other, the way we used to.

Standing there in that chilling evening, as the stars illumined the heavens while the Wicklow Mountains darkened like the spines of prehistoric creatures, we turned to talking of other things. Rob wondered why we were here. 'The ultimate question,' I said.

'No, not here as in why do we exist, but here in North Wales. What's it all about, this bit of our lives?'

I struggled for an original response, considering feeble alternatives such as 'It's better than living in a city' or 'Well it's a good place to bring up children, living off the land'. But I supposed he meant the way of life, hard as it could be. 'It's probably my favourite way to waste a bit of time.'

'What, living here at Dyffryn?'

'No, leaning over a gate watching the twilight unfolding.'

Then, from an upstairs window, came the call that we had heard far too often. 'Dad, there's a pig out.'

And off we ran, yet again armed with a broom and shovel, pushing the sow back up the drive, cursing the beast for breaking our reflective mood. Nothing could bring you back down to earth like a straying pig.

Harry rang that evening, surrounded by noise and music.

'I can't hear you,' I said.

'I said it's ours. I got it for a hundred and fifty. The sausage-making machine.'

'Oh, good. Where are you?'

'I'm at the left-handed charity darts match in Caernarfon. You sponsored me three quid if you remember.'

'Oh, right. See you tomorrow.'

Harry had never let go of the idea of making sausages, always convinced they would be a money spinner.

Evan Evans, who, without fail, called at least once a week, had not informed me that he would be bringing his regional sales manager, Reg Dyer, to pay us a visit. Evan greeted me as if I were a close friend, with a familiarity I had not seen before. He even handed me a bag of sweets, saying, 'You know who they're for, wink, wink.'

I shook Reg's hand. 'What beautiful views you have up here,' he said, drawing in a deep breath. 'Such wonderful clean air.'

'You can't live without it,' said Evan, laughing loudly at his own joke.

Reg ignored him. 'You know, if I lived up here I'd be a happy man.' In his late forties, he was straight out of the office, wearing the uniform of a company man: navy blue blazer, white drip-dry shirt, striped tie and grey flannel trousers. Evan had told me he had worked his way up from the milling machines.

We ambled around the buildings looking in on the pigs, Evan speaking for me, saying how pleased I was with the service I got from Crosfields. I was also apparently impressed by the fantastic food-conversion rates, the high numbers of porkers that graded A at FMC. It became obvious then why Evan felt it so necessary to portray us as such good buddies. They were looking at his performance. It could have been to do with his sales figures, or maybe something else was going on, but it was clear that Evan had to justify certain things to his regional sales manager. Maybe

I was just one of several clients they would be calling on today.

Reg pulled out a customer information sheet from his briefcase and said he thought I could save at least £1,000 a year if I installed a silo and had my concentrates blown straight into it.

'Gets you away from the tonnage rate,' he said.

'I'll have to think about that. It's a big chunk of capital expenditure. I'm still paying for a cold store.'

'Well don't say I didn't tell you; it would be paid for in three years.'

I wanted to change the subject. I had no interest in buying a silo. 'So, what brings you here today?'

'We're looking at what's going on out in the field, as we do from time to time.'

'Some change is afoot, you mean?' I said.

'Could be . . . could be.'

Evan, now with a wrinkled frown, had lost his joviality.

'By the way,' said Reg, 'you are invited to the Royal Hotel in Caernarfon. It's the annual dinner, when all our customers get together. You know, swap ideas. Your friend Josh Hummel is giving a talk on how to improve food-conversion rates.'

What other subject could Josh talk about? 'Are you sure I'll fit in? I'm an outsider when it comes to these dos.'

'We'll arrange it so you're seated next to Josh.'

'No, please don't,' I found myself saying, 'not for a whole evening.'

The difficulty I had with the pig industry fraternity was my unconventional approach to it. When people share a common belief you have conformity. I lived outside the circle, hence the wide berth Josh Hummel now gave me. He wouldn't want to be seated next to me any more than I did to him.

Halfway up the drive Evan and Reg stopped their car and reversed back to allow an old Austin A60 van to get past them. I knew that van. It was the one I had driven to Caernarfon the day of the WH Smith incident.

'I've got it,' said Harry.

I followed him into the barn, where he bolted the sausage-making machine on to a slate slab, tightening the screws that secured it while I fetched the finely chopped off cuts of meat we'd already prepared from the cold store. We bulked out the meat with sage and onion and a few secret ingredients Harry claimed were handed down from his grandmother. He then slipped on to the metal tube what looked like a huge Durex, but was in fact the hog-gut sausage casing, and began to turn the handle. So we watched Dyffryn's first sausage come into the world. It was a moving experience even if somewhat pornographic. We decided that before we launched them for public consumption they should pass the taste test at supper that night.

We all agreed we had another success on our hands. Sam and Lysta covered theirs with baked beans, soon asking for more. There was a succulence to a Dyffryn sausage you would not find in a commercial brand.

'Maybe a little less salt,' Harry thought.

When I drove up to the Nichollses' bungalow in Bontnewydd, with its manicured lawn, clipped box hedges and a topiary of what I assumed to be a heron, I was impressed by an overwhelming neatness and the effort required to keep it just so. And Gwenda too, opening the front door, was immaculate and well fronted, with rounded breasts under a Bri-Nylon pullover. She liked gold, a glittering light coming from her necklace and earrings. A bracelet of leaping deer encircled her wrist. She stood on the 'Welcome' mat inside the conservatory, beside an umbrella stand full of walking sticks with carved handles. Above her a bright plastic parrot swayed on a brass perch. I was holding two polythene bags of jointed lamb that I placed on a glass table.

We sat amongst the pot plants beneath an old, leafless vine fastened by loops of wire to the white beams. As was often the case with first meetings, I listened to anecdotes of a long-standing friendship between the Nichollses and my in-laws.

That done with, she talked of her own life, her work with the Women's Institute, the Rotary Club. Here I sniffed another business opportunity, as I spelled out what we were doing at Dyffryn. How modern farming methods, through the over-use of chemicals, would turn the earth into a dust bowl. That we couldn't go on taking from the planet, we had to give back. She listened intently, seemed to be interested in my ideas. I even said how important it was to educate our children about these things too, that schools should have at least a bit of land where pupils could connect with the earth and get their hands dirty. She was so enthused she suggested I give a talk on the subject to the WI, which I agreed to without a second thought.

'There will be about twenty of us; can you stretch it out for half an hour?'

'Of course. It's a big subject.'

I was rather pleased with myself as I drove back to Dyffryn. I could see the WI of Caernarfonshire spreading the message, converting to organic produce. But Ros pointed out that to speak for half an hour I was going to have to write a lot of words, pages of them, and not repeat myself. I usually made things up as I went along.

Seeing Jack approaching me with a black eye, my first thought was that he had been head-butted by the ram. It was the tupping season, and the testosterone was raging. But that was not the case; far from it. He'd been on the receiving end of a well-aimed punch, bestowed upon him by a ruffian shepherd over in Rhyd-Ddu. The man had been beating his dog, and Jack couldn't tolerate it. They fought together in a pen full of sheep, swinging punches at each other, whilst the dog fled and the sheep panicked, breaking down the hurdles and scattering across the fields. Idris Owen was the shepherd's name, and he had a reputation for burning a short fuse, spending more than the odd night in a police cell.

After the fracas they lay breathless, their faces caked in mud. But Idris Owen had thrown the first punch and knew he was in trouble. There were no witnesses, and they were out in the wild with the light fading. Owen went on cursing Jack, spitting blood from a cut lip, saying it would be Jack's word against his. But Jack's only care was for the dog, a young collie bitch who had suffered a merciless thrashing. Little did I know, as Jack described her condition, that what followed would have such an effect on my own life. For out there, as darkness gathered around them, Jack and Idris Owen did their own deal. They agreed that if Jack was given the dog, nothing further would be said.

'So you've got another dog,' I said.

'No. I want you to have her. She's traumatised. She can't work; she needs a home.'

I didn't know what to say. A shocked silence followed.

'Where is she now?' I asked at last.

'In the back of the van, shaking, scared out of her life.'

I wanted to say well of course, bring her in, but Ros was over at Trefanai and it needed to be a joint decision. I asked Jack how on earth he'd caught her. It turned out it was Meg who had brought her back; Jack had seen them coming down from the hills together in the falling darkness.

When Rob heard the story he said she could live in the caravan with him. But Ros's heart went out to her straight away, while Sam wanted to hit Idris Owen over the head with a shovel.

Jack carried her into the sitting room. From then on we spoke only in whispers. She never stopped shivering, although not from the cold. Ros fetched blankets, and we made a bed in a corner behind the sofa. She hid herself away as animals do when they're ill.

It was an unusual Saturday night. There was no music, and we said just the minimum to each other. At midnight she had not reappeared, showing no interest in the bowls of food and water we'd put down. Jack slept on the sofa, believing she would take some comfort from Meg's being in the room. In the morning we tiptoed around the kitchen and ate a quiet breakfast. We grimaced at each other if we suddenly raised our voices, and left the house hoping for the best.

As we walked along the footpath beside the Menai Strait, a low mist floating over the still waters, Gwyn told me that the long goodbye was beginning in his life. He said there was a hook on the back of his surgery door where in less than six months he would hang his white coat for the last time. I was never to use the word retirement, or dare suggest that he should be looking forward to it. The thought of holding his last clinic on the last day of his working life depressed him. He'd already heard of the big farewell that was being planned, the local health authority organising an evening when he would be presented with an award. He was a self-effacing man and loathed the idea of having to make a farewell speech. Eryl, who basked in her husband's reputation, was not holding back, dismissing his sensitivities, saying that his lifetime's work should be recognised and applauded.

'The paediatric world will be a poorer place without him,' she said, miffed he had not been considered for an MBE.

That Sunday morning, watching the sea birds floating on the strait, disturbed only by the weekend rowers, he told me things he would never have said in the library, where we spent most of our time together. About his work, the struggle to eradicate tuberculosis from the villages of North Wales. He was a doctor of the people, wanting no accolades for what he had achieved. We walked for another hour, turning back too late to arrive at Trefanai for a one o'clock lunch. Eryl complained that the roast had dried out, and although Ros calmed her down she still scolded us. 'Thoughtless, the two of you, just thoughtless.'

She banged plates down on the table, kicked the oven door shut. As she put the meat in front of Gwyn for him to carve she said, 'Don't blame me if it tastes awful.'

'Nan's so grumpy,' Lysta whispered to Ros. But Sam lightened the mood by reciting his six times table in Welsh and Lysta, not to be outdone, played 'Greensleeves' on her recorder after lunch.

When we returned to Dyffryn the vet, Barry Evans, was just leaving. Jack had got him over to look at the dog, who still lay unmoving on her bed. He had given her a shot of adrenalin, telling Jack it was in the lap of the gods whether she was going to make it.

'Let's give her a name,' said Lysta, suggesting immediately that Poppy would suit her. Ros thought Bryony, while Sam liked Lulu. Later that evening Lysta handed everyone a piece of paper, making us write down the name of our choice. She put them all into a basket and asked Ros to shut her eyes and pull one out. Jack did a drum roll to add to the suspense.

Ros unrolled a piece of paper. 'And the winner is . . . Moss.'

'Moss!'

'Who chose that?'

'I did,' I said. 'It's a lovely name for her, in keeping with Dyffryn. We've got moss everywhere.'

'I like it,' said Jack.

In the days that followed she gradually improved. At first it was no more than tiny things: an ear would prick up when anyone entered or left the room. We hand fed her little bits of chicken; she wouldn't eat from her bowl. She lifted her head whenever Meg came near and they touched noses. She let the children stroke her gently. She wasn't shaking any more, and sometimes she would look out at us from behind the sofa.

I knew for certain that the worst was over when she barked for the first time. She had heard Dewi pull up in his van outside the house. Although she remained hidden, I knew then she would survive. We'd had her for nearly three weeks, and when I told Jack he agreed she was on the way to making a full recovery. We needed to get her outside; she wasn't house-trained, and the sitting room smelled like an old kennel. Ros wanted to open the windows and disinfect the whole place.

So Jack and I walked her on a lead with Meg across the field to the boundary wall with Llwyndu Canol. There we sat with Moss at my feet sniffing the air, her coat ruffled in the breeze.

Only a small circle of bluish purple remained on Jack's eyelid, and a scab on his knuckle, where his fist had connected with Idris Owen.

'I feel we have lived a bit of life now,' I said.

'I suppose we have.'

'Would you want to live any of it again?' I asked.

'No. What about you?'

'Some of it, but only the nice bits.'

Frieda walked towards us, nosy as always, curious to find out what was going on. When she saw Moss she picked up speed, even at her age, her udder swinging from side to side. This aggression was out of character.

'Pick her up,' said Jack. 'Quickly! I'll deal with Frieda. Walk away, or we'll be back to square one.'

So I scooped Moss up into my arms, and turned my back on the stampeding Frieda, while Jack, flailing his arms, managed to stop her just a few feet from us. Moss was calm, completely unaware that half a ton of cow had been charging down on her. It goes to show that even the sweetest creatures will not tolerate an intruder on their territory. You wouldn't have expected it from Frieda, who ambled round the place as a pet. But no harm was done. Walking Moss quietly to the gate I came across Hughie, giving Bryn a dressing down. I might just as well not have been there for all the notice they took of me. But Moss panicked at the raised voices, pulling on the lead, terrified. It was going to take a long time for her to forget the beating she'd received. Idris Owen had a lot to answer for when his day of reckoning came.

Ros's head was thick with cold, giving her the perfect excuse not to accompany me to the Crosfields dinner at the Royal Hotel. I wanted to cry off myself, but Evan Evans had rung the day before, saying how much he was looking forward to seeing us there.

I owned one suit that I'd bought in Kensington High Street years ago. It had flared trousers, with faint stripes running through the cloth. It still fitted me well, but I looked as if I belonged to a bygone era. I'd never mastered the art of fastening a tie, but I didn't want Ros leaning over me with her germs so Rob, who claimed to know what he was doing, half throttled me with a Windsor knot.

My first impression, walking into the dining room under the crystal chandeliers, was that everyone around me was overdressed. There was no mistaking the fact that I stood out, when I would have preferred to be anonymous. To those who filled the glittering room, I must have looked like someone who had just come from a jumble sale wearing second-hand clothes.

I looked for a face I knew, but there wasn't one. I walked around the circular tables searching out the place names, wanting to know who I would be sitting next to. A girl with teenage spots, wearing a flowery apron, offered me a glass of sparkling wine, which I sipped as I stood alone. In a gold-leaf mirror I came face to face with myself and saw just how out of place I looked.

A hand came on my shoulder. 'Perry, good to see you. Where is your wife?' It was Evan Evans, and after I told him Ros was unwell he took me into the throng, introducing me one after another to the valued Crosfields customers.

These weren't real farmers, I could tell by their soft handshakes. No dirt had ever got under these fingernails. They were factory farmers, no more than businessmen, with huge intensive units far removed from my world. After 'Pleased to meet you' no dialogue followed. Having scanned me with indifferent eyes, they turned back to whoever they were talking to. Only the wives smiled, but none would break away and talk to a total stranger. Especially one dressed the way I was.

I noticed Reg Dyer walking towards me, on his arm a redheaded woman, wearing a low cut dress revealing freckled breasts. 'My wife, Rebecca,' he said. She looked at me quizzically.

'You remind me of the singer in Fleetwood Mac.' Nobody had ever said that to me before.

'It's the suit.'

'I love "Albatross". You can float away on that guitar,' swaying as she spoke, closing her eyes dreamily. But Reg took hold of the conversation, keen to get my reaction to the evening.

'It's marvellous.' What else could I have said?

I told them of Ros's head cold, and when Rebecca Dyer realised I was on my own she said, 'There's a band playing later. You can dance with me after we have eaten.'

'No thank you,' I said. 'I have absolutely no rhythm.'

Sitting next to me as we ate our prawn cocktail was a turkey farmer called Hywel Thomas from Criccieth. He reared three thousand birds in air-conditioned sheds with automatic feeders.

'Most people are ignorant about turkeys,' he told me. 'They think they're only ready to eat at Christmas. Nothing could be further from the truth. If I ruled the world turkeys would be on school menus, part of a good hospital meal. As an industry, we don't advertise enough. One day I'll dress as a turkey myself, stand outside the Co-op, see if that improves awareness.'

To my right Isobel Hobart, a bookkeeper on the Glynllifon estate, blew gently on her watercress soup. 'I always feel I'm here under false pretences, not actually being a customer,' she told me. 'Todd, the farm manager, can't stick these sorts of occasions. I suppose it's because he has a speech impediment, a stutter you could say. So they send me along as a sort of representative . . . I've been coming for years now. I even put it in my diary in case I double date.'

After a main course of pheasant, we finished with crème brûlée. Then came the speech from the managing director, who spoke to the audience as one would to a brotherhood, with the sinister embrace that large corporations like to wrap around their customers. What do they really care, as long as we pay our bills?

'To you all,' he concluded, 'a heartfelt thanks.' As he raised his glass, people applauded, rattling their cutlery.

Then the band started up, too loud for anybody to hear a

word being spoken. For the first time that evening I saw Josh Hummel, as he and his wife took to the dance floor.

Now, with all the strobe lighting flashing, I saw my chance to slip away unnoticed. But Isobel Hobart's hand grabbed me and pulled with a strength that belied her petite build.

'Come on, let's twist. It's a silly dance, I know, but I don't care,' she said.

Just as I was leaving I bumped into Evan Evans and his wife Eleri, and lied that I had been looking for them to say goodnight.

When I eventually crept into bed at twelve thirty, the room smelled of Vicks vapour rub. I could hear Ros's congested breathing, and managed to get between the sheets without disturbing her. My eyes closed with the music playing on in my head, images whirling, Isobel Hobart dancing. I didn't have to wait until the midnight hour, or for my love to come tumbling down. I put my arm round Ros's waist and just dropped off.

8

Mirror in the
Bathroom

It was May again, the most wonderful month of the year. Deep green grass, rich in protein, flecked with daisies and purple clover, white trails of blossom scattering across the fields. The air warming. The smell of bread baking was coming from the house.

Shirtsleeved, with Moss walking beside me, Rob and I made our way down to the lower fields to round up the bullocks. Beneath the larch trees dappled light played upon our feet. Dragonflies zipped through the air, hovered over the ivy-clad gatepost; our ears rang with the raucous cry of rooks, busy in the tree tops feeding their young. We were going to move the bullocks up to Cesarea and rest the tired fields where they had spent the winter. Give them the luxury of tasting spring grass, roaming free in their new surroundings.

In the distance we could see them grazing on the raised bank of grass above the bog and heather, a narrow green plateau that ran across the land. I put my hands to my mouth, shouting 'Come on then', and almost as one they lifted their heads. 'Come on then.' Always when they were called they followed their leader, a Hereford-Charolais cross, who walked ahead of them through the ferns, along the track between the clumps of gorse, a mixture of mottled colours, their heads swaying as they lolloped, keen and hungry, expecting to be fed.

We swung open the gate, Moss tugging on the lead, barking. 'Quiet!' I snapped at her, for I wanted them moving slowly, to where Gitto's lorry waited with the ramp down, but it was not to be. They stampeded, running up the lane several yards ahead of us.

I reprimanded Moss as Rob ran after them. 'No! Now stay there!' taking off the lead. 'Stay!' raising my finger. I walked a few yards away from her, watching her, until I told her to come, which she did slowly, her head down, looking miserable. There were good and bad days with Moss. She had to learn, had to be disciplined. I wasn't being hard on her; she was progressing every day. Sometimes she just happened to take a few steps backwards.

'I counted twelve,' said Gitto.

'What? It should be thirteen.'

'I promise you, twelve.'

'There are thirteen.'

'I'll count them,' said Rob, climbing on the back of the lorry, leaning over the barrier. 'I make it twelve.'

'There are thirteen,' I said.

'I'll count them again,' offered Gitto. 'God! I've been counting cattle in and out of lorries for years!'

'Well, how many?'

'Hang on. Stand still you buggers.'

'Well, how many? Come on, Jack's waiting up at Cesarea.'

'There are twelve, on my mother's grave.'

'Well, get going,' I said. 'Count them when you're unloading them.'

'I'll have a bet with you,' said Gitto. 'There are only twelve.'

'OK, you're on. A quid.

'You know,' I said to Rob as Gitto drove off, scraping another layer of paint from his lorry, 'we should have counted them as they came through the gate. Maybe we've left one behind down there.'

'Don't worry, Jack will count them. There'll be thirteen, you wait and see.'

Frieda let me know she was waiting to be milked. Her udder looked heavy. Amazing what happens when spring comes around and the grass perks up; no wonder our spirits rise. Harry swished by on his bike, whistling cheerfully, on his way to butcher the meat ready for my round tomorrow.

Recently back from California, Rose Tobias, wearing a summery blouse that announced it was the weather for flirting, coo-eed for me, asking 'Where's your brother?'

'He's up at Cesarea,' I told her. I hardly ever saw Jack during the working day. He followed his own routine. 'There's every chance you'll see him before I do.'

She went off to see Ros. 'I need to get some of your delicious vegetables.'

I never knew what went on between Rose and my brother. It

could all be a game she was playing. The older woman teasing a younger man. Jack just shrugged his shoulders when Ros asked him about it.

When I had finished milking Frieda and was carrying the milk down to the kitchen to filter it through a fine sieve, Ros came running from the house wearing an apron, her sleeves rolled up.

'All of you come now. There's a bullock in the bathroom!'

'What? How the hell did it get in there?'

'Looks like you owe Gitto a pound,' said Rob.

It wasn't hard to work it out. Before we caught up with them, it had run through the gate into the old garden beside the house. Being such a warm day the back door was open, and the beast had strolled in and wandered into the bathroom. We found it wedged between the wall and the bath, staring at itself in the mirror above the wash basin. My first thought was, how on earth are we going to get the thing out? It seemed to be fascinated by its own image, probably wondering who was looking back at him. For how often does a bullock find itself staring into a mirror? Rob thought it was in a trance, that on seeing its own reflection it had entered an altered state of consciousness. Whatever was going through its head, it at least had a calming effect. Its docility gave us time to work out what we were going to do. Somehow we were going to have to reverse it out. If it panicked we were in for trouble.

Rob suggested fetching the mirror from the hall, believing it would indeed panic if it could no longer see itself. So I crawled along the bath holding the mirror in front of its face, Harry gently tugging on its tail as step by step we eased it out. A deluge of the brown stuff splattered onto the floor. I wanted to, but I didn't let myself laugh, or even smile. Once out of the bathroom we steered it into the garden and back down the drive. Harry said he would be putting in a dry cleaning bill. It took Ros an hour to hose down the bathroom and clean the rugs. It made me wonder whether this sort of thing happened on farms across the country every day, or whether it was just us.

Of course, as Harry was leaving to go and get himself cleaned up Dewi was on his way to the house and got the full story from him. As he handed me the post he gave me that knowing smile. 'Who writes your script, boy?' I knew when I went on my delivery round the next day word would be out. 'Is it true a cow got into your bathroom?' I suppose in a funny way it was good for business.

Evan Evans turned up on Friday morning, just as I was rubbing Ambre Solaire into Dave's pink skin. We were in the middle of a hot spell. I could tell straight away the rep was suspicious of my sexual proclivities. It was written all over his face. I explained to him that pigs suffer from sunburn, and are susceptible to heat stroke.

Evan Evans had come for commercial reasons, to give me, as he said, 'the inside nod' that feed prices were going up eight pounds a ton and suggest, as a friend, I get an order in quickly, before the end of the month. When I asked him to justify another price hike when last year's harvest had been so good, he moved to the safe excuse of world markets. These companies relied on the ignorance of their customers.

'Oil prices,' said Evan.

'I doubt that very much,' I said.

But I would have been a fool to fall out with Evan over such matters. He was, after all, the obedient messenger. However, there was nothing for me to lose by telling head office that I failed to see how they could justify such a price increase, that I might take my business elsewhere.

As I continued to massage sun cream into Dave's back, I told Evan it was my intention to approach BOCM or maybe Spillers. He was aghast, turning away in disgust. 'It's not the end of the world, Evan.'

'It's not that.' he said, 'I can't watch you exciting that boar any longer.'

In the villages now they would wait for me; a lot of them pre-ordered their meat. In the early days I didn't think about the time, often stopping for a cup of tea. But now all that had changed. I could afford no more than five minutes with each customer, otherwise I wouldn't get home until midnight. Sometimes they crowded round at the back of the van, turning it into a social gathering.

I got the stories of their lives in weekly instalments, and although I couldn't speak Welsh I would chuck in the odd word. Those that I could pronounce without swallowing my tongue. They didn't mind, finding my attempts humorous.

'Diolch yn fawr, Mrs Hughes, and don't forget dim parcioyn Castle Street,' as I handed over the meat.

Bit by bit I entered their lives, getting to know their hardships and struggles. The history of those who worked in the slate quarries, why some despised the English who lorded it over them. Every week I found out more about the folk who lived in the remote villages of North Wales. But it was Dorothea that brought it all home to me, the haunting atmosphere amongst those derelict buildings. Everyone in Talysarn had a relative who had laboured there.

When I returned on Friday nights, the first thing I always did was empty my pockets on to the kitchen table. Sam and Lysta made columns of coins, whilst I counted the notes. It was a time of great excitement; when the twins saw all this money they thought we could buy anything we wanted. Lysta couldn't wait to have a pony, Sam a flashy bike. They got neither, instead had to go through the ordeal of inspecting what I had brought home in the 'bartering box' full of children's clothes swapped for meat. No sooner had they grown into something than they grew out of it, but they were at school now, and how they looked was crucial to their self-esteem. So when I showed them the crocheted ponchos Mrs Hughes from Talybont had exchanged for a couple of lamb shanks it was too much for them to bear.

Ros told me bartering was only appropriate when we received something that was actually useful. 'Please tell Mrs Jenkins we only have one teapot. She doesn't need to knit us another tea cosy.'

But I couldn't tell them. These dear ladies were bored, lonely widows in terraced houses, living on state pensions. I told Ros I wasn't just doing a meat round, we were a social service. They'd be very disappointed.

'Well, get them to knit socks. We always need socks.'

'Bobble hats in Tottenham Hotspur's colours,' suggested Jack, the team we had supported since childhood.

Arfon was a rare visitor to Dyffryn. I couldn't remember the last time I'd seen his Land Rover pulling up outside the house. He was a skeletal figure with a sunken face, one cloudy eye half closed, the other darting about the place. Trouble was coming, I could tell.

'Someone has poisoned Mac,' he said, in his hollow, hoarse voice. 'It's not you, boy, I know that.'

He fidgeted, leaning forward, putting his full weight onto his crook. Moving from foot to foot every few seconds, drawing in deep breaths. As well as all his other ailments, he was asthmatic. 'It's been brewing for some time, and I'll get to the bottom of it, you wait and see.'

'Is he dead?'

'Dead as can be. Likely rat poison.'

'Who's behind it?'

'Him over at Cae Uchaf, of course.'

He said I would do well to stay out of the matter, that he would take his revenge. I wondered if he knew that Gethin hadn't spoken to me for months, that I had no dealings with the man. I asked him why he thought Gethin had poisoned his dog, what proof he had.

'The man's a liar. He was brought up on lies.' So I asked him again, but he struggled for breath, unable to speak. Before he could answer Ros appeared from the vegetable garden, pushing a wheelbarrow. With a nurse's eye, she saw the state of him. She put her arm round him and walked him slowly to the bench below the kitchen window.

'Go and get a glass of water,' she said, giving me a look, as if I wasn't dealing adequately with the situation. She sat with him while he drank, and in a few minutes he'd recovered. Speaking to her in Welsh, getting animated, his breathing becoming more strained, he stood up holding onto Ros with both hands and made his way back to the Land Rover.

He hadn't told me what proof he had that Gethin had poisoned his dog. What drove him on I did not know, let alone where he would find the energy to take revenge. Maybe any man is loath to go to his grave knowing old scores have not been settled.

I had now finished writing my speech for the WI. When I read it to Ros she timed it at only eighteen minutes, well short of the half hour Gwenda Nicholls had suggested. Ros said I'd rather raced through it; I should speak more slowly. I did, stretching it out to twenty-one minutes. So I added some dramatic rhetoric about the coming of Armageddon, the opening of the seven seals, the four horsemen of the apocalypse, and the wrath of the Almighty if we did not stop using modern farming methods. I said that the individual can do something about it. Everybody can play a part, buy British, buy organic food. Look after Mother Earth. Then I crashed my fist down on the table, Ros looking up from her watch, saying thirty-one minutes. 'Good. That should leave them reeling in the aisles.'

'If you don't mind me saying, you sound a bit like a religious fanatic.'

As I sat down again in Winford Hook's Porthmadog office, every feeling I'd had on my first visit rolled back over me. I sat in the gloom like a castaway, with my only hope of rescue lying at the bottom of the profit and loss columns. Despite his suggestion, we hadn't taken on a bookkeeper, Ros thinking it another expense and herself more than capable of organising the necessary files. She had filled in the ledgers, showing every transaction clearly in neat handwriting. Every transaction, that is, that went through the books. Some cash had gone into my back pocket, but it hadn't found its way there by some clever plan to deceive the taxman. It was out of laziness more than anything.

Mrs Hook, for that unfortunate woman was indeed his wife, traipsed across the room rattling the tea cups. I thanked her and emptied the saucer, while the cat still slept in the fireplace. Everything was exactly as it had been before, except that Winford was wearing a yellow V-neck pullover under his tweed jacket as he went through our accounts.

The longer I sat there waiting for him to lift his head, the more I rehearsed my responses to his opening salvo. It was a year since I had left here disconsolate, thinking my world was coming to an end. Winford was an unemotional man, adrift in a sea of numbers. My gaze was drawn to the large aspidistra on the windowsill, to the delicate cobweb quivering between its leaves. I was about to walk over and dust it when Hook at last grunted beneath the tweed.

'Well well,' he said, 'the man who reversed the tide . . . well, well. The man who tied the tourniquet around the haemorrhaging wound.'

'Thank you, Hook. Words I can tell you I was not expecting. But as you can see we've worked hard, and the improvement, without doubt, is because I'm selling at a retail price.'

'Duw, Perry, I cannot fathom you. You come over in many different guises.'

It was hard to tell from his expression what he thought. Maybe he was genuinely mystified. He lived in a room of panelled mahogany, tieback curtains, moulded ceilings. It was as if he never left the place, had grown into his furniture, and Mrs Hook was really the dominant one keeping him prisoner. I imagined they lived in a Hitchcock film, his view of the world coming from his clients, the weary hill farmers, pouring out their woes and struggles. I knew all too well his depressing monologue: give it up, son, go and take a job down in the Firestone factory, all is in decline. It made me wonder if he had seen anybody reverse a trend before.

'You have made a profit of four thousand two hundred and eighty-six pounds. The tax man will want some of that.'

After I left Winford Hook's office I went to the Cob record shop, where I spent an hour going through the second-hand LPs, wondering whether they would consider bartering. I eventually came home with six new albums, bought at a knockdown price. It was strange that a shop with such a huge record collection should be found in Porthmadog, but there it was, right on our doorstep.

Sam and Lysta were both down with chickenpox, so Sunday lunch at Trefanai had been cancelled; instead we invited my mother to join us. We hadn't seen her since her holiday in Cyprus. When Moss heard the droning insect sound of her moped outside, she was up at the window scratching at the glass. Fearless now, she ran out barking at the alien with the huge bright cherry on its head.

My mother's skin never tanned, but reddened into a mass of freckles. She'd brought presents for the children, and from her saddlebag produced a bottle of Metaxa brandy. Jack came by with a bandaged hand, fingers crushed stonewalling. Meg and Moss adored each other, and sprinted joyfully up and down the drive. Rob was asleep in the caravan. There was enough noise being made to have woken him, so we sat down to lunch without him. We all thought he must have a hangover.

Dinah was in a particularly happy mood, girlish in fact. Laughing at the most trivial things, even things that just weren't funny.

'What's going on?' I asked.

'Yes,' agreed Jack, 'you're behaving like a teenager.'

'Am I?' she said, pretending to be taken aback at the very suggestion of it. 'What do you think?' she asked, turning to Ros.

'You do seem to be in an extremely good mood.'

'One can surely be in a good mood, can't one?'

'It seems out of character,' I said, 'that's all.'

'Well, maybe I'm in character,' putting her knife and fork firmly down on her plate. We sat in silence, waiting for my mother to gather herself.

'I've met someone.'

Through the rest of lunch we heard the story of her passionate holiday in Cyprus, spent in the arms of a fisherman called Stavros who took her out on his boat and threw his nets into the clear blue seas of the Mediterranean; of cooking *barbounia* over an open fire, drinking the local wine. He had proposed to her, and when she left had cried his eyes out. She passed round photographs of them together, this bearded man who looked like Anthony Quinn in *Zorba the Greek*.

'I think we all need a brandy,' I said, opening the Metaxa, raising my glass, proposing a toast. 'To our mother!'

Rob then appeared with a hangdog expression and slumped down in the chair at the end of the table, head in hands, apologising for his lateness.

'Water, water,' was all he said, and drank straight from the jug. 'I'm sorry. I shouldn't have done that. Bad manners I know.'

'So what happened last night?' I asked. 'Was there a girl involved? Was there any passion?'

'I'm not sure, but I remember she couldn't swim, and when I ran out into the waves to grab her she wasn't there.'

'Where was she?' asked Jack.

'Back on the beach.'

So after my mother's, we had to listen to Rob's story. Saturday night on Dinas Dinlle beach, dancing in the moonlight with the hippies who had camped there for the summer. He could only tell us her name was Kate and that she came from Lancashire.

Then from upstairs came the cry, bringing our lunch to an end. 'Pig out, Dad.'

And like firemen who scramble when the alarm bell sounds, we rushed from the house to deal with another marauding sow out for a Sunday walk.

That evening Ros rubbed a soothing lotion into the back of my neck. I'd suffered two bee stings, even though I'd worn protective clothing. Every time I checked the hives I came away stung. Moss and I were pursued by our attackers and no matter how far we got from the hive they still followed, dive bombing us. In the end I stopped taking Moss with me, after picking several bees out of her coat.

When Jim Best first spoke to me about the life of a bee it quite uplifted me. He told me I would discover some secret understanding of this highly evolved creature. I wasn't so sure now. He was obviously a man at one with them, whereas I'm sure they saw me as an invading predator. Although I approached them calmly, something in me triggered off an aggressive response.

I always lit the smoker and wafted it over the hives, but it never once sedated them. We had a lot of honey, but my only hope of extracting it was to ask Jim Best again for his help. The thought of it pained me, for his health had deteriorated; he could only walk with the aid of two sticks. I was telling Ros all this as she kissed my stings, stroking my hair.

'What do you think your mother will do about her Cypriot lover?'

I had no idea, thinking that although my mother was in her fifties it couldn't be more than a holiday romance. Surely it would fade away after a few tearful love letters. Ros, with her feminine intuition, thought it went deeper than that.

'Anyway, I have something to tell you. I nearly mentioned it at lunch.'

'Don't tell me you're having an affair.'

'I'm pregnant.'

I'd only ever heard that once before in my life. On that occasion, a cold river of fear had swept through me, just as it did now. I lay on my back looking at the ceiling, mentally numb. So I lied, because it is best to lie rather than be dismissive or show little emotion on hearing something Ros was delighted about. And besides, just as before, the thought of it would eventually please me.

'But I'll be glad if it's only one this time.'

So we lay together, with bee stings throbbing in my neck, my thoughts hopping between my mother, my wife, and my two children lying next door with chickenpox. Seven years ago I was a free man without these responsibilities. But temptation is there for a bloody good reason. Without it the journey would never begin. Mind games. I was playing mind games with myself.

'Do you want a boy or a girl?'

'I don't care. One or the other will do.'

It was a blustery night, as I pulled up at the Nichollses' bungalow in Bontnewydd. Gwenda Nicholls introduced me as a young man with alternative ideas concerning the future of farming. As luck would have it, I had developed a twitch in my left eye, a symptom of tiredness which unfortunately coincided with my standing up in front of the Caernarfon WI, a gathering of well-fronted women whose polite applause echoed around Gwenda's conservatory. The flickering of my eyelid made reading my speech difficult, but I'd rehearsed it so many times I could almost remember it line for line. After starting at a gallop I settled into a calmer rhythm, managing to get the pauses between my words just long enough to add the impression of weight to what I was trying to say.

'We cannot continue like this, using more and more nitrates. The earth is a living body, and the over-use of fertilisers will lead to a breakdown in the ecosystem. The delicate balance of Mother Nature will be tipped over the edge. We cannot go on taking, we have to start giving back.'

I went on about pesticides, the damage being done to the micro-world.

'Everything from earthworms to bees, all going about their work, suffering in silence. They need a voice!'

I watered down the Armageddon bit, and the four horsemen of the apocalypse. Ros was right, I sounded too much like a religious fanatic. In the end, although they remained seated, they gave me quite an ovation. And Gwenda, as she passed me a cup of tea, whispered, 'Usually half of them would have fallen asleep by now.'

It had been a successful evening. I was quite pleased with myself. I whistled a lot on the drive home and felt relaxed. My eye settled down; maybe it had flared up because of all the tension I had been feeling.

Frieda was bulling. Her whole behaviour had changed. Restless, flashing her tail, her milk yield had fallen off considerably. I got Barry Evans out and he artificially inseminated her back to a Friesian bull. Vida wasn't sure how many calves she'd had, but we thought this would be her fourth. Now we'd have to start buying milk again down at the Co-op. Or maybe, as Ros suggested, get some from Hughie, who was milking every day. This could be my chance to do some bartering with a neighbour. What did we have that Hughie and Myfanwy needed? Well, meat for a start, and bread, and vegetables. They didn't grow any.

I went over early one morning, when Hughie was having his breakfast. I'd never been in their kitchen before, but there he was sitting over a bowl of cold mashed potatoes with a little pinch of salt added. That, and a mug of tea, was all he put in his belly before he went out and laboured in the fields. They only ate meat on a Sunday; the rest of the week they fed themselves on a stew, kept warm on the old black-painted cast iron range.

Hughie wasn't prepared for my approach. He had no tactics, as Gethin would say. He was sitting down for a start, putting a spoon in his mouth. I was standing up and, besides, Myfanwy would hear every word and hill farmers don't do deals in front of their wives.

I suggested two pints of milk for a loaf of bread, three pints for a pound of potatoes. 'Myfanwy can come over and pick vegetables, if you'd rather, or of course there's the meat. A Sunday joint's got to be six pints, depending on the cut.'

'Duw, boy, I've got gallons of bloody milk . . . she can come over and sort it out with you.'

'It's a deal, then, Hughie?'

'It's woman's stuff,' he said. 'I want nothing to do with it.'

England were playing Australia in the first test at Lord's, so I had a portable radio strapped to my belt as I walked around with Rob doing what we always did: mucking out pigs, emptying wheelbarrows, making a huge manure pile. We moved pigs from their pens, got Dave out on the lead to stretch his legs and changed the bedding, carrying bales of straw over our shoulders.

Moss had taken to nipping at Dave's trotters and stalking the chickens, rounding them up into the corners of buildings. We would find them huddled together in little groups, Moss lying down watching them. It was Harry who first noticed it, that natural instinct in a collie to work, to round up anything that moves. What he said was plain to see, if I'd paid more attention. She was ready now, needed training as a proper working dog. So Jack said let's take her out with Meg tomorrow, up to Cesarea, and see what she can do.

It was late summer, when the grass has slowed and hazy evenings filter the light over the Irish Sea. The combine harvesters were far below us, crawling along in dust clouds across the lowlands. There was a hum at this time of day, when the tiniest things come out to dance. Around us swallows fizzed through the air picking them off, speeding past in the blink of an eye.

Ros, I knew, would be in the kitchen cleaning earth from vegetables, preparing supper. That's when Rob and I liked a quiet smoke. Still warm, in our shirtsleeves, talking about whatever came into our heads. Absorbing the last heat of the sun's rays, pointing out to each other the wisped clouds, the reflecting light on a patch of sea. These moments were never arranged, we just seemed to end up there after the evening feed, leaning over a gate, quiet and contemplative.

When Jack sent Meg off to gather the ewes and lambs up at Cesarea, I kept Moss on a lead. She was keen, pulling hard, wanting to follow Meg, who went off in a wide sweep, lying down behind the flock, watching them run, before Jack moved her nearer on the whistle.

'Slowly, slowly, lie down now,' he shouted at her.

Whenever I watched Jack working Meg it put me on edge: tense, as if witnessing an unfolding drama. There was an unpredictability about it. Sheep live close to a panic button, can scatter easily. A man and his dog are only ever a split second away from losing control. But Meg moved with assurance, reacting to every command in an instant, for she and Jack had trust in each other. I realised Jack had discovered who he was, what he wanted to do with his life out here, in the remoteness of wild places, not needing to be with his fellow men. My brother, happy in a landscape of rock and grass, where the wind has swept back the trees with their branches like witches' fingers, tangled up by the north-westerly gales. The gorse bushes swaying, their yellow flowers iridescent under the racing clouds; a half moon appearing in momentary gaps to be swallowed up in the gloom.

Jack grabbed my arm, drawing my attention to Meg, how far she had hung back from the flock, now gathered up and moving towards us. 'You can't teach a dog that,' he said. 'She just knows it.'

Moss was sitting at my side, her head still, concentrating hard, watching every movement, looking up at me as if to say, 'When is it my turn?'

Then Jack said, 'Let her go.'

I undid her lead. 'You tell her, give her the command.'

'Get away,' and she was gone in a moment, speeding across the field, black and white, curving through greenness, lying down just inches from Meg. Jack on the whistle, edging the two of them forward with short sharp blasts, bringing the flock closer and penning them. He went amongst the sheep, checking the mouths of some, turning over others, shouting to me things that hardly reached my ears in the incessant wind.

Afterwards we sat in the Land Rover smoking, Moss and Meg between us, and talked about how far Moss had come. Jack could tell she was ready by her behaviour today, attentive and keen, and said I should spend time with her now, half an hour a day, bringing her along step by step.

Vida Koeffman, who had become a friend and ordered a box of vegetables every week, suggested we exhibit at the Caernarfon flower and vegetable show next year. She thought it the best way to reach a wider audience, knew of no one who entered organic produce. We were building a reputation, thanks mainly to Gwyn and Eryl's friends. And now, following my successful speech to the WI, we were making inroads into the middle classes of Caernarfonshire.

But the villagers were on low incomes, struggling to make ends meet, and found Dyffryn's organic vegetables too expensive. Sales were stagnant, but meat sales, on the other hand, went on expanding. We were competitive with the local butchers, had the edge on quality and freshness. Eventually I stopped putting vegetables in the van, filling the space instead with mince and sausages.

Occasionally Vida brought up the idea of keeping goats, selling the milk to people who suffered from skin problems. At one time I would have been tempted, but not now. There was enough to do. My days were full, and I could see no return in milking a few goats. Harry gave the idea a big no-no, because goats love to hop over walls and would certainly find their way amongst the vegetables, cleaning us out of everything as we lay asleep in our beds. 'As for those billy goats, they piss all over themselves.' I dropped any idea of it. But we did have some newcomers: four geese who patrolled the farm, letting out a racket when anyone approached. Instead of a turkey we could kill one for Christmas.

'Can't beat a goose on the Lord's birthday,' was how Harry saw it.

As Ros left to drive to Gwyn's farewell do at the Royal Hotel, I watched the thunderstorm over Dinas Dinlle lighting up the sea; those first gusts do not give a clue as to what will follow. Soon the strengthening wind was cracking branches in the larch trees; I could see their roots being lifted out of the ground. It was the increasing force that scared me. I was used to storms but not ones of this intensity. I thought of Ros driving on the Caernarfon road. We were in for a battering, no doubt about it.

Harry rang, warning me we would be blown away that night.

I gave Rob the news and we decided he should sleep in the house. Maybe Jack would come down, I didn't know. Things were already rolling around. Sheets of corrugated roofing that we kept at hand to turn back loose pigs were tossed up by the wind and disappeared over walls. Sam and Lysta were at their bedroom window watching the lightning, counting the seconds before the thunder. It wasn't dark yet, but under the passing gloom of heavy clouds, the whole landscape suddenly lit up. I knew the crash that followed would have terrified the animals out in the fields. I put on a raincoat and ran up to check on the pigs, asking Rob to stay with the children. The infrared lights still glowed over the litters, but I wondered for how much longer. I knew we'd lose some piglets tonight. The wind wasn't constant, but came in ferocious gusts. Doors banged; rain swept into the hay barn, soaking the bales. This was the worst storm we'd had.

I saw car lights turning into Dyffryn, hoped it was Ros coming back. I looked in on Dave, who stood in his run letting the rain lash him. Manly, I thought, but stupid.

I fetched Frieda from the field, moving her into the old milking parlour. It was impossible for me to carry a bale of hay for her; I couldn't walk into the wind. I looked into each farrowing pen, shining my torch. The lights were flickering. There was nothing more I could do, just wait for the storm to blow itself out. And count the cost.

Jack's van was parked outside the house. He too had heard we were in for trouble, with eighty-m.p.h. gusts expected. I rang Eryl; Ros had made it to Trefanai. Gwyn's farewell evening was still going ahead. It was raining in Caernarfon, but there were no strong winds. Ros was going to stay the night at Trefanai.

While we cooked supper the lights dimmed. We lit candles, and as we sat down to eat we lost our electricity. It was eight o'clock, and I wondered what damage was being done outside.

We certainly did not go gentle into that night.

After we'd eaten, Jack and I ventured out. We climbed over the larch trees that now blocked the drive. Only my torch guided us, a single beam of light through an impenetrable darkness. Water flowed at least two inches over our boots. When we managed to reach the farrowing pens I yelled to Jack that we needed to get more bedding for the piglets. We broke up fresh bales of straw, building a protective wall around the litters in an attempt to keep some of the warmth from escaping. We did it with faint hope that it would work. Wanting to feed from their mother, they would wander off to look for her in the cold and damp. Restless, knowing they were scurrying around, the sow could lie down, crushing her own offspring. We had done everything we could; it would be the weakest who would perish.

In the morning the storm had passed. We were still without power, but remarkably the telephone was working. Ros rang, telling me the road from Caernarfon was impassable because of flooding in Groeslon. Gwyn's farewell gathering had gone ahead, although some guests couldn't make it from the outlying areas. Caernarfon had not borne the brunt of the storm.

Gwyn had given an emotional speech and had been presented with a carriage clock in recognition of his thirty years of heroic work for the people of Caernarfonshire. He opened the dancing with Eryl, gliding across the floor to the accompaniment of Percy Faith's well-known adagio 'A Summer Place'.

Sam and Lysta told Ros of the most exciting night of their lives while I went up to inspect the carnage from the night before. This was going to be one of those days when the hard reality of farming delivers a heavy blow to the heart.

In every farrowing pen, Rob and I found dead piglets lying in wet straw. As we carried them out and threw them into the wheelbarrow, the misery of it consumed us, while the sows showed no sign of noticing their loss.

We cleaned out each pen, sweeping them dry, filling them with fresh bedding. Only the strong had survived. By the time we'd finished, we counted thirty-eight who had not made it. We dug a grave using pickaxes and spades, and buried them in a quiet spot away from the buildings. How indifferent Mother Nature is to the destruction she causes.

We'd lost several tiles from the barn roof. Half-fallen larch trees leant against each other, their branches entwined. Plastic buckets rolled around, to-ing and fro-ing with the monotonous clink of metal handles scraping on concrete.

After seeing to all the animals and milking Frieda, it was hard to know where to begin. Harry appeared and walked around the place. 'Could have been worse.' He got out a chainsaw and cut up the trees blocking the drive. Jack went down to the lower fields where we had sheep grazing. The only damage was to the beehives. They'd all been blown over and were lying on their sides. He picked them all up and reassembled them, without any protective clothing. Never got stung once.

'Where were the bees?' I asked.

'Climbing all over the hives, thousands of them.'

The morning was calm and blue, only a few puffs of clouds, like scoops of ice cream, moving from north to south. Evan Evans, anxious to see what damage had been done, called in offering to help. In the boot of his car he had overalls and wellingtons: 'I'm here to get my hands dirty.' My mother had telephoned. She too had no electricity and would come up to make lunch. So an army of us worked together, putting everything back in place. After Harry cleared the trees, Jack left to go up to Cesarea. Sam and Lysta busied themselves with their wheelbarrows, sweeping up anything that moved. Evan Evans, not a man used to physical work, held ladders that Harry climbed to begin replacing the missing tiles.

At four o'clock in the afternoon our power was restored; at last the piglets slept in warmth. At six Ros returned home, and after a disruptive twenty-four hours a word I rarely used, 'normality', tiptoed back into our lives.

I checked the freezer: everything had remained frozen. The

meat hanging in the cold store, although no longer chilled, Harry assured me was still fit for human consumption. So we had lost only the piglets, but in four months from now, when they would have been ready for slaughter, a gaping hole would appear in our cash flow.

Dewi walked into the kitchen at 6.45 p.m. saying he could murder a cup of tea, telling us of the devastation he had seen. Raif Williams, down in Pant Glas, had lost six cows, electrocuted when a power cable came down from a pylon. Caravans in Pontllyfni had been seen somersaulting across the fields. In Penygroes high street a lamp post had crashed into a window of the bank, setting off the alarm.

How were his Welsh Blacks, I asked him. 'Duw, they stood single file below a wall all night. Not stupid, you know, a Welsh Black.'

After he'd carried on for another twenty minutes I said, 'Dewi, what post have you got for us?'

'No post today,' he said, 'desperate I was for a cup of tea. I need the toilet, then I'll be off.'

Dinah rang, and I thanked her for making lunch. The children were in bed, and I was alone with Ros. It felt as though I hadn't seen her for days. She told me she'd had morning sickness at Trefanai. As we lay on the bed I kissed her, felt her stomach. A slight swelling was now visible.

'When is it due?' I asked.

'The First of April. A spring baby.'

The day before, the world had gone mad; now everything had given way to its opposite. Not a murmur to be heard anywhere.

'I feel like saying I love you.'

'Well, say it then.'

So I whispered it. And with the lights still on she fell asleep, while the image of electrocuted cows hung over me, along with somersaulting caravans and a lamp post crashing through the window of the bank.

In my head I was with Otis, and like him I knew a change was going to come.

9

A New Arrival

Jack and I came down out of the clouds above Cesarea with the Land Rover crammed with ewes and entered the blue October morning, past the barbed wire fencing glistening with frost, knotted fleeces freezing in the biting wind. Neil Young was singing 'Out On The Weekend' and we were bringing down the last of the stock for the winter. Jack told me he'd heard that Gethin Hughes' dog Don had been shot and dumped out on the Carmel road. He thought we should protect ourselves, meaning I shouldn't let Moss out of my sight. Again Mrs Musto's words came back to me.

I was sure it must have been Arfon taking his revenge, but I wasn't going to let the pristine beauty of the day be tarnished by the act of a callous heart. We descended into the autumn light of soft blues washing over the metallic-grey sea as the white foaming waves broke along the shoreline of Dinas. The heat from the woollen throng behind us wafted over the back of our necks.

Floating up over Cwm Silyn a flock of birds emerged from the spilling cloud, speeding away towards the Wicklow Mountains.

I told Jack, as I had the previous week, that we needed to sort our mother out, that we should say something. She had read me a letter from her Cypriot fisherman Stavros in which he asked her again to give up her life in Wales, to come and sit on a beach helping him mend his nets. He was ten years younger than she was, and I dared not tell her he was only after her money. Dinah was prone to falling in love; Stavros was not the first. She was attractive, though not in a Rose Tobias way, flirty and leading from the front. My mother had a girlishness about her, and a sensitivity that appealed to men with an extrovert nature who would take on the world, then cry like a child when defeated. To this type my mother offered sympathy and a listening ear.

'She'll be unhappy in six months,' I said. 'We've got to say something.'

'Hatch a plan, you mean, to keep her here?'

'Yes, so she doesn't make a fool of herself.'

'Well, we need to think about it.'

I could tell by that remark it was the last thing Jack wanted to do. It would be me who would have to talk her out of it. I doubted whether she would listen, especially as I had told her once that holding back will get you nowhere in life.

Rob certainly wasn't, now disappearing every Saturday to be with Kate in Chorley. I couldn't let him have the Land Rover at the weekends so Ros gave him the Hillman Imp whenever she could. Now I was really waiting for a change to come; not only might my mother disappear, but Rob as well.

Meanwhile, our four geese patrolled the farm, hardly goose-stepping, but certainly with a threat about them. They were constantly out on manoeuvres, hassling everyone who came to Dyffryn. If they annoyed Frieda she would throw her head about and kick out with her back legs. Moss would have none of their nonsense, but they provided excellent practice for her, because she could not scatter them, only turn them this way and that, zigzagging up the drive.

They chased Dewi's van every time he delivered the post, and terrorised Evan Evans, who never got out of his car until the coast was clear. I told him they were harmless, but he went on about his high blood pressure. They would rush up to him, their necks stuck straight out, honking, their wings flapping.

'I really don't like coming here any more. Can't you shoot them?'

Poor Evan, having to deal with that, and then being told I was going to trial some food with Spillers. At the end of his protestations, accusing me of turning my back on him, he said, 'I thought we were friends.'

'We certainly are,' I said, 'but Evan, they are eight pounds a ton cheaper.'

Hughie would only come to Dyffryn if it was important. It had to be a serious matter.

'Perry, in all the time you've been here, I've never seen you plough a field.'

'That's because I haven't.'

'Well I have a plough that will do the job for you. Three shears.'

'Harry does all the ploughing.'

'Duw, boy, how can you call yourself a farmer if you can't bloody plough?'

Maybe I couldn't, but Hughie was there to give me the hard sell. I remembered that first deal with him, Gethin's words: show you're not interested. So I half turned away, stuck my hands in my pockets, stared at the ground.

'Fifty-five is all I'm asking.'

'I'll think on it. I'm not ready to do a deal now.'

He shook his head, wiping his brow. 'You're not the man you were. Know what they call you around here now don't you?'

'I've no idea.'

'The housewives' farmer.'

It was true, that was where we made our money. It was said as an insult, but I felt no need to defend myself. All I said was, 'I consider that to be a compliment.'

After we'd got the children to bed I told Ros I was going to see my mother, to tell her not to throw her life away on a Cypriot fisherman. Ros thought it was best to let love run its course. It was odd how I felt about it, as if I were dealing with a teenage daughter, not my mother at all.

She was putting the telephone down when I entered the sitting room at Hendy.

'That's it,' she said, with a gleaming smile. 'All done. That was Stavros. Do you know, he rings me from the taverna, and has to book the call four hours in advance.'

'What have you arranged?' I asked, knowing full well I was too late to stop her.

'I'm going next Tuesday. You will look after everything, won't you? Here, I mean. I'll be gone for the winter.'

So I never said a word about what I felt. It was pointless, and would have caused a rift between us. I didn't stay for the cup of tea she offered me. I felt a mixture of anger and sadness. But how did I know what goes on in a fifty-four-year-old woman's mind? Was I being judgemental, or maybe just disappointed that my mother was not content living here with us, and Ros with a baby on the way. Then I realised I was just being selfish. 'Let her go,' I said to myself. 'What's it got to do with you?'

I don't know the origin of the word 'bodge', but we certainly used it a lot. Harry mentioned it often when coming down a ladder. I would ask him, 'How's it gone then?' and he would say, 'You know, I've managed to bodge it.' Make do, is what he meant; nothing permanent, something for now. That's what held Dyffryn together. I wondered when it had entered everyday language.

Much of life on the farm was spent doing running repairs. Since the night of the storm we had cut down the uprooted larch trees, and the old hovel was completely full of logs.

We saw more of Gwyn since his retirement. He would come over in his VW Beetle, after Sam and Lysta were home from school. He loved being with his grandchildren, walking with them round the farm if the weather allowed. Although he did some locum work, sometimes standing in for a colleague, he had time on his hands; after mornings in the library he took the air along the Menai Strait. He wrote essays on spiritual matters, attended Quaker meetings. Eryl continued to play golf, leading her own independent life. He still pursued his interest in the occult world. But it must have taken some adjustment, making changes from a way of life he had followed for thirty-odd years.

Ros detected a sadness about him, and why on earth wouldn't he, a man who had given everything, regret finding himself no longer useful. He would stay as long as he could, the time dictated by Eryl's demands, which he conceded to without complaint. Sometimes when I watched Ros and the children waving him goodbye, I thought it would be for the last time. I don't know why; it would float up in me, a little cloud of its own making. There was no reason for it.

I was now trialling my new 'grow fast' pig nuts from Spillers, a controlled experiment on a batch of ten weaners. It required self-discipline on my part to record the daily feeds, writing down the exact amounts. Spillers offered me discounted rates, and their rep Arwel Jones, a progressive thinker who spoke with a fast tongue and a self-assured cockiness, said the result was a foregone conclusion. He was careful not to criticise Crosfields, instead elevating Spillers as market leaders, ahead of their competitors not only in scientific research, but also in the all-important factor, price. He was one of those new breed of salesmen who didn't offer you a cigarette when they turned up but a Wrigley's spearmint gum.

Evan Evans, still somewhat subdued, paid his weekly visits, but was a wounded soul now. He told me head office were reviewing my account, and Reg Dyer was intending to call on me, no doubt to offer a better price. Rob thought I'd been hard on the man, and maybe I was, but I had to do what was right from a financial point of view. I told Evan how things stood, that at the moment I was a Crosfields customer, and hoped that's how it would stay. But I had to try new products, to find out if I could improve my food-conversion rates. I was sounding like Josh Hummel again.

'I can't go blindly on; sometimes we all have to make changes.'

Then the geese caught sight of him, and he was back in his Austin Maxi, winding down the window. 'You've changed, Perry. You've developed rough edges, man.'

'No longer a pushover, you mean.'

As he drove off, Rob said he felt sorry for him. So did I, but I wasn't going to let it rule my head. Crosfields was a large nationwide company; they were bound to come back and offer me something. Besides, we wouldn't know the result of the trial for nearly three months.

Dewi handed me an envelope addressed to Mr and Mrs Perry, hand-written in italics using a fountain pen. 'Very smart,' Dewi said, hoping I would open it in front of him. 'It could well be from the Queen, asking you to attend one of her garden parties.'

The geese surrounded him, but he stood his ground.

'Open it, Perry. Duw, man, aren't you curious?'

'It's not from Her Majesty. It's got a local postmark.'

'Feel it, there's a card inside. It's an invitation to something.'

'Dewi, it's a personal private letter. Now leave me alone.'

He had this trait, when he got his mind set on something; he couldn't resist worrying away at it like a terrier. It made me think he must have been a horrible child, pestering his parents if they refused him something. His eyesight was deteriorating even further; I'd noticed we'd been receiving other people's post. He read everything with his glasses pushed back on his forehead.

'Dewi, your eyesight's getting worse. When did you last go to an optician?'

'It's only close up stuff. I can see for miles.'

Ros took the letter and opened it in front of us. Dewi's curiosity was satisfied. 'Oh, how lovely. It's an invitation to Tom Felce's wedding.'

'Well, man, what did I tell you? I said it was an invitation.'

Ros grabbed his hand. 'Come on, Dewi, come and have a cup of tea.'

Sam came and asked me, 'Dad, what's a bra?'

He was at that age now, noticing the differences between the sexes.

'Your mother knows. It's something women wear under their blouse.'

'Why don't men wear them?'

'Ask your mother, she'll have a good idea.'

Frieda let me know it was milking time, repeating her party piece of kicking out her back legs and scattering the geese, who had gathered around the gate when Dewi and Ros went inside.

When I got back to the house, Dewi was still at the kitchen table. Ros had removed his glasses and was holding up a piece of cardboard on which she had written letters of the alphabet like those you see at the opticians.

'Duw, I'll be honest with you, they're all a blur.'

'Dewi,' she insisted, 'you must take an eyesight test. You might well be able to see for miles, but close up you can't see further than your nose. What happens if the post office finds out? You'll lose your job.'

Sam told me he now knew what a bra was and why girls wore them. Lysta had told him.

'Oh, good. That clears up one of life's mysteries. Dewi,' I said, 'you do know it's twenty to six?'

'Duw, man, is it? I had no idea of the time. Your wife really knows how to talk.'

'There, it fits you perfectly,' said Mrs Mostyn, her hands smoothing down the front of the pullover she had knitted for me. 'What do you think of it?'

'I like it,' I said, though I was doubtful about the sheep.

'That's a ram. Masculine like you.'

Mrs Mostyn, who occupied her time knitting various garments in exchange for cuts of meat, was one of my regular customers. She was a lonely widow who shuffled around her bungalow in her slippers, her ankles swollen because of water retention. She was a cheerful soul, housebound most of the time, apart from a weekly trip to Caernarfon to play bingo. She had fast hands. In the bottom of our chest of drawers lay the results of her previous efforts: a bobble hat that I was sure I would grow into some day; a scarf that would make a Christmas present for someone. Her family, who lived in Chester, were coming for Sunday lunch and she looked at me pleadingly. 'Could you stretch to a leg of pork?' Of course I could. 'I'll start on some thick woollen socks for you. There's cold weather coming, we don't want you getting chilblains.'

I left, wearing the pullover until Brian the tiler, the Talysarn Celts centre forward, saw me and burst into laughter. 'You look like one of those half-vacant geeks out of the asylum.' So I took it off and put it in the glove compartment of the van.

Friday was always a demanding day. Selling required an enormous amount of energy; you're on show, an entertainer. I would get in and out of the van at least fifty times, going round to the back to open the doors as the housewives came down their garden paths with their shopping baskets. And there the chinwagging would begin, the unfolding stories of their lives. It was difficult to break away and despite my best efforts the round was taking longer each week. It never ceased to amaze me what people had to endure, and the good humour they showed. Living on the breadline, counting the pennies. The sadness of a loss, or a loved one going downhill. The more I got to know them, the more I cut the price when they came up short, rather than let them owe me. I didn't want to call with a notebook of names that were running up a debt. It was a social thing, but now I understood why Dewi would turn up late having been held up chatting. I was not one for gossip, telling Ros only some of what I had heard.

On Friday evenings, with an exhausted tongue and weary legs, it would take an hour or so slumped on the sofa for me to recover, for all those conversations to clear from my head.

Ros knew the history of some of these families. She was never judgemental, and sometimes she would say that many things were predestined, that people were condemned from birth to a future they could not escape from. To me their existence seemed so dreary, surrounded by those great piles of discarded slate. But the rounds were fun, as well as melancholic, and we laughed a lot, especially in the dull dark days of winter when life was at its hardest. Sometimes when I drove through Talysarn on a winter's evening, past the lit terrace cottages, my heart went out to the occupants. I could see them in their kitchens, living out their modest lives. All had become individuals, people I knew.

Dinah rang that Friday night from Cyprus. It was not a clear line, her voice hiccuping, cutting her words short. There was a background noise of bouzoukis, what sounded like plates smashing. I was not sure what she was saying. I kept losing her, getting half sentences before she faded away. With the delay on the line we spoke over one another. I could only guess what she was trying to tell me. If I'd heard correctly, she was coming home on the twenty-sixth. I remembered that schoolboy joke about the army captain who was thought to have said 'send three and fourpence, we're going to a dance', when what he actually said was 'send reinforcements we're going to advance'. Maybe it was over with Stavros, the passion spent. Or the opposite, that she was returning home to tidy up her affairs and would go back to him permanently.

Sunday: a rare day out with Ros and the children, made possible because Rob was not going to see Kate and could look after things at Dyffryn.

It was a bright morning with a sun that needed a shielding hand. Ros had made a picnic. We were on our way to the zoo at Colwyn Bay. Above us the darkened summit of rock cast a weight of shadow that contrasted with the green fields, the whitewashed cottages above the Caernarfon road. You could pick out the underbellies of gulls floating on the currents, while the ebb and flow of light swept over the conifer plantations.

We played I Spy, and for some reason Ros and I sang *We're all going on a summer holiday*, which we weren't: we were going out for the day, and it wasn't summer. But it felt like it, as we all teased each other. It felt good being away from Dyffryn, not thinking about the farm, being a family man. The twins, sitting behind me, let me know they could see a thin bald patch on the back of my head.

'Daddy, did you know your ears stick out?'

Ros suggested we should count how many caravans we could see. There were plenty in this part of North Wales, parked in gardens, rented out to tourists who came from the Midlands and Liverpool for their two-week annual holiday.

At the zoo Sam and Lysta looked at the animals in wonder.

'What is it?'

'It's a porcupine. See all those spikes? They get stuck into whoever threatens them.'

'It's like a hedgehog.'

'It's bigger than a hedgehog.'

'Dad, come and look at this bird.'

'That's an Amazon parrot.'

'Look at the beautiful colours, Mum.'

We watched the gibbons swing through the trees, the sea lions being fed. For Sam the lasting impression of the day was a Burmese python, which slid over the stones through the foliage, flicking out its tongue. I told him how it crushed its prey to death and swallowed it whole, animals as big as a pig, because it had a mouth that could open extremely wide. My son disappeared into an imaginary world, and as we ate our picnic he said not a word to any of us. Eventually he remarked, 'So you would see the shape of the thing it had swallowed moving down its body.'

'Yes,' I said, 'you would.'

'Supposing it swallowed a chair?'

'Why would it bother to swallow a chair?'

'I don't know, but you would see the shape of it.'

'Yes.'

'Imagine being crushed to death and then swallowed.'

When we put them to bed, Sam asked for the light to be left on, and could Moss sleep with them. As Ros and I ate supper he came down, worried, asking if pythons could climb stairs. So Ros went and read to him until he fell asleep.

At six thirty in the morning, when the alarm rang, I saw Sam had crawled into our bed. He'd slept between us.

I dressed and swigged a cup of tea downstairs, waiting for Rob to appear, bleary-eyed after his weekend exertions. Surprisingly he fairly skipped into the kitchen, even gave me a hug.

'Come on, let's get on with it. Wagons roll!'

I asked him the reason for the extremely good mood on a dark Monday morning. He smiled. Something had happened over the weekend. 'Rob, you're not hiding it very well.'

'What?'

'That you've got something to tell me.'

'You'll find out. Come on, let's go and feed the inmates.'

On the way up to meet the school bus Sam was half asleep and Lysta lagged behind, followed by Moss and four geese who thought they were chasing us off the property. Sam was grumpy, not wanting to go to school, stamping his foot, breaking the frozen puddles.

I saw Reg Dyer and Evan Evans driving down the track towards us. They must have had an early start, for I knew Reg lived in Rhyl. Why were they here? They didn't have an appointment. I told them to go and make themselves a cup of tea, that I wouldn't be back for twenty minutes. Evan looked sombre, Reg not his usual friendly self.

'*There may be trouble ahead*,' I sang to myself.

When I got back to the house, I'd brought Sam with me. 'Look at him, Ros. He's not going to get through a day of school.' She picked him up as Evan and Reg finished their tea.

'I hope he's not ill,' said Reg.

'No, just a troubled night with a python sliding through his dreams.'

They had no idea what I meant.

'We went to the zoo yesterday. A python left quite an impression upon our dear son,' explained Ros, carrying him out of the room. I told them they had come at a bad time. I had work to do.

It wasn't a story I wanted to hear. Reg Dyer spoke of the changes Crosfields were making. Things had been under review for some time, he said. Geographical areas were being merged and North Wales would now be part of the north-west of England. A new rep would be looking after me a month from now.

'So what's happening to Evan?' I asked.

'Evan is going to take early retirement, spend more time with his wife and grandchildren.'

They were dumping him. I felt as if I'd betrayed him. It was a sad day for a company man when he found himself on the scrap heap.

'I'm not happy with it,' I said. Not that it would make the slightest difference. I was just a customer with a cheque book, but I could still say what I wanted.

'It's a younger man's work nowadays,' said Reg. 'This decision has not been taken lightly. Evan doesn't want to be on the road driving thirty thousand miles a year. It's time he put his feet up, slowed down.' Nothing else was said. Reg shook hands with me. 'We've taken up enough of your time.'

I put my arm round Evan. I wanted to offer some comfort to him. What a lousy, painful day for him, travelling from customer to customer breaking the news. I regretted the Spillers trial, the unhappiness I had caused him. He'd been good to me. I rang him that night, telling him I thought I'd let him down. He remained friendly, convincing me he thought he was better off out of the place. His wife was pleased. I only saw him once more, when he came with the new rep, a fresh-faced chap in a herringbone suit.

'I've heard a lot about you, Mr Perry,' said Crispin Thomas, firmly gripping my hand.

At least I was now a Mr in someone's eyes. He was English, lived in Tarvin near Chester. They came off the conveyor belt, these salesmen, having learnt the talk in hotel conference rooms. All the keywords of seduction, the generous discounts for new customers. It had come over from America and was now polluting the hill farms of North Wales. The likes of Gethin Hughes and Hughie Catchpole, laconic at the best of times, would give short shrift to this new breed of flashy men in their saloon cars.

When I finished the trial with Spillers and totted up the sums, there was indeed a gain to be had by changing my supplier, all of thirty-six pence per porker. I told everyone the results, and Ros in particular was keen for us to take our business to Spillers.

'That means,' she said, 'if we're selling a thousand porkers a year, an extra profit of three hundred and sixty pounds.' She was right. But before I told Reg Dyer of my decision I rang Evan to let him know my intentions. He was indifferent.

'What do I care? You do what's right for you.'

He sounded depressed, unwilling to pursue a conversation. I wished him well, hoped he would drop by and bring his grandchildren. They were the same age as Sam and Lysta. That was the last time I spoke to him. He died of a heart attack in a bumper car at a funfair in Pwllheli with his grandson beside him.

Tom Felce's marriage to Agnetta, a sparkling blonde Danish ice skater, brought the small population of Clynnog Fawr to gather at St Beuno's church in the March sunshine. The couple arrived in a pony and trap, preceded by the Talysarn brass band, who had added a hit from the sixties to their repertoire. Agnetta was four inches taller than Tom, which I could be precise about, because Tom had asked me what I thought of a man marrying a woman taller than himself. I'd said to him, is life really measured in inches? And he'd laughed and said there's more than one way to take that. Watching them walk down the aisle I must admit it did take my eye, though no doubt their height difference was exaggerated by her high-heeled shoes. She was slim and long-legged, and six feet tall.

Tom had become a regular visitor to Dyffryn. He liked to dig his own vegetables and kept me up with what was going on in his life. He told me how he and Agnetta had met at Birmingham fish market, a slightly incongruous place to find a Danish ice skater. She had been there with her brother filming a documentary, following fish that had been caught on a trawler in the Atlantic all the way to the plate. Tom it was who bought that particular box of fish, so they filmed him returning to North Wales, where the fish was finally eaten by a chap called Wyn Evans in a caravan in Llanrug.

The party that night in the village hall in Penygroes was unfortunately gatecrashed by some of the locals and the place became overcrowded. The vicar grabbed the microphone and asked those who had not been invited to please leave immediately. The doors were then locked, and the celebrations resumed. Harry carved the hog roast that we had donated to the feast.

Tom opened his speech by saying, 'I hope I'm not skating on thin ice, but I'm looking forward to a long and happy marriage to this beautiful girl. Luckily for me she loves the smell of wood smoke and kippers.' Agnetta's father told everyone he had never seen his daughter so happy, that the warmth he and his wife had received from the Welsh people was overwhelming. Then he invited everyone to their village in Denmark, a remark I hoped he was not going to regret. After the cake was cut the dancing began.

Ros, due in two weeks and feeling too uncomfortable to take to the dance floor, sat in a corner with an iced ginger beer. Sam and Lysta were spending the night at Trefanai, so there was no hurry to get back to Dyffryn. Ros pointed out to me a girl she used to go to school with, Sian Richards, expelled for having her breast tattooed. Jack was dancing with the girl who worked on the cooked meats counter of the Co-op, and played in the Talysarn band.

Then suddenly I saw Rob banging on the window. He should have been in Chorley. I told Ros it must be over, that was why he was back. But I was wrong, for in they walked, the two of them. At last we were going to meet Kate. A slim figure in jeans, with long dark hair halfway down her back, blue eyes and a broad smile. They didn't just walk in: he grabbed her round the waist as the band played 'Yeah, You Really Got Me'. It was an impressive entrance, clearing the dance floor as everyone crowded round the late arrivals. It was a pity Rob went for a move too far by trying to pass Kate between his legs and fell forward, hitting his head on a wooden upright. Although dazed, he managed to bow to the rapturous applause they received. The band played on into the night.

It was lunchtime on Sunday when Rob and Kate emerged from the caravan. They wandered into the house as Ros and I were eating roast lamb. Rob had been seeing Kate for months, so why he had decided this weekend to invite her down I didn't know. Maybe he felt there was some permanency in their relationship. She had a self-assured confidence, was good fun and easy-going.

When it was feeding time, she came and mucked out the pigs with us, happy to get her hands dirty. She would have fitted in well at Dyffryn, pushing a wheelbarrow to the dung heap, chasing a porker out of the stream or breaking up a bale of straw for the sows. No doubt Rob would be leaving Dyffryn soon to live with her, but there was no talk of it that afternoon. In the evening he drove her to Bangor station, where she took a train home.

I had noticed an increase in the rat population at Dyffryn. There were two ways to deal with it. I could poison them with warfarin, which would be dangerous if other animals were to eat it, or, as Harry suggested, I could shoot them with an air rifle. They were living around the feed store, where we kept all the concentrates in twenty-eight-pound bags. I'd watched them disappearing down various tunnels they'd dug into the rendering of the stone walls. Whenever we frightened them off, they scattered in all directions. There seemed to be no pattern to their escape routes. Dewi told me that if I turned a blind eye to them, they'd overrun the place in weeks. 'They breed every month, and with more mouths to feed more food will disappear.' Hughie said we'd never get rid of them, that all we could ever do was keep their numbers down. They ate into the bags, and each time I carried one out over my shoulder I left a trail of pig nuts behind me. At night I shone a torch into the store and watched them flee, at least thirty of them, fat buggers, eating into our profits. The only way to protect the feed was to empty it into metal containers, or have it blown into a silo.

I didn't like the idea of warfarin, so I thought I'd try to pick them off with an air rifle. I'd never shot anything before; shooting didn't appeal to me. Harry brought up a gun, and I hid out of sight as the light was fading, waiting for them to come scurrying.

What I saw was a rat rush hour, all of them busy, coming and going under the feed shed door. They were getting fat on my food, so I took aim and fired. I missed, and missed again, never hitting one, until I gave up because it was too dark. Rob told me he was a dead-eye shot, boasting that he had once won a goldfish by shooting a plastic duck at a village fete. Prove it, I said, so he had a go the next evening, but did no better than me. Maybe Harry should finish them off with a machine gun.

So warfarin it was, which we put down in handfuls. Every morning we found it had all been eaten. We never found a dead rat, but gradually we saw fewer of them and for a while they disappeared, giving the impression we had killed them off. Then suddenly I would see one, its whiskers twitching out of a hole in a wall. They were regrouping.

Dinah was back from her odyssey. She telephoned from Bangor station asking where I was. She had been expecting me to pick her up and had been waiting half an hour. I explained I hadn't been able to hear a word of her last call. Now she was too tired to wait any longer and was getting a taxi. She was going straight to bed, would speak to me tomorrow. She sounded fed up and didn't ask me how Ros was.

In the morning as Rob and I were feeding the pigs, Lysta came running to tell me, 'Mum has started to have the baby.' We had always planned to have a home birth.

I rang Anna Westphal, the matriarchal midwife. She'd already been out to the farm to lay down the law. She was a force to be reckoned with. It seems to go with the job, the high handedness, the bossing of a vulnerable patient. She'd made it clear she disapproved of home deliveries, saying to me 'I suppose you want to be present at the birth'. To which I had promptly replied 'I certainly do not'. Ros knew I wanted to be around, but not at the actual birth.

'So you're not one of those modern men then.'

'I'm probably quite modern,' I replied, 'and I'm looking forward to the birth of the baby. I just don't want to witness it.'

Ros was lying on our bed, being cared for by Sam and Lysta.

'I've gone into labour. The contractions have begun,' she told me. It was the first time I asked Sam and Lysta to walk on their own to catch the school bus. But they didn't want to leave their mother, asking to be allowed to spend the day at home.

'Shall we?'

'Oh, let them stay for a while.'

Forty minutes later Anna Westphal pulled up in her Volkswagen Passat. Four aggressive geese followed her muscular calves to the front door. I was there before her hand had reached the brass knocker and showed her in. She strode past me, holding a black leather case.

'Where is she?'

'Upstairs,' I said.

'Children out,' she said, sitting on the side of the bed and preparing to take Ros's blood pressure. 'How often are the contractions?' I left the room and rang Gwyn, telling him what was going on. He, of course, knew Anna Westphal, saying that Ros was in good hands. He would come over anyway. Meanwhile I drove Sam and Lysta to school, both pleading with me to let them stay at home to see their brother being born.

'How do you know it's going to be a boy?'

'Of course it will be, Dad,' said Lysta.

'It's going to be a girl,' said Sam. 'I want a sister called Lucinda.'

'I want a brother called Horace.'

How bizarre. What on earth had my children been delving into? Where had those names come from? Certainly not from the Carmel playground. Horace and Lucinda were two names that I could safely say were unheard of in North Wales.

When I returned I sat with Ros, holding her hand. Anna Westphal had laid her instruments out on the top of the chest of drawers. I offered her a cup of tea which she accepted. As the kettle boiled on the Aga, in walked Gwyn. I hadn't seen him in over two weeks and I thought he'd lost some weight. There was a look to him that I hadn't seen before. His face seemed thinner too.

'That stomping around you can hear is Anna Westphal attending to your daughter.'

'Herr Doktor,' she said as we walked into the bedroom.

'Pa, how nice of you to come,' said Ros, taking Gwyn's hand.

Ros eventually gave birth to a boy, weighing in at seven pounds six ounces. I had stayed downstairs catching up on paperwork, my only role taking up kettles of hot water. But I was with Ros until the birth was imminent.

When I saw our son for the first time, he looked like an ordinary baby to me. I was stuck for words, searching for something original to say. 'Seems like a nice chap. Let's hope he's good at football.'

When Sam and Lysta got home from school, they went straight to the bedroom, tiptoeing to their mother and whispering, 'Is it a boy, Mum?'

'Can we call him Horace?' said Lysta.

'Where did you get that name from?' Ros asked.

'He's the hero in a book I'm reading. He can tame tigers and ride on the back of swans.'

As Gwyn was leaving I asked him, 'Are you all right? Are you feeling well?'

'Of course,' he said, dismissing me. 'Be ready for your mother-in-law. She's on her way from Harlech.'

I thanked Anna Westphal for all her help and presented her with a leg of lamb, which was gratefully received. I shooed the geese from the front door and they immediately turned their attention to her front tyres. One day soon they would misjudge it and get run over. They were more irritating than ever, always annoying people. I wondered if I should have a word with Harry, get them ready for the oven.

I rang my mother and gave her the news. There was no sparkle in her voice. I needed to find some time to talk to her, hear about her trip to Cyprus. Eryl pulled up outside the house with flowers and a box of chocolates. Our eyes meeting, she smiled and kissed me on the cheek. I'd never had a greeting like that before.

That night in bed, Ros and I listened to Radio Luxembourg, just like we used to. It was Dusty Springfield closing her eyes and counting to ten. I loved it back in '68, and loved it just as much now.

10

Eryl Moves In

When Eryl announced she was coming to stay for a few days to look after Ros and the baby, I knew this would make or break our relationship. I was going to have to invent a new version of myself that would be acceptable to her. She knew nothing of my habits, the routine of the house, how the farm dictated our lives, what time we were up in the mornings, when we went to bed. She didn't know I liked to lie on the sofa listening to music every night. I wondered what Gwyn thought about her coming to stay. She was confrontational, and it was me who was going to have to acquiesce to keep the peace.

We lived in a farmhouse that wasn't particularly tidy. It was clean enough for us, but mud got carried in on our boots, and often we had to chase chickens out of the kitchen. Moss slept on the sofa. Dewi would turn up unannounced, make himself a cup of tea. There was goose dung in the porch, where the geese gathered when it rained. These were just a few of the things I knew she'd dislike. She lived in a spotless house, with a cleaner coming in twice a week. It wasn't going to work. What did she mean by a few days? How long is that? I didn't mention these anxieties to Ros, but arranged with Rob that I'd go to the caravan when I needed a smoke, then clean my teeth, or suck a Mint Imperial. 'She'll smell it on your clothes,' he said. So I'd spray myself with an underarm deodorant.

Meanwhile my mother too was wanting to play her part, telling me she would come up and make meals, help out where she could. I foresaw an outbreak of granny warfare, the two of them squaring up to each other. I sensed my mother was fragile, and I needed to find out what had happened in Cyprus. Having a new grandson to dote on could be the distraction she needed.

Sam and Lysta were insisting we name their brother Horace, but we settled on Seth Orion, which they hated.

It was the end of April, and though the air was still cool Eryl opened all the windows. She said the place was stuffy, smelled of wood smoke, needed a full airing. She got Mrs Reece, her cleaner, to come over with a mop and disinfectant. Our first skirmish was over Moss. 'Dogs don't sleep on sofas. Dogs sleep in kennels, outside the house.'

When my mother arrived, Eryl welcomed her warmly. 'Dinah, how wonderful it is, we're grandmothers again!' Their cheeks touched with pretend kisses while their eyes looked away. My mother disappeared upstairs where Ros lay in bed breastfeeding Seth. She appeared unaware of the atmosphere that was already building up in the house.

Eryl announced supper would be ready at seven, and asked if I could make sure the children were out of the bath by six thirty. 'Would Dinah like to join us?'

Harry waltzed in wearing a pair of cowboy boots. Eryl told him immediately to take them off and leave them by the back door. I whisked him out of the kitchen. 'Don't say anything, just be polite. She's only here for a few days.' He'd come to butcher the meat. We usually had a joint on these occasions (not of meat); he preferred to work through the evening stoned. 'You can't tonight, Harry. Go down and have one later with Rob in the caravan.'

'OK, man.'

Dinah stayed for supper, and after we had eaten I managed to grab a few minutes alone with Ros.

'How's it going down there?' she asked.

I didn't over dramatise the situation, saying only it was getting difficult. 'She's rearranging the house, but apart from that everything is fine.' Seth lay asleep in a cot beside the bed. He had wispy golden hair, looked like a cherub. 'Have you any idea how long she'll be staying?'

'Another day or two. Surely you can put up with her?'

But the conversation came to an end when Sam and Lysta arrived and got into bed next to their mother. They were gripped by the excitement of the day, and I wondered if there would be any sleep in them tonight. My mother was washing up. There had still not been an opportunity to speak to her and as I dried the dishes I said we would talk tomorrow.

Eryl went to bed at ten o'clock with a hot chocolate and Tony

Jacklin's autobiography. Leaving the house quietly, I went to see Rob in the caravan. He had a joint rolled and ready waiting for me. Moss would sleep with him until Eryl had gone. My mother-in-law continually turfed her off the sofa. It took all my self-control to button my lip, for no other reason than that I didn't want to upset Ros. I told Rob that the plain truth was we just didn't like each other.

'It's a common thing,' he said, 'the mother-in-law problem.'

I changed the subject. 'How's Kate?' but before he could begin to tell me there was a gentle tapping on the door. It was Jack, then ten minutes later Harry joined us. The four of us spoke quietly, passing the joint to each other. Eryl slept at the front of the house with her window open a few inches. I told them she had a sense of smell like a sniffer dog's. The light was still on in her bedroom. It would be just our luck if clouds of smoke drifted in through her window. We giggled, whispering like schoolboys in a dormitory. When we tiptoed out into the night, Harry pushing his bike up the drive with Jack and Meg walking beside him, the light was off in Eryl's room. We'd got away with it.

Gwyn came over the following day, giving me the time to go to Hendy to talk to my mother. She was indeed unhappy. She said she had been a fool to herself to have believed she and Stavros had a future together. 'You don't just marry the man, you marry the whole family,' she said, and what a large family it was.

Stavros, being the breadwinner, was away fishing two or three days at a time. My mother could see herself spending her days doing domestic chores, waiting for her man to return from the sea. And when he did, he drank retsina and then slept for twenty-four hours. The women gossiped all day, while the children threw stones at the feral cats. They washed their clothes by hand, talking about their neighbours and menfolk, while the sheets hung beneath the pine trees drying in the Mediterranean sunshine. It had taken her two weeks to realise that nothing was ever going to change, that this was how it would always be if she accepted his proposal of marriage.

Stavros broke down on hearing the news, then raged and ranted that she had insulted him, let down his family. They all turned against her and she had to go and rent a room in the town to escape their threats. Unable to get an earlier flight, there she remained, eating alone in the tavernas, being ogled by the men while they fiddled with their worry beads and played backgammon. It had been a horrible few days culminating in an embarrassing scene in a café on the seafront, when Stavros came and pleaded with her to change her mind. After her refusal, he hurled a mouthful of abuse at her as the other customers looked on.

I gave her a hug. My mother had been through an unhappy marriage with my father. He ran off after some pretty blonde turned his head, leaving her with four children to bring up in the nineteen fifties. She was young; he was gone before she was thirty. 'Come on, let's go for a walk at Dinas. Moss needs a run.'

That night at Dyffryn the atmosphere had changed because Gwyn was staying for the evening. Eryl was mildly welcoming when I entered the house. Or maybe Ros had said something. No matter what the reason, she had backed off, sitting on the sofa with Sam and Lysta either side of her, the three of them speaking Welsh. Her austerity disappeared when she played with her grandchildren, but Gwyn had a weariness about him, his eyes dull. He wasn't well, I was sure of it now.

It was rare for a sow to rear more than twelve good-sized piglets, so it surprised me the next morning when I counted a litter of sixteen. Remarkable that all apart from two were fighting for the teat. It was the mother's fourth litter, and when I checked the records she had already raised an impressive thirty piglets.

If all my sows could perform so well I'd be smoking cigars and driving a Ferrari. It was her genes, of course, and it occurred to me that I should keep back her female piglets for breeding stock. They would have to go to a new boar. I couldn't have Dave shagging his daughters. But now, with the pig herd established, it made sense to hold on to the strong gilts from good mothers rather than continue buying in from Josh Hummel.

I worked out with a calculator that our average litter size was eight. Not bad. No doubt unimpressive in the world of highly efficient modern units, but up here in the blasted landscape of North Wales it was pretty good. Ros always said I had no regard for detail, but I would dispute that now. There were scraps of paper everywhere with little sums on, my workings out of percentages. Rob was impressed, seeing it as a radical change in my character.

We had a foothold now in the local community. People knew we produced quality meat and by word of mouth our reputation had spread. It was not unusual for people to ring, or call by and pick up half a pig or a lamb. Our beef was just as popular, but this we sold as joints.

On the fifth day after Seth's birth Eryl packed her bags and at last headed back to Trefanai. It had been the longest five days of my life. I exaggerate, but all we had discovered merely reinforced the feeling that we were incompatible.

She got Mrs Reece to clean the house from top to bottom on her final day, to emphasise that we lived in filth, well below her standard of cleanliness. Every time my mother rang, she told her there was no need to come and help, that everything was under control. I was pleased Dinah came up anyway and sat with Ros, and spent time with Sam and Lysta.

The night Eryl left, my sense of freedom returned. The house seemed bigger, Moss was able to relax on the sofa and I could lie back and have a roll-up. What's more, I'd never said anything I might now have regretted. Later, after Sam and Lysta had gone to bed, Ros told me Gwyn was ill and they were awaiting test results from Bangor hospital.

The police had never turned up at Dyffryn before. The panda car stopped outside the house. Bryn Thomas was a young constable in uniform, stationed in Caernarfon. He could have been the same age as me. He had that unfortunate look the ginger-haired sometimes have. Needing to compensate for a lack of masculinity, he became very serious, trying to defy his inexperience by slipping immediately into the jargon of a TV detective.

'We need to have a word about a case of sheep rustling.'

He had already got his pencil and notebook out, waiting to take down every word I said. But before I could open my mouth the geese spotted him. They hadn't seen a uniform before. To them this was more than an ordinary threat. This was a red alert!

They lined up next to each other and charged. Their wings outstretched, they made an increasing din as they picked up speed, nearly becoming airborne. As they got closer, Moss decided she was having none of it. She got it into her head they were going to attack me. Bryn Thomas fled to his car as Moss tore into them. Suddenly everything became quite brutal. If I hadn't grabbed a broom, which was enough to scatter them, I feared we might have witnessed a fight to the death. I picked up Moss, who had a mouthful of feathers, and calmed her down. The whole incident lasted less than a minute. Then Bryn Thomas was back in front of me and resumed his questioning. I told him I knew nothing about sheep rustling, but that it didn't surprise me.

'Yes,' I said, 'I do know Arfon Williams, and where he farms. No, I haven't seen anything suspicious.' Bryn Thomas was too inexperienced to understand the goings-on in the hills of wild Wales, the scores needing to be settled, the never-ending feuds that ran between families. It would do no good if I said what I really thought, or pointed an accusing finger. He'd only been in the force a year. It was like sending a boy to do a man's job. If anybody knew anything it would be Dewi. It would come to nothing, nobody would be arrested; the case would go unsolved. As he left I said, 'By the way, do you have a deep freeze?'

'Yes. Why do you ask?'

By chance I saw Arfon the next day on the Carmel road. The radiator had blown on his Land Rover and I offered to tow him back to his farm. He was reluctant to accept my help, something I could tell he was uncomfortable with, but I insisted this time.

We tied a rope round my tow bar and slowly we crawled to Henbant. He lived in an old rundown farmhouse, curtains drawn across the windows, paint flaking from the woodwork. A rusting Fordson Major and a muck-spreader without tyres stood in the yard, in the Dutch barn a few bales of hay. Penned at the far end were a handful of Welsh Black calves. What keeps him going, I wondered. We untied the Land Rover and I waited to hear what words would come from those thin lips. At first just a faint smile, then 'Diolch yn fawr' (Thank you very much). If there was ever a time when I wanted a man to open up and for God's sake speak to me it was now. To give something of himself, break the silence, spit out the truth of who he was. What was this feud with Gethin all about?

'Duw, Duw, I'm too old for all this now,' he said, sitting on the bumper of the Land Rover. 'Do me a favour, boy, on the dashboard, get me the bottle of blue pills.' I handed them to him and he chewed them before swallowing. 'Don't judge me by the state of the place. I haven't laid a finger on it for years. Not since she died.'

He farmed above Dyffryn and looking down I could see the sloping fields criss-crossed with stone walls, the pylons stretching away towards Caernarfon. I'd not been up here before; his view was broader than the one Rob and I saw when we leaned over the gate and had a smoke after the day's work was done. The place had an abandoned atmosphere, as if no life was being lived here any longer.

'It's not how I wanted it to be,' he said. Beyond him I could see a recess in the wall, the metal chain that once tethered a dog. The wind rattled loose corrugated sheeting on the roof of the barn. 'When we worked it together, it was all tidy then. It was she who cared for the look of the farm.'

A bank of cloud had thickened on the horizon; a black cat slunk down from the straw bales in the lean-to.

'I said to her when she was taking her last breaths, I would leave it as it was.' All around the yard were half-dismantled machines, never to be put together again. The formaldehyde bath the sheep used to run through, full of leaves. The whole place felt it belonged in the past. As he raised himself up he said, 'I can't remember the last man who walked through the door of my house, but come in and let us take a drink.'

We went together into a dark kitchen, he sometimes leaning on me, or stretching out his hands for support. I found the light switch.

'Don't bother with that. All the bulbs have blown; I haven't replaced them.' He made his way to the cupboard, pulling out a bottle of whisky.

'Say what you will, boy. I know what you're thinking.'

Through the cracked walls, spindly plants were creeping over the damp surfaces like withered fingers. Grass was pushing up between the flagstones under my feet. A spider's web clung to a lampshade. Broken crockery lay strewn across the floor; in the corner a dustbin full of empty whisky bottles. He filled two glasses.

'Have it out with me, then.'

Have what out with him, I asked myself. What was I meant to be saying? The black cat ran into the house and I heard the scream of a kill in the next room. Arfon filled his glass again. Then I asked him what I always wanted to know, the question that could never be asked, nor maybe answered.

'What about him over at Cae Uchaf?' I said, waiting for an explosion of anger, half expecting his body to rise up in fury and fall across the table and that would be the end of him. But he swigged back another measure before he replied.

'Him over at Cae Uchaf, you say?'

'Tell me what happened there.'

He was getting drunk now. 'Go back to our fathers, for that is where it begins,' he said, emptying the bottle. 'Two brothers who fell out over each other's wives.' He became silent, with the vacant look that too much alcohol can give you, holding his glass before his mouth, staring as if reliving the horror of a dark secret.

'Bloody fools, all of them . . . they never knew who fathered who. And then the place left to one, and not the other. What would you expect, they who had farmed as brothers, even shared their womenfolk? He who was cast out had to raise money and fell into debt.'

'So he over at Cae Uchaf, is he your cousin?' I asked him in that dank kitchen, with the dripping tap, and the trail of ants making tracks across the stone floor.

'He could be, who knows, boy, you the outsider who has come in with your fancy marrying.'

'Maybe he is your brother.'

'Yes, but she, my mother, said no. But there is five years between us.'

I left him there and went into the yard, putting together a roll-up. An hour had passed; the spring air carried the smell of fresh grass. As I sat there, surrounded by the desolation of Henbant, I tried to understand the lives that had been lived up here, the history in these hills, beyond forgiveness. The scarred hearts, the barren attitudes, as bleak as the harsh landscapes.

It left no room for hope, for new beginnings. Most of them lived in the Old Testament, an eye for an eye. So Arfon's father, if he had indeed been his father, was cast out from Cae Uchaf, forced to borrow money to buy Henbant. While the other brother, favoured by the father, inherited Cae Uchaf, where Gethin Hughes now farmed. This thing called bad blood has a lot to answer for.

When I went back, he was asleep, an arm spread out on the kitchen table. I walked through the downstairs rooms, into the once cosy lounge where a cuckoo clock hung on the wall, three ceramic ducks flew away on another, and a sad framed piece of needlework read *Home Sweet Home*. On the hearth of the tiled fireplace was an empty brass coal scuttle; cobwebs floated in the chimney. When was the last time they had sat in here together, husband and wife?

As I left, an early swallow swooped through the yard. If only it could have been an optimistic omen, that better times were on their way to Henbant. But I was fooling myself.

I drove away along the track and stopped to open the gate, where built into the stone wall was a length of pipe stuffed full of post, the mail he had never collected: brown window envelopes full of unpaid bills.

From the road above Henbant you could see over to Anglesey, as far as Holyhead, where the overnight ferry sailed to Dublin. Such a vast, unspoilt landscape with no industrial buildings, just as nature had created it. A small speck on the map of the world. Here I stopped for a while, trying to understand the tragedy of a man tangled up in family history he had never been able to break free from.

There is a comfort in the smell of baking bread. It filled me with a sense of security, making me feel at home. Ros said Seth had a huge appetite, glugged at the breast rather than sucked on it. I thought it a good sign, showing a hunger for life, suggesting an enthusiasm, that he would get stuck into things. He had put on a considerable amount of weight. In his baby bouncer, with a nappy wrapped around him, he looked like a sumo wrestler. When Ros was out working in the vegetable garden, he was strapped to her back in a harness. There he slept, rocking to and fro as Ros bent over the seedlings, thinning and transplanting them.

Harry had given me the nod again on a deal worth doing, with a mate who drove a ready-mix concrete lorry. The drive down to the house had only a hard-core surface that turned into a river whenever it rained heavily. For a few quid in cash, he would come and empty what remained from his last load of the day. We would be able to concrete the drive cheaply, run two gullies either side to carry away the surface water. It sounded like a good idea.

'Any hidden costs?' Always my first question nowadays.

'None. Not a penny.'

So in the evenings, foot by foot, we gradually laid a drive, smoothing down the concrete with lengths of three by two, hoping no escapees would wander down, leaving their footprints to harden in the night.

Hughie came over, giving me the last chance to buy his plough, which was now £40, down from his original asking price of £55. On top of that he said he would teach me how to plough, asking me again how I could call myself a farmer. Rob was keen, whilst Harry was against the idea. He saw it as a lessening of our dependence upon him. He couldn't stomach Hughie's showing us how to plough. I'd never thought about it before, that it suited Harry for us to be at arm's length from our neighbours. It meant he could play his role here with freedom and influence, and no one questioning him. He'd done us well, and had the just rewards of a man who had given good advice, although without always being aware of the financial consequences. But then Harry was a practical man. He liked to see a job done, even if it had to be bodged.

A clear, soft, June morning buzzing with insects, the air full of swallows, the breeze warm enough to tempt you to take off your jacket, a day when any man would feel good about the world. That is, until the terrifying roar of low-flying jets from RAF Valley shattered the peace, stampeding the animals, frightening some into instant heart attacks, so that they dropped dead on the spot. These unpredictable occurrences enraged everyone, for the MoD never gave us prior warning of such manoeuvres, saying it depended on weather conditions. The planes appeared literally out of the blue, flying no higher than two hundred feet through the valleys. The Farmers' Union of Wales complained bitterly, but were always met with the same response: it was an essential part of a pilot's training, necessary for the defence of the country.

Once, when they came swooping low over the fields of Dyffryn, sheep ran into the barbed wire fencing, climbing on top of one another, tearing their fleeces and getting their heads stuck in the netting. Farming was hard enough without having to suffer an aerial threat from the RAF. I got on the phone and asked if they were aware of the effect these training flights were having on our livestock, only to be told that any complaint should be put in writing. Their written responses were always sympathetic, but we never received a penny in compensation.

I sat with Gwyn one Sunday before lunch. Behind him a rose bush pressed its pink petals against the library window. I could hear the children laughing in the garden. He told me what I feared without emotion, as he would have done had he been giving a diagnosis to the relative of a sick patient. He had bowel cancer, no more than three months to live. He had no intention of going on a prolonged course of treatment, and would let the illness run its course with, as he put it, the minimum of fuss. He knew it was going to be harder for those around him than himself. He would talk of practical matters later, but the care of his books was what concerned him now.

'There is,' he said, 'a weight of responsibility in looking after books. I want you to consider these words.'

He went on to tell me how we were to treat his dying, that it was not to be a topic of conversation. He wanted no sympathy from those closest to him. It was as if we were to remain indifferent during his gradual decline. I told him this would not be possible, even daring to say that showing our sadness was the natural thing to do. I suspected there had been too many years of having to suppress his emotions, sitting with the parents of sick children, being the bearer of bad news. Even in this he was trying to protect us. Or maybe it would be too much for him to witness the grief of his loved ones. He would rather have everything dealt with now, wanted to tidy things up.

'No loose ends. I have decided on everything.'

Then he touched on Eryl, for although nothing had ever been said he knew full well the state of our relationship. But it was me who pulled back, saying we didn't need to talk about it, that things would never be resolved. No warmth would ever exist between me and my mother-in-law. He said only one more sentence on the matter.

'She always wanted Ros to marry a Welsh doctor. She knew a young man she thought would make the perfect husband.'

So I could never have won her over, however much I tried.

We shed tears that night, Ros and I together in the sitting room. Moss, sensitive to the mood in the house, spent the evening behind the sofa.

We decided not to tell Sam and Lysta everything, just that Taid (Grandfather) was ill, that he had asked everyone not to make a big fuss about it. I told my mother, whose spirits were now restored. She'd joined an art history course at Bangor university. Every Tuesday evening she caught the bus to Caernarfon, where someone on the course drove her to Bangor.

'He's a charming man, fascinated by British railway timetables.'

'Sounds just up your street.'

Hughie was good to his word and came over to show Rob and me how to plough. We took it in turns to work an acre of land, which we split into a half acre of wheat and a late crop of potatoes that Tom 'Tatoes had recommended. Our old Fergie tractor pulled the three-shear plough with ease, to a depth of nine inches. It was pleasing on the eye to see the furrows turning over behind us, the stones glinting, worms wriggling through the soil. Earthworms, a good sign that the earth lacks nothing in minerals. From time to time a chap would come from the Ministry and take samples away, a service we paid for. We never once had to add any nitrates or the like to the land at Dyffryn. Every year after we had moved the sheep up to Cesarea we spread well-rotted manure on the fields.

It shocked me when Jack turned up and threw a dead ewe on the ground in front of us.

'That's what a dog can do when it's on the rampage,' he said. 'That's why farmers shoot dogs.'

'Is it one of ours?' I asked.

'Yes it's one of ours, and we're lucky it's only one.'

Jack told us what had happened. A group of ramblers from the Wirral, camping over in Rhyd-Ddu, had been out walking on the footpath towards Nantlle. They had a dog off the lead and while they were climbing over a stile it was gone in a flash.

'If I hadn't been there and sent Meg out, more would have been killed.'

'Did they pay for it?'

'I got thirty quid out of them, told them if I had a shotgun I would have killed the dog.' Jack rarely got angry. I had not seen him like this since his punch-up with Idris Owen. 'It's not the dog's fault, it's humans and their bloody ignorance!'

From time to time in the summer months we heard of dogs killing ewes in remote places. It is surprising how irresponsible people can be, not shutting gates on footpaths, leaving litter in fields after they've had a picnic.

I hadn't seen Jack all week. I told him about Gwyn and his mood changed quickly from anger to sadness. He put the dead ewe back into the van. 'How old is he?'

'Seventy,' I said.

Later that evening, with the children in their beds, I asked Ros, 'Who's this man your mother always wanted you to marry?'

'How do you know about that?'

'Your father told me.'

To speak of past lovers serves no purpose, and can wake a jealous heart, from which I do not suffer, but I wanted to know not so much Ros's feelings as the qualities this young man had that so appealed to Eryl. What was it I fell short of in making a good husband? There were no surprises: he came from a solid Welsh family of doctors and lawyers, played rugby for his public school, went to a good university and supported the eisteddfod with generous donations. But for Eryl his crowning glory was that he owned a large house on Anglesey, overlooking the Menai Strait.

'Hmm,' I said. 'So what have I got that he hasn't?'

'A sense of humour, a buccaneering spirit for adventure.'

'Thank you, Ros.'

'He was in fact dull, and very predictable, and he had the whole of his life mapped out to the finest detail. His wife would have merely been an accessory.'

So that pretty much summed up our little excursion into Ros's past. You would have thought that Eryl would have taken into account the obvious fact that her daughter was happy.

As I was filling up the Land Rover at the Paragon garage, Trevor Thomas, the owner, a second-hand car dealer with a forecourt full of used cars, made his way towards me in some haste. He knew who I was, having made several attempts to corner me in the past. This time there was no escape. 'Perry,' he said. 'I heard all about your speech to the WI. Won a few hearts that night, didn't you?' He was softening me up. He had a car coming onto the market that would suit Ros down to the ground.

'I've noticed that Hillman. A bit tatty for a doctor's daughter, isn't it?'

There was certainly rust along the bottom of the driver's door and blotchy patches had started to appear on the boot. But all cars around here rusted, being exposed to the sea air.

'It's had one woman owner,' he said. 'She only drives it thirty miles a week, to Caernarfon and back to do the shopping.'

'I wasn't thinking of buying another car until we've run this one into the ground.'

That was our philosophy on cars, or rather Harry's, who said let them go to the scrap heap having given their all, or sell the body parts, as he called them, to somebody trying to keep the same model on the road.

'No, I really cannot agree with such methods. Have you not heard of part exchange? We could allow you something on your wife's car.'

'I'll think about it.'

'It's an Opel Kadett coupe, a lovely deep blue. I'll have it in at the end of the week. Come in for a test drive.'

'I'll be in touch. Thank you Mr Thomas.'

'Call me Trevor, please.'

I spent some time in Penygroes that morning. I needed to buy a birthday card for my youngest brother, four years younger than me, who lived out in Darwin. It took ten days to get a letter to him. I was wearing wellingtons and a pair of corduroy trousers. I'd come straight from the farm after mucking out the porkers and moving a load of bales into the farrowing house. I tried the chemist, knowing they sold hand-painted ones by local artists. I'd only been there a minute or two when Maimee Jones, a delicate woman who was not only the chapel organist but also captain of the Penygroes bowls club, came up to me and did not mince her words.

'A bit high today,' she said, holding her nose with her fingers. An elderly couple in the shop were looking at me distastefully, as if I were a tramp.

'Do you mean I smell?' I asked.

'To high heaven – not to put too fine a point on it.'

'Really?' I was genuinely shocked. I had no idea.

'I must ask you to leave. This is a chemist, not a pig farm.'

So I apologised, deeply offended, and watched her from the street spraying air freshener around the shop. I still had to go to the Co-op to get a few things. Ros wanted a sheet of stamps from the post office, I needed to buy some nails, and I stank. Why had nobody ever told me before? I remembered the advert about someone who had an underarm problem. It began with the words 'Even your best friend couldn't tell you'. I smelled of pig and nobody had ever mentioned it. I decided to give it one more try. I'd go into Griffiths, the ironmongers, and if I was on the end of any strange looks I'd leave immediately. I made my way through the domestic area, where they sold lighting and crockery, to where Arwel Watkins, chairman of the Penygroes Allotment Association, looked after the DIY stuff. Behind him were lots of drawers full of every size of nut and bolt, screws and nails, staples and curtain hooks. You name it, Arwel would find it in a split second. It was his boast to say there was no man quicker on the draw in this town. As I stood in front of him he greeted me in the way he always did. 'Perry. How is the world of swine?'

'The sun is shining on the world of swine,' I said, and asked for two pounds of six-inch nails, which he poured into the metal bowl of his scales, placing the brass weights until they balanced. Not once during this mundane activity did he sniff the air, or give a clue that I was giving off a pungent aroma.

I asked him, 'Arwel, do you notice anything unusual about me today?'

'You have always been of an unusual disposition since the day I met you.'

'I want to ask you, man to man, do I smell of pig? I need to know. I've been thrown out of a shop this morning.'

'Duw, Duw, boy, there's a turn up for you, and I bet I could tell you which shop.'

'Which shop?'

'The chemist, of course. You're not the first; she doesn't like the agricultural type.'

'So there is a smell to me.'

'Well, yes, I suppose so, but if I threw out all those who smelled of their profession, hardly a customer would come into the shop.'

I managed to get in and out of the post office without any adverse comments, but at the till in the Co-op, as I paid for shampoo, I was sure Mrs Angwyn was holding her breath. I told Ros about it, and she didn't deny it for a moment, but said she was used to it. In the clean environment of a chemist's shop of course the smell of pig would be quite overwhelming.

Sam and Lysta were now at that age when friends had become the most important thing in their lives. After school in the summer months they would often go home with classmates and play until eight o'clock in the evenings. It was usually me who picked them up, Ros having to stay with Seth. Lysta's closest friend was

Eleri Topliss, the daughter of the Hotpoint engineer who lived over in Nebo. He sold reconditioned washing machines for cash and was a suitable target for me to home in on to barter some meat. Our old Bendix had a life of its own. When it went into its spin cycle it made its way across the kitchen floor like something out of *Doctor Who*, Dalek alert! Dalek alert! He had saleable machines piled high in a disused chicken shed, and while Lysta pushed Eleri on the swing hanging from an old pear tree in the orchard we talked business. He was an Englishman who had fled Stourbridge after spending five years working in a glass factory. I'd met him a few times, usually outside the school gate. The only other time was when I beat him in the parents' sack race on school sports day.

'It's Allen, isn't it?'

'Yes, to you it is. To the others around here it's Topliss with no Mr in front of it. Then of course to the children it's Topless. It's hard for Eleri having to bear the brunt of it.'

'Do you have a deep freeze?'

'Yes, half empty at the moment. Why?'

Twenty minutes later the deal was done. I'd got a reconditioned Bosch with a year's warranty, he a whole porker for his freezer. Another successful transaction, bartering at its best, pleasing both of us. As Lysta and I drove home, after she had given up trying to play 'Frère Jacques' on her recorder, for the road was bumpy, she brought up the subject of her pocket money, telling me that twenty pence was a lot less than some of the other girls got. She didn't ask for more, not directly, but if she did extra work, could she be paid for it?

'I want to get a pound a week, Dad.'

'That's quite a lot, Lysta.'

'I know, but I need to save up.'

'What are you saving up for?'

'Dad, it's a secret. Don't make me tell you.'

'Well, I'm sure we can arrange something. Let me talk to Mum.'

Coming into Dyffryn when the sun was setting you could not help but stop and stare at the opaque cloud formations folding over one another, like high waves tumbling in a sea of sky, while the mind's eye invented the faces of Greek gods, or stampeding animals rushing across a blue desert. Lysta knew this game well.

'What can you see?' I asked her.

'I can see Taid's face. He's looking down on us.' Maybe she could, but we didn't talk about it. She got excited as Moss came running towards us.

Mrs Mathias at Banc-y-Celyn thought she was trying her luck until I agreed to swap a shoulder of lamb for her old cast-iron bath. She wanted a leg, but it wasn't worth it. I knew she would have to pay someone to take it away. It was just what we needed to cure the lamb skins in. It was another idea that I'd come up with. I'd researched it in a book from the library called *The Curing of Sheepskins*, and although there seemed to be a lot to it, Ros agreed that we should give it a go. We were wasting an asset. We currently got no more than a few pence for skins from FMC, who sold our fleeces to a woollen mill for a pittance. Jack wasn't interested in the idea at all. After he had done the shearing, back-breaking work even for a young man, he told me to forget about it. 'Look at the state of them,' he said, all torn and knotted with burrs and dirt, caked-in dried dung around their rear ends.

'Stop always looking for ways to make more money, when it's best to get rid of them with as little effort as possible.'

That was the difference between me and my brother, he contented as a shepherd, me always sniffing an opportunity. When I brought the cast-iron bath back in the Land Rover it took four of us to carry it into the barn.

The first thing to do was to scrape away the actual muscular layer on the underside of the skin using a serrated knife. After nearly an hour Seth needed a feed so Ros left me to it. It was laborious work, but eventually it was done. The fleece was pretty dirty, so as Ros wasn't around to see me I ran the Hoover up and down it. One has to improvise; there was no mention of this in the book. I then soaked the sheepskin in alum, covering it completely and, returning to the instructions, left it for six days.

Harry disapproved of this latest venture, saying it was time-consuming, and none of the locals would buy a sheepskin. I told him that the real potential lay in finding someone who could make sheepskin jackets. There was a huge market for them in London, down the Portobello Road. We could dye them purple, sell them to the hippies.

Dewi sat in the kitchen eating a slice of bara brith. His new spectacles, which magnified his eyes, gave him the look of a bushbaby. He was passing Sam and Lysta photographs of himself dressed as a druid, sitting on a golden throne. A far cry from being a postman who drove a mud-splattered van. Other photos showed him white-robed, at the Llangollen Eisteddfod, followed by a procession of acolytes. It was then he told me that Arfon had been taken to the cottage hospital in Caernarfon. 'All collapsed in and fatigued' was how Dewi described him. 'The man can't weigh more than a sack of grain.'

'Who will look after the livestock at Henbant?' I asked.

'There's a cousin over in Beaumaris; he'll be the one who tidies up the mess.'

I couldn't imagine Arfon recovering; his days were done with. It saddened me to think of him facing a lonely death. I knew that day at Henbant would remain with me for ever.

Rob interrupted us, telling me to come with him, that he had made a remarkable discovery.

I was about to follow Rob up the drive when I noticed that Frieda was not leaning over the gate. She was always there, keeping an eye on things. So I went to look for her and found her licking her bull calf, which had slithered out into the grass, a dull grey colour with patches of white on its flanks. She gave out a series of gentle moos as I stroked her back. She had just got on with it, not needing help from anyone. 'Well done, girl.'

Rob was waiting with a weaned sow standing quietly beside him. 'Watch this.' In his hand he held a rope, secured by a slipknot to one of the sow's back trotters. 'If only we had found this out years ago. The misery it would have saved us.'

He whacked her ham and she walked on, not bolting or charging away as they usually did, but with a steady stride that was easy to keep up with.

'See what I mean? It's amazing, all controlled by just a tug on the rope.'

'How do you turn round?' I asked.

'I haven't worked out that bit yet. But watch, I can stop her.' He tugged back on the rope, keeping it taut, and she stopped in an instant. 'What do you think of that?'

All that energy we had spent chasing after pigs, when they could be subdued by a single piece of rope round a trotter.

'Rob, I don't know what to say. I want to kiss you.'

'You can, but not on the lips.'

My mother telephoned, inviting herself up for supper. We were enjoying a spell of weather when we were hardly in the house. Even at twilight the air was warm, a song thrush giving its all in a larch tree.

Dinah, with her Cypriot experiences now behind her, had brought some wine. It was Thursday and Harry joined us before he butchered the meat.

'We've got three more days of this, then the heavens will open,' he said.

We carried a rug out into the field in front of the house. Jack, who could see us through his army binoculars, came down with Meg, and there we lay sprawled out in our shirtsleeves, watching the abstract forms, random shapes of clouds, floating like a white hedge across the horizon. Black-tipped birds scribbled a signature along a ribbon of light. We ate our home-grown salad, savoured the taste of Ros's bread, beetroot and mayonnaise, the home-made pâté, baked potatoes with melting butter. Seth sat on Ros's lap like a baby Buddha, while Sam and Lysta ran around in circles, throwing dandelion heads, holding buttercups beneath our chins.

'You like butter.'

We chatted on, our heads in the grass, carefree, as the evening slid away, feeling that the night would be for ever fixed in the memory. Maybe it was because we were all together, friends and family. But my heart was low as I thought of Gwyn.

As the colours darkened a great splodge of sunlight glowed on the sea, theatrical but muted, as if curtains were about to close over the whole scene.

We could hear the telephone ringing in the house.

'I'll go,' said Lysta.

'No, I'll go,' said Sam.

And they raced one another to answer it. Rob, still basking in his amazing discovery, teased Harry, asking him if he was aware of the 'pig on a rope trick'.

'What do you mean?'

'It's impressive, Harry, although I don't think Rob will get a worldwide patent on it.'

Harry was baffled, not having a clue what we were talking about.

'Don't worry yourself, we'll show you tomorrow.'

'Mum, it's Nain [Grandmother] on the phone, she wants to talk to you,' Lysta shouted.

'I'll ring her back in half an hour.'

So we stayed until night fell, no one in a hurry to go back into the house. My thoughts drifted to the continual interplay of life and death. Ros having brought a new life to us, Arfon who would not be around much longer. Frieda with her calf at foot. This is it, I thought, all of us stepping in and out, guests for a while here on this earth. As I gazed at the darkening sky, I started to sing Don McLean's 'Vincent' while the day's last light faded across a rippled sea.

11

Price Fixing

Some friendships are like Guinness, they just don't travel; where they were made is where they taste best and should always remain. Through the years at Dyffryn many people had come to stay with us, and waving them goodbye I knew they wouldn't be returning. For who we were then was certainly not who we were now. We'd taken different roads, and the closeness formed in the 1960s at all-night parties, stoned in London bedsits, rock 'n' rolling, was in the distant past.

They came and hung around, wanting to smoke and listen to music into the early hours. Even long after we had gone to bed, they raved on downstairs. I resented it, because they had not moved on. We did smoke, but it never stopped us getting on with what needed to be done. For them it was a way of life. In the end I put a stop to the visits, and after five years at Dyffryn everyone we had known in our London days had faded away.

This is what I said to Rob when he read out a letter from an old friend, a Scotsman who had lent him a kilt in Liechtenstein, as they hitchhiked around Europe back in '67. Hamish had tracked him down, and wanted to come and stay for a few days. Rob remembered the hours stuck on lonely roads as the cars whizzed by ignoring him, no doubt because of his long-haired appearance. Hamish never waited more than a few minutes before he got a lift, putting this down to the kilt and sporran he wore. To prove his point he lent Rob his kilt for a day. It was Rob who was picked up, the talk in the car always about the kilt. So they became friends, travelling for three months from country to country, kilt-swapping as they went.

'Long time ago,' I said to Rob.

In the letter was a telephone number for Rob to ring. In two weeks Hamish would make the journey from Fort William down to the mountains of North Wales.

Meanwhile Tom and Agnetta were hatching plans, sounding us out about inviting people to come and camp for a long weekend to see what we were up to regarding self-sufficiency, our organic garden, my interest in bartering. I hadn't realised how much this way of living interested them. The idea of forming a community of like-minded people appealed to them both, and when Agnetta inherited a large amount of money she started to get serious about it. She wanted to buy a farm, following the teachings of Rudolf Steiner. What did we think, would we have anything to offer? We shared the same philosophy, she said. I was non-committal, whereas Ros was enthusiastic, keen to pursue the idea.

When the Seaview Hotel in Llandudno ordered fifty pounds of sausages from us, the largest order we had ever taken, I dressed up for this special delivery, putting on a shirt and tie. Ros, who cut everyone's hair, gave me a trim, and I had a shower before I left. It would be a disaster if I turned up smelling of pig.

The hotel was fully booked for three days, with fifty-odd psychiatrists attending a conference on mental health in the family. Tom 'Tatoes had dropped our name, saying we produced the best quality meat in the whole of North Wales. It presented us with the opportunity to break into the hotel market. The margins were not as good as selling door to door, but they were still way above what we got on our meat contract with FMC.

I had been told the owners of the Seaview, a husband and wife team called Graham and Wanda, were prompt payers but wanted a discount. So I gave them five per cent and they handed over a cheque for thirty-eight pounds there and then. I produced a leg of lamb free of charge, telling them that it was from our own flock, fattened on organic land in the hills above Penygroes. It did the trick; they were on the phone by the end of the week. I knew this breakthrough would lead to supplying other hotels in Llandudno.

Off I went to pay my annual visit to Winford Hook. This time, with Ros's help, I had sent the accounts on ahead of my appointment. When I entered his office, I was confident that I could deal with him. I had finely tuned my defence mechanisms, and only hoped I could stop myself from drifting off while listening to his dreary talk of accountancy. All was just the same in this timeless zone. The cat hadn't aged, or moved from the fire grate, and the delicate one with the nervous disposition traipsed across the carpet in her slippers, holding the teacups with an expression of intense concentration. I emptied my saucer back into the cup. Old Winford Hook, with a weight of eyebrow, raised a look as if lifting up two giant caterpillars.

'It has, I have to admit, been a good year for you,' he said grudgingly.

I let the pleasure wash over me, almost saying, 'Sorry I couldn't hear you. Could you say that again?' As self-satisfaction welled up inside me, I stretched out my legs and folded my arms. All of a sudden I had become terribly relaxed. Was it because the tables had been turned?

'Well, I'm not going into the nitty-gritty . . .' but before he could finish I said, 'Winford, please do. I want to hear the fine detail. Why has it been such a good year?'

He sighed, not once but twice, and went back to sipping his tea, a long noisy sip, from the very edge of the cup.

'Your margins have risen considerably, and of course you have reduced your overheads.'

'Ah, that's what I wanted to hear.'

'But be careful, boy, more than ever have fallen by the wayside. The cock doesn't crow for long.' Slamming shut the ledger, he said, 'You have made a profit of eleven thousand two hundred and eighty pounds.'

'Hmm. Pretty good, don't you think, Winford?'

Then, predictably, he said, 'The tax man cometh, my boy, the tax man cometh.'

After leaving, I did what I always did when I found myself in Porthmadog. I went into the Cob record shop, this time knowing I could afford to spend a few quid, and bought LPs of JJ Cale, Van Morrison, Eric Clapton and Cat Stevens.

When Ros came into the sitting room after saying goodnight to the children, I knew she had been crying.

'What's up?'

'It's Lysta, and that extra pocket money she wants.'

Our daughter was saving up to buy her grandfather a pair of walking boots for his birthday. Gwyn had told her he needed some new ones, had jokingly said that since his retirement he would have to save up. The sadness of it was he was unlikely to see his next birthday.

It had been arranged with Eryl that I could go and see him the following Sunday. He was now very tired, spending most of his time in his bedroom, reading between long periods of sleep. Eryl protected him from visitors and apart from relatives he saw no one. Ros, taking Seth with her, went to sit with him every day. We decided now to break the news to Sam and Lysta. Gloom hung over the house. The twins talked about their dying grandfather touchingly, asking those big questions about life after death, and what part Jesus was playing in the whole affair.

'Surely,' Lysta said, 'he will be with Jesus, and will get well again, even though we won't be able to see him?'

Hamish arrived from Fort William, wearing not a kilt but tartan trousers. He had an abundance of red hair and heavily freckled skin; one could imagine that too much sun would burn him to a crisp. He did not have a harsh Glaswegian accent, but the soft lilt of a Highlander. On his back he carried a bulging rucksack and a rolled-up sleeping bag. He'd been on the road for three days, sleeping out under the stars.

'This is a grand place,' he said. 'Rob's given me the lowdown, and I want to muck in. I'm ready to work.'

The following day Jack and I had arranged to drive over to a farm sale in Garndolbenmaen. Another farmer gone bankrupt, with all the equipment laid out in a field. As we arrived, the auctioneer's hammer came down on £11,000, sold to Gwynthor Jones, who would apply for planning permission to add a wing to the house, put in a nice front lawn and sell it to someone looking for a holiday home. A group of farmers walked around eyeing up the lots, agreeing not to bid against each other to keep prices low. One man's loss was another man's profit in these sell-offs. We knew many of the faces around us, most from our visits to Bryncir market. It was the first time we'd seen Gethin Hughes for months. He was there with others to fix the prices, but they kept their distance from Jack and me.

We were after some troughs to feed the sheep, rather than sprinkling concentrates on the fields. We fed them only in the winter, after lambing. We had noticed how much food was lost through being trampled into the snow and mud. There were six troughs and we had put a ceiling price of three pounds on each. When the auctioneer eventually came to the lot, asking if he could hear ten pounds for six metal feed troughs, there was a stony silence before he said, 'Come on, surely eight, come on, boys, who'll start me at eight?'

'Eight pounds,' I said, and why not as an opening bid? But it didn't go down well with Gethin and his crowd. They encircled Jack and me, letting us know that these troughs were theirs for ten pounds.

'Back off, boy,' one of them said, so close to my ear I could feel his breath.

'Ten pounds,' another shouted as they pushed against us, not using their hands but with the weight of their bodies, jostling us away.

'Twelve pounds,' I yelled but I could hear Gethin shouting in Welsh, and the auctioneer knocked down the lot to one of them. Then they broke away, moving on, bidding for certain lots, leaving others to fail to make a price at all.

'I'm not going to let them get away with that. We can't let them bully us and do nothing about it,' I said to Jack.

'We're outnumbered.'

Back in the Land Rover I was shaking so much I couldn't put a roll-up together. I told Jack I was too angry to drive away.

'Calm down. They're not worth it, and besides, what good will come of it?'

But I didn't calm down, and before Jack knew it I was gone, charging through them as they counted out the cash, passing bundles of notes between them, settling side deals they had made with each other. I grabbed Gethin Hughes by the collar and threw him over the bonnet of a parked van.

Someone got a crook round my neck and pulled me backwards. Suddenly I was lying on the ground with a boot on my chest. That was when Jack got stuck in, pulling them off me and giving me a chance to pick myself up. As one of them came running towards me I swung a punch, perfect in its timing, and watched him go down, out cold, flat on his back.

It stopped the whole fracas. I'd 'put his lights out', I think is the expression. I could see Jack, breathless, with a bleeding nose, while the dishevelled mob had gathered in a circle and were staring at the crumpled heap that lay before me. Others who had been attending the auction stood only as onlookers. No one moved or uttered a word. But it was time to say something and I spoke out so everyone would know why the brawl had taken place.

'What's going on here today is illegal price fixing, the greedy lining their own pockets. You know who you are, and you'll suffer the consequences.'

There was no response, so Jack and I walked through them and drove away. In the rear-view mirror they were still watching us as we disappeared out of sight.

After we had driven a mile or so without a word passing between us, I pulled off to the side of the road. That was when I told Jack the secret I had kept hidden for so long. How I had found Daphne Musto's note the day we arrived at Dyffryn. The suspicions I had always felt about Gethin, that he was playing a dirty game, knowing he was trouble, up to no good behind our backs. I reminded Jack it was he who had stolen our water. Then I let it sink in, everything I had just said. I felt a tremendous sense of relief. Then both of us burst into laughter.

'And where did that little monologue at the end come from?' asked Jack, still unable to stop laughing.

'I think it was Gary Cooper, in *High Noon*.'

It wasn't really funny, none of it was funny. When I swallowed, my Adam's apple ached, bruised by the shepherd's crook. My knuckles felt the pain of the punch I had thrown. My ribs hurt where the boot had stamped down on me. Blood had congealed inside one of Jack's nostrils, and there was a blue swelling on his bottom lip. Our war wounds. I wondered if reprisals would follow, or whether my accusing words would break the ring. At least they knew we were aware of what they'd been up to. And where did the auctioneer stand in all this? Was he in the pocket of the mob? I was certain he was. They were vultures, picking over the remains of a hard-working man who had gone under.

That night at Dyffryn as we sat round the supper table, Jack and I told the whole story. Hamish must have wondered if he was staying with a bunch of roughnecks. I told him not to form the wrong impression of us, that what had happened had to be faced up to. Rob thought they could come after us, while Ros was more worried about the fellow I'd knocked out pressing charges for assault. Jack thought they could poison our dogs, or run our sheep from the fields. The whole incident created some unease. The conversation went round in circles as we weighed up the possible outcomes.

As I was falling asleep, I decided on one last course of action. The damage had been done, so it could not make matters worse if I paid an unexpected visit on Gethin Hughes.

When Harry came by in the morning, he told me the story was out. He'd been playing darts in the Quarryman's with Boomer Harris, who had described it as the punch-up at the Garndolbenmaen corral, adding that the chap I had laid out was Will Hughes who farmed over in Criccieth. He'd been taken to hospital to have his jaw X-rayed.

'What do you think they'll do, Harry?'

'They'll come after you in some dirty way to get revenge.'

Once the morning feed and mucking out was over and I'd seen Rob and Hamish going down to the lower fields carrying bales over their backs to feed the bullocks, I took the opportunity to make my way over to Cae Uchaf. I didn't tell the others because I felt they would be against it. I wanted to defuse any plotting and planning for revenge.

As I climbed the stile in the boundary wall, Gethin was driving up the track in his Fordson Major, his rear-end loader stacked with bags of phosphates. Rather than wait for him to see me, I walked to the yard, where his wife was hosing down the flagstones. The water sparkled as it splashed on the ground. She seemed away in a world of her own. Not once did she look up as I called out to her. Only when my shadow fell across her did she jump with fright, throw down the hose and run into the house, leaving it wriggling like a snake until I turned off the tap. I couldn't see her anywhere, staring from a window as she had done before. I wondered if she was stone deaf. She must have heard me calling.

I could hear the tractor coming into the yard. Gethin was about to discover me standing there in front of his house, on his land, where he had once said I must never set foot again. In that minute I prepared myself for what was to follow. As he got closer, I stood with my feet apart, arms folded across my chest. An aggressive stance to show him I was ready and not going to back down.

When he saw me he hit the brakes and came to a stop no more than a dozen feet in front of me. He sat in his cab glowering, with the engine still turning, his hands gripping the steering wheel. What was going through his head, I wondered. Maybe his dominance of the mob, which as far as I knew could have begun years ago, was at last threatened. And here I was, confronting a way of life that didn't allow for strangers coming in with new ideas. Everything following a code of behaviour laid down by previous generations: this is how it has always been, and this is how it will remain. Had they made the Mustos' lives a misery too? I suspected so from the note Daphne had left.

Was he rattled? How was he going to deal with me? Had anyone defied him before? I couldn't remember the last time I had lost my temper. Strange that I felt no fear, none whatsoever. Maybe he would pick up this fearlessness like a scent, backtrack and concede. Perhaps I would detect in his turn of phrase a hint that he wanted to make peace, a radical undertaking for a bully who was used to getting his own way.

At last he turned off the engine, climbed down from the cab and slowly made his way towards me. When he was no more than an arm's distance away, I saw in his eyes the look of a man no longer brazen and domineering, but toppled and exposed.

'Here to finish the business are you?' He spoke as if resigned to a fate already decided.

'The game is up,' I said. 'All your dirty tricks, your conniving, your arrangements, your price fixing, all out in public now. And there's nowhere for you to hide.'

I told him I was considering going to the police (I wasn't, but I thought I'd chuck it in for good measure), intended to speak to the FUW (Farmers' Union of Wales) to seek advice on the matter, would have a serious word with the auctioneer. 'He was certainly in your back pocket.' Gethin's reign was over and he knew it. 'And tell your boys they are as guilty as you.'

He said nothing, just stood there with his hands in his pockets, spat at the ground to show his defiance.

'Do you remember the first words you said to me?' I asked. 'Good walls make good neighbours. Well, you've been a lousy one.'

As I walked away, having said what I had to say, an unfamiliar feeling came over me. I had taken the high moral ground, but who was I to appear so righteous? I who dealt in cash and had my own secret stash in a shoe box under the bed? Was I a hypocrite, laying down the law to him? But there was no one around here who didn't keep a certain amount of income back from the tax man. It was because so much was dealt with in hard cash. It's in your hand in an instant. The animal you have just sold might be dead the next day. Cheques take days to clear and could bounce; where would that leave you? And if the boot was on the other foot, it was pointless going after the man who had sold you the beast to ask for your money back. We already knew that from our own experience with the dealer in Devon: 'They were fine when they left here.'

Most people didn't trust banks after the financial crashes their fathers had lived through. The hill farmers saw them as institutions with smart carpets behind frosted windows, not places for those covered in earth and dung. Here everyone survived on subsidies and hid what cash they could. 'Who will feed the family if I go under?' The answer was 'No one', so life was hard and you lived on your wits. That's what Gethin Hughes had always done, and his father before him. The difference between us was that the way Gethin survived in the world was at the expense of his neighbours, who struggled by his side on the same hills. It was malicious, unfair, and had made their lives harder. All this went through my mind as I walked back to Dyffryn, feeling for certain that there would be no recriminations, that they would not be coming after us.

Dave was chewing the metal bars of his pen, his twizzle fully extended, smelling a sow, wanting her to be let in. How many times had he done it? He was always ready to perform; nothing ever diminished Dave's appetite for a good shag. He never turned his snout up at any sow; even in sub-zero temperatures he showed the same enthusiasm. Where would I be without his extraordinary sex drive, his amazing sperm count?

We'd been at Dyffryn more than five years. How many weeks is that, the days, the hours? It felt as if I had learnt something every single minute. Or maybe it was just today, trying to put a value on everything that had happened. Who did I think I was, speaking to Gethin Hughes so self-righteously?

Ros realised without my saying a word that I was preoccupied. I was never in the house mid-morning, making a cup of tea.

'Where have you been? What's going on?'

So I told her. She wasn't sure I had done the right thing, or that they would let the matter lie.

'Gethin Hughes is an unpredictable man,' she said. 'We will know the consequences soon enough. Anyway, we have other things to think about.'

'What do you mean?'

'You have to wean Frieda's calf.'

Another one of those jobs I find painful and emotional. I carried the calf into the old milking parlour and bedded him down on some fresh straw. I would have to hand feed him, but at least he would still be drinking his mother's milk, even if it was from a bucket. We no longer reared calves and would be selling him in a couple of weeks. Frieda bellowed her unhappiness around the farm. In the evening I turned up the music; I couldn't bear to hear her. I hated myself for causing it. In the morning, when I milked her, she just stood there and let me get on with it. 'Why do you let these things affect you so?' asked Harry, immune to such feelings.

'Because I care about her, that's why.'

Sunday, and we drove to Trefanai with the children. Our journey was delayed by a herd of Friesians blocking the main Caernarfon road. Sam had earache and was short tempered with his sister and brother. A cow pushed its wet slobbery mouth against the window of the car, while Glyn Roberts, a farmer I knew well, waved his arms, cursing in Welsh, trying to turn his herd into a field where they had bottle-necked. When we got past them we were running fifteen minutes late, and I knew it would irritate Eryl. Even if we explained the reason for our lateness she would say 'You should have allowed for it.' What's more, there were slots she had allocated when Gwyn could take visitors. She was frosty when we arrived, telling Ros she needed to speak to her. She pushed me upstairs, letting me know I could have no more than ten minutes with him.

When I entered, Gwyn was reading, his half-spectacles balanced on the end of his nose.

'You should read this. *The New Man*, by Maurice Nicoll.' He took a pen from the bedside table, wrote my name inside the cover and handed it to me. 'You'll get a lot from it. He was a disciple of Jung's.'

He was slipping away, his eyes sunken, cheeks hollowed, a yellowish hue to his skin. I offered him a glass of water that he sipped at only once before waving it away.

'It's only an ending here. A new beginning somewhere else,' he said with a smile. 'You are to share the books with Rhys [his son]. Those are my wishes.'

I walked to the window overlooking his beloved Menai Strait, the wide gap of sea that separates the mainland from the Isle of Anglesey. Guillemots landed clumsily on the calm drifting waters. A rower's oars broke the surface with a splash of whiteness that came and disappeared after each stroke. All were passing down the river of time, while on the footpath where we had walked so many times a Labrador barked at a ball floating away on the tide. I turned back and sat beside him on the bed.

'Gwyn, is there anything you need me to do?'

For a few moments he looked at me, reaching out his hand, almost whispering to me. 'You're not a Welshman, my boy, and this is not your home.'

'What are you saying to me?'

'When you know it's time to go, do not stay for the sake of others.'

I didn't know what he meant, neither did I find out, for Eryl, after a gentle tap on the door, entered the room, saying he needed to rest now.

'You can come again during the week,' she said to me.

I hadn't thought of it before, his ending, the closeness of it. Throughout the house there were cards from well-wishers; on the hall table, along the mantelpiece in the dining room, filling the kitchen shelves, even on the ottoman upstairs.

Eryl displayed the equilibrium of a woman in control of her

emotions. Her outer persona showed a gracious attitude to the sympathetic feelings of all who knocked at the door, and it must have required an inner strength not to be pulled down into a world of tears. For those who knew him had come laden with their sadness, with gifts of flowers, too many to find a place for in the house. Some were in vases in the conservatory, others she sent to the cottage hospital. She declined Ros's offer to come and stay with her. She preferred to sit alone in the evenings, watching television with a glass of sherry. A nurse now slept in the room next to Gwyn's, while Eryl slept at the far end of the landing. The chime in the grandfather clock had been turned off. At eight o'clock in the evening she took the receiver from the phone, and the house fell silent. At ten she went upstairs, opening his door the necessary inches to see if he was sleeping. She left the bedside light on, entering the room only to remove his glasses, or to take a book from his hands.

In the morning I arranged with Rob and Hamish to look after things, and left to say goodbye to Gwyn. It was autumn and after the chill night a warming sun rose over the fields, vaporising the dew in little mists not even knee-high, a layer of whiteness covering the grass at Dyffryn. The mountain peaks sharpened in clear skies. Down on the Caernarfon road I drove with my headlights on, stuck behind Gitto's cattle lorry. Between the gaps in the woodwork I could see the eyes of Welsh Blacks looking out, their wet nostrils breathing heavily. The hedges were thick with blackberries and wild honeysuckle. Stray sheep grazed the verges, three feet from certain death if they decided the grass was greener on the other side.

Eryl was in her dressing gown when I got to Trefanai, carrying a handful of letters in one hand, a cup of tea in the other. She told me to go up, that he was awake and knew I was coming.

'Remember, no more than ten minutes,' she insisted. 'He'll lose concentration anyway.'

'Who's looking after things?' he asked, as I pulled up a chair beside the bed.

'Rob,' I said, 'and a Scotsman called Hamish.' I told him the story of how they had met, the advantages of hitchhiking around Europe wearing a kilt.

'I want you to take Gilbert White's *Natural History of Selborne*, and here,' he said, 'I've made a list of others for you to read. Take it, take it.' He handed me a piece of paper. 'How's Jack? Has he got himself a girlfriend yet?'

'No, he seems more interested in sheep.'

He laughed. 'And your mother, does she still pine for her Cypriot fisherman?'

'I think that's far behind her now, but you know my mother, she is naturally romantic.'

'Now, I've written you a letter to be opened after I've gone. Here, put it in your pocket.'

'Gwyn, thank you for your friendship is all I can say. I don't know what . . .'

'Enough said. Leave it at that.'

I got up and walked over to the window, looking out over the Strait.

'Tell me what you can see.'

'Far off in the distance, above the blur of mist, I can see an unclouded day, and the white peak of a mountain, veined like marble. The trail of a high-flying plane, no more than an inch long in a huge sea of blue. I can see the stonework of the Menai Bridge. There are three cormorants flying east to west. And below, on that bench where we have sat so often, a woman is throwing bread into the water. There, that's a picture of the day painted for you, my dear friend.'

When I turned back to face him, he had fallen asleep. For a minute I stood and watched him, his chest barely rising, his eyes light-lidded, his head lolling gently to one side.

'Goodbye, Gwyn,' I whispered tiptoeing from the room.

Later that morning in the warmth of an autumn day, Ros and I stretched out our sheepskins to dry in the sun. Six of them nailed to sheets of chipboard, clean and brushed, they looked like works of art. The plan was to find somebody who could make jackets from them. Hamish, who was leaving later in the week, said there were crofters all over the Highlands who made garments for the London trade.

'I'll be your Scottish representative,' he said.

He seemed serious about it, and when he mentioned it again I said, 'What's the deal?'

'Ach, I want no money for it. I'll get you names and addresses.'

His plan was to join his uncle, who had a trawler in Mallaig, go to sea for three months, then head off to Kathmandu.

'In a kilt?'

'Aye, in a kilt.'

After lunch Ros left, taking Seth over to Trefanai. Jack and I went to check on the hives. They never got the attention they needed, out of sight, never part of our daily routine. If Jim Best knew he would be disappointed, for though I had a genuine interest in bee-keeping I just did not have the time. Besides, as Jim had said, they are the most highly evolved creatures on the planet; surely they could look after themselves.

So I put on the moon suit, making sure the gloves were over the cuffs, pulled the veil down over my face, and lit the smoker. Jack hung back while I lifted the roof of the hive and puffed smoke over the frames, whereupon an army of bees appeared, preoccupied, taking off and landing, and, dare I say it, extremely busy. We lifted out one of the frames, which were overflowing with honey, masses of it, set in the hexagonal cells.

Jack had carried down Ros's jam-making pan. He was wearing no protection whatsoever and once again bees were crawling all over his hands, but not one of them stung him. The secret lies in the chemicals the body gives off. That was my theory. Or perhaps Jack, being at ease, gave out no threatening messages. For some reason I spoke in whispers. Can bees listen in? Or are they on some other frequency, listening to cosmic radio waves, all highly tuned into a celestial world?

'How many are we taking?'

'Don't let's be greedy. Just the one.'

I replaced it with an empty frame, one of many Jim Best had given us. Did they notice, I wondered, or would they, being of one mind, just work that little bit harder to fill it again before the cold weather set in. It felt as if we had burgled somebody's house. Well, we had; it wasn't as if they had given it up for some greater good. We were petty thieves.

But the golden honey looked wonderful. I got out of my space suit and sat down with Jack on a rock in the afternoon sun to stick our fingers into the comb.

'It's the elixir of life,' I said. 'Maybe we will stay for ever young.'

'Never get arthritis.'

'Never go bald.'

'You're halfway there already.'

Back at the house, Sam and Lysta were home from school. I told them to get Rob and Hamish; I had a special treat for everyone. I toasted the bread Ros had made from the wheat grown on the farm, spread it with the butter we'd made from Frieda's milk and placed the honeycomb in the centre of the table. It was another of those satisfying moments that lifted the soul. We had achieved so much from what had all begun as a simple dream. It was a pity Ros wasn't there to share it with us.

I got the call when I was back in the house having breakfast. Gwyn had died at five o'clock in the morning, with Ros and Eryl at his bedside. I put my arms around Sam and Lysta, told them their grandfather, their taid, had died and gone to join the angels.

It was unusual for Jack to come by so early. The geese chased him, running down behind the van, their wings flapping, honking, as they always did. We ignored this daily occurrence. Only Meg took any notice, trying to scatter them, until Jack called her. I told him the news.

'He was a good man. I'll miss him . . . I hope Ros will be OK.'

'Why are you here so early?'

'I need fifty quid in cash. Have you got it?'

'Yes, of course.'

Jack knew of a weighing machine for sale over in Capel. A 'run through', as he called it, with the scales above, fixed to a metal frame. You let the sheep in one end and out the other, better than suspending them in a canvas harness until they were quiet enough to take an accurate reading.

'Fifty quid,' I said. 'Is that a good deal?'

'They're a hundred-and-fifty new.'

'Offer him forty.'

'God, you can't help it, can you?' Jack said, shaking his head.

'What?'

'You know what . . . just leave it to me.'

I got the cash, giving him an extra five pounds.

'What's that for?'

'Can you get some flowers for Eryl, from the florist in Caernarfon? You know the one near the cinema. They'll deliver them.'

'Yes, I'll send them from us all.'

After I told Rob and Hamish of Gwyn's passing, we had to move thirty porkers into the holding area, to wait for Gitto to take them to FMC. He had already quoted me forty pounds cash. It annoyed me that he had no sense of time. I'd known him be over an hour late, for which he would say in passing 'Sorry for the few minutes' delay', always putting it down to a mechanical problem. Whenever he left Dyffryn he would leave behind a puddle of oil. Once he left a wing mirror swinging on the five-bar gate at the end of the track. There was a tight turn there; he wasn't the only one. The walls showed the tell-tale signs of scraped paint, all the colours of the rainbow. These roads were built when the mode of transport was a horse and cart.

As we stood there waiting, Dewi came down the drive; surprisingly early for him. Opening the back doors of the van, he let two ewes jump out.

'They're yours,' he said.

'Where did you find them?'

'I didn't, Gethin did. Out on the Carmel road, where else?'

'Gethin Hughes found our sheep, and gave them to you?'

'He did, told me to bring them down.'

I could not put into words what I felt. I stood in a daze, speechless.

'Duw, you look like a man who's just received the most astonishing news.'

'Who would have believed it?'

'There's a man, I tell you, who has changed his ways. And that's not all: he's working a new dog now, Spider. A few rough edges, but a good dog in the making.'

Before Dewi left, I told him that in all the years we had been at Dyffryn, I'd never met Gethin's wife.

'What's wrong with her? Why does she never leave the place? I saw her the other day, couldn't get a word from her.'

'You and everyone else. She hasn't got a word in her. She's deaf and dumb, that's why. Born like it.'

'How did she meet Gethin?'

'Duw, now you're asking. That's before my time.'

'Dewi, before you go, there's something different about you today.'

'Surely you can tell? I'm wearing new glasses. Ma says I look like an owl.'

What strange lives we live, and what strange relationships we form. What on earth went on in that house at Cae Uchaf, between the two of them? Why had they married? Maybe Gethin learnt sign language, and that's how they courted. Who knows? I remembered he told me once that children 'hadn't come along with them'. And what had brought about this act of kindness, returning our sheep? What had turned the man from his malicious ways? Was it the fracas at Garndolbenmaen, or my going to him, telling him his dirty tricks were out in the open?

Or maybe lying beside his silent wife he had become aware of a new door opening, that it was time to step through. All this swam around me as we waited for Gitto. That and the passing of Gwyn, wondering how Ros was coping.

At last, and only forty-five minutes late, Gitto's lorry appeared, the old rickety wagon swaying from side to side. When he got to us he jumped down from the cab, and before we could get in a word said, 'You'll never believe it, it's that bloody clutch again.'

Ros returned home as the last light of day slipped into the depths of a calm sea, squeezed between a bank of cloud that drifted along the horizon's edge. Autumn's bite was in the air, adding to the melancholy of the shortening days. She looked drained. We hugged, a long hug. I held her close with her head on my shoulder.

'You're not doing anything tonight,' I whispered, leading her to the sitting room as Sam and Lysta came running in with Moss. We sprawled out on the sofa, each of us full of our own silence, remembering Gwyn.

Seth crawled over Ros, trying to open his mother's eyes. The day would not be forgotten. On any other night I would have told her about the remarkable change in Gethin Hughes. But there was no talk in me and Ros did not have the energy or the will to listen to something so dramatic.

Together we fell asleep in the sitting room. Cat Stevens summed it up: it is indeed a wild world.

12

Do We or Don't We?

The funeral had the feeling of a state occasion. Caernarfon came to a standstill. The streets were lined with people who bowed their heads as the hearse passed on its way to Christ Church in North Road. All the dignitaries filed in, including the mayor and his wife. A constant stream of cars pulled up, doors opening to let out the well-to-do. There was not enough room for everyone inside the church, as the milling crowd around the entrance inched forward under the stone arch. We made our way through them, to the front pew where the rest of the family sat; Gwyn's two sons Ian and Rhys, his brother Robyn and his children, nephews and nieces whom I hardly knew.

The pall bearers carried the coffin down the aisle, followed by Eryl, her face veiled, wearing a black woollen coat. She acknowledged everyone at the ends of the pews with a polite smile as she came to sit next to Ros, who had Seth on her lap. There was no heating in the church and we shivered as we stood while the music resonated around the building. The acoustics confused me, as I could not see the organ pipes, or the organist or where the sound originated from. Gwyn's coffin, covered with flowers, rested on a plinth draped with the Welsh flag. I wondered whose decision that was, for Gwyn was no nationalist, but a citizen of the world.

Of those who came to the lectern to give a reading, or recite a poem, it was Dai Ellis who best summed up the man they all admired. He spoke of the selfless doctor who drove one winter's night on the icy roads to Blaenau Ffestiniog, to see his sick boy suffering from tuberculosis, and in a snowstorm followed the ambulance back to Bangor hospital. His care had touched the family, who owed their son's recovery after months of treatment to this man. 'I'm just one of many who are indebted to the doctor. Byddwn yn gweld ei eisiau.' We shall miss him.

After the service there was a buffet lunch at the Royal Hotel. It was a muted affair, filled with the drone of sombre conversations between Gwyn's acquaintances. For he had never, in the time I knew him, spoken of friends or mentioned an individual he was particularly close to. For his work colleagues he had, I think, not a fondness, but a feeling of mutual respect. Many would probably have said you did not get close to the man. But in his self-contained world, I always thought he had a place for me. He adored his grandchildren. The only sentimental quirk in his nature was the Valentine's cards he sent every year to Ros.

At the Eifionydd Farmers' shop I saw Gethin Hughes loading his trailer with railway sleepers and I took the opportunity to go over and thank him for catching the ewes out on the Carmel road. I didn't overdo it, neither did I hold back in showing genuine appreciation. He dismissed it, giving it scant regard, so I decided to say no more about it. To have forced a conversation with him, or tried to pursue a friendly chat, would have fallen on deaf ears. After I said hello to Spider, his young Border collie, I left him, bent over the sleepers in the cold drizzle of a February day. I would never get more than a few words out of the man, but at least the hostilities had abated.

Several weeks had passed since the funeral. Eryl had gone on a cruise with a lady friend to the Canary Islands. Dewi told us that Arfon now farmed the Elysian Fields. He died in the cottage hospital with no meat on his bones, his heart worn out. I remembered that day at Henbant with him so clearly; I always would. Seeing his frailty then, I didn't know what kept him going for so long. The farm would be put up for sale, the equipment auctioned.

It was April 1976 when Tom and Agnetta told us their plans. They often dropped by, as friends do, never outstaying their welcome. During the day we had only minutes to spare. It was spring, everything in a rush; even the grass was in a hurry. Again we were growing wheat and potatoes; crops had to be rotated. Rob and I ploughed the top fields on the Massey. We worked into the evenings, with flocks of seagulls following the tractor. Cloud formations had changed in the lengthening days to wisps of silk that floated in the sky; over Cwm Silyn the light darkened, mauve upon the summit. The air was green with leaves unfurling, while dawn with its gathering brightness would wake us early with a chorus quite different from the one at dusk when the birds settled in the trees, until only a single thrush could be heard in the fading light. As one of these sweet evenings crept towards its quietness, Tom and Agnetta told us the scale of their adventure.

Agnetta, ex-ice skater and full-time Danish beauty, was keen to get on with it. This plan had been a long time in the hatching. Having come into money, she wanted to spend it for the benefit of others and form a community with like-minded people here in North Wales. 'People like you, who live off the land, growing your own food.'

'I suppose in some ways we are a community,' I said.

'Yes, you are,' agreed Tom.

'But there's more to it now,' Agnetta went on. 'We've worked out the details.'

That was the beginning of a long night. We went through the practicalities of such a venture, who was going to do what. There would be a central pot, the bank, each person taking what they needed to pay their way in the world. Rob and I would run the community farm, Jack would look after the sheep, Ros would oversee a herb and vegetable garden. Everything in fact, that we did already. Tom would continue selling fish. All the income from Dyffryn and Tom's business would go into the community bank. Agnetta would finance the whole project. We would trade as a limited company, in which we would have shares. It had come to the point where we had to decide whether we were interested in getting involved. We all looked at each other, not knowing really what to say.

'It's a lot to take in and just come back with an answer here and now,' said Rob.

'And you, Ros?' asked Agnetta.

'There's so much to think about.'

'Jack, does it appeal to you?'

'I'm a bit of a loner. I'm not sure if I would have much to contribute.'

'We need to consider it,' I said. 'You are asking for a huge commitment.'

'Well, we've talked about it enough tonight. Why don't we meet again in a week?' suggested Tom. 'It's late. I've got to drive to Birmingham in about three hours.'

So we agreed we would meet again, talk about it further.

'We want you to be honest with us, otherwise it will never work.'

In the morning, Harry cruised down the drive with two dead rabbits hanging round his neck, showing off to Sam and Lysta, 'Look, no hands,' skidding to a halt outside the kitchen door. He teased Moss with the kill he had brought for Ros to make a stew. He put his arm round me and pulled me to one side, whispering in my ear, 'I've done it.'

'Done what?'

'Got engaged to Bronwyn Jones.'

'The blonde barmaid at the Quarryman's?'

'Indeed.'

'Congratulations, Harry! When's the wedding?'

'Hopefully before the baby's born, which is in six months. Now I need to make some money, buy somewhere.'

Harry lived with his parents on the edge of Penygroes, in an ordinary stone-built semi-detached house. They scraped by, his father living on sickness benefit, having been laid off with a lung disease caused by breathing in slate dust over the years in Dorothea quarry. His mother worked three nights a week in the fish and chip shop, which seemed to provide most of their diet. Every week Harry took home a basket of vegetables, but whenever I saw his parents they looked unhealthy. Their skin had a pallor, lacking some vital vitamin, or maybe just sunlight. Harry told me the 'old man' sat at home most days, reading the racing form, getting a neighbour to place his bets, not attempting to walk the few hundred yards to the betting shop in Union Street.

'I'd marry her anyway. We've got a lot in common, you know: darts, shove-halfpenny, playing cards . . .' he laughed.

The news came as no surprise to Ros, who had heard snippets from Harry when he butchered the meat in the barn. He would confide in her, telling her things that men would never talk about between themselves.

On the way to Pant Glas to get six more point-of-lay pullets, I called in to see my mother. I wanted to talk to her about joining forces with Tom and Agnetta, hear what she thought about it. When I walked into her kitchen, because I never knocked, she was having a cup of tea with Owen Bethel, who seemed embarrassed, as if I'd caught them up to something.

'Darling, I wasn't expecting you. Is everything all right?'

'I'll come back. It doesn't matter.'

But Owen stood up, his tea unfinished, saying, 'No, no, it's inconvenient, I can see that.'

My mother didn't try to stop him, telling me she had some news, wanting me to stay.

'I'll see you tomorrow evening, Dinah,' he said, pointing to the box of Cadbury's Milk Tray on the table. 'I do hope you enjoy them.'

'I will, I'm sure, and thank you for the book of crosswords.'

We waited for him to put on his coat, passing the kitchen window, raising his hat as he disappeared down the garden path.

'He's a lovely man,' she said. 'Interesting and well read.'

'I told you he would come calling.'

My mother smiled and cleared the table, removing the evidence as if Owen's gifts were better out of sight. She showed certain traits when something serious had to be discussed. Sitting upright in her chair, clasping her hands together, as if about to utter a prayer, or say grace before a meal.

'It's your sister. Her marriage has broken down, and she's coming home.'

Dale, two years older than me, married to a Canadian university lecturer, had gone to live in British Columbia and now had a three-year-old daughter, Freya.

'It's irretrievable,' she went on. 'He's a philandering rogue, who would rather lecture his students in their bedrooms. It's such a pity. I never thought he was that type of man.'

On hearing this news I decided to keep quiet about my own. I knew my mother well enough. She would get flustered, believe the world around her was crumbling into uncertainty.

'Of course, this changes my whole life, you realise that, don't you?'

'I'm not sure how it does.'

'Well, she wants to return to Westbourne and study law. I shall have to help her. She's a single mother, and she'll need me to look after Freya.'

I kissed her forehead, saying it was too early to decide anything. 'Sit tight,' I said. 'Let things unfold. A direction will reveal itself.'

I drove to Pant Glas with Moss to deliver half a pig to Rhona Gasgoine, who taught religious studies at the primary school. It was warm enough to lower the windows. As I passed down Penygroes high street the shop doors were open, and Morgan the Butcher, a competitor of mine, was winding down his awning. It was warmer than usual for this time of year. It felt like a summer's day. As I filled up at the Paragon garage Trevor Ellis came over to me.

'Well, Perry, you missed out on that Opel Kadett, didn't you?' he said.

'I'm sure it won't be the last car you try to sell me.'

'You're right there. I've got a lovely Cortina coming in shortly. One owner, three years old, forty thousand on the clock.'

'Not yet. I'll let you know when.'

'It's yellow,' he shouted after me.

'Yellow doesn't suit me,' I shouted back.

In the spring of '76 we had little rainfall. The arable farmers down on the lowlands were taking water from the rivers. Already the scaremongers on television were warning of a hosepipe ban, unless the heavens opened up. We had the occasional passing shower, but no heavy downpours. It held back the wheat and potatoes, both of which needed a good drink. The water level had dropped in the stream, but not enough to cause us any real concern. The automatic water feeders in the farrowing pens still had sufficient pressure to ensure that when the sows pressed their snouts onto the metal flaps water oozed into the trough.

Every night the six o'clock news showed pictures of half-empty reservoirs, telling us the many ways to conserve water. The long-term weather forecast was for continuing dry sunny days and no rain. What concerned me now was how people's eating habits change when the temperature rises. Less meat gets eaten. No one wants to cook a joint, preferring salads and cold foods. Pork sales started to fall, and as the warm weather continued, the demand increased for lettuce, tomatoes, onions, everything that we now struggled to grow in the dry earth.

Tom and Agnetta came to get our response to their proposals. There was a subdued atmosphere when they arrived full of expectations. Although Ros and I had spoken about it from time to time, we hadn't found out what Rob and Jack really felt. Neither of them had turned up, which said it all: they weren't that interested. Ros apologised and asked for another week. They stayed for supper, telling us more about their plans. Agnetta now wanted to start a school based on the ideas of Rudolf Steiner.

It wasn't until we were having breakfast the next morning that Rob told me.

'Kate and I have been making plans. I've decided it's time to leave. I'm going to move in with her, in that town you say no one has ever heard of, Chorley.'

'For sure? It's definite?'

'Yes, it's definite.'

'What will you do?'

'Find a job somewhere.'

'What do they do in Chorley?'

'Make cakes.'

Rob was so much a part of the place; through the years we had become close friends. No, more than that, he was like another brother.

'And Kate, has she got a teaching job?'

'Yes. She'll start in September.'

'So the end of an era.'

'In some ways, but I'll be back. Dyffryn's in my blood.'

There was nothing more to say. Now it really was a matter for only Ros and me to decide, for we knew that Jack would prefer to be on his own. It would be too complicated for my brother to deal with all those relationships. We had a week to make a life-changing decision.

Ros and I talked every evening, agreeing and disagreeing about the several ways we could get involved.

'Surely,' I said, 'there's no point in joining Tom and Agnetta unless we're better off? I don't just mean financially, but as a family.'

The prize for Ros was the children going to a Rudolf Steiner school. She made that quite clear, saying it was me who couldn't make up my mind.

'I don't understand why we have to make such a drastic change. We have a farm that makes enough money for us to live on. We are self-sufficient in food, and we have our freedom. That's a lot to give away. Let's send the children to the school, and just help in any other way we can.'

We flopped back on to the sofa, both of us staring at the ceiling. Was that our final decision? We certainly didn't say so to each other.

Hughie was stacking his churns on the stone platform beside the Carmel road, waiting for the milk lorry to take them to the creamery in Bangor. It was yet another cloudless day as we watched the slow progress of the school bus climbing the hill. Every morning I listened to it groaning round the bends, wondering if that day would be its last. One day it would give up the ghost, stop in the middle of the road, its engine expired. Hughie told me in all the years he had farmed, this was the driest he had ever known it.

'We'll have no harvest if it continues like this. Prices will soar, hay will go through the roof. Everyone will sell their cattle, cut their losses.'

We had now been over a month without any rain. There was a nationwide hosepipe ban, not that it meant much to us. Farmers short of grass had started to bring their cattle to Bryncir market and each week saw a further drop in prices. The summer of '76 was a hard time for pigs, who suffered in the extreme temperatures. I could feel the resentment building up amongst the herd. After long periods of close contact they would turn nasty and bite each other. All of them sought a cool spot, which is hard to find under a hot tin roof. They had become disgruntled sunbathers. As soon as they had eaten, Rob and I would run from either end pouring water along the trough. Their antisocial behaviour had got worse since we had stopped hosing them down. They were simply overheating. Pigs burn easily; Dave's skin I could scratch off with my fingers.

From the cities of England, people made their way to the coast to enjoy the novelty of a summer holiday full of sunshine. I'd never seen so much traffic passing through Penygroes, on its way to Butlins in Pwllheli. However, at Dyffryn our situation was worsening. The stream that we relied on was drying up and we were having to restrict our water, which was now coming through the taps discoloured and undrinkable. Every day I drove to Trefanai with ten-litre plastic containers, which Eryl let me fill from a standpipe outside the garage. The government appointed a minister for drought, showing the country how seriously they were taking the situation. Rob suggested that at the next full moon we should go out into the fields and perform an ancient Inca rain dance. The gods needed to be appeased.

That summer a lethargy set in. By midday our brains were cooked and we started to take after-lunch siestas. We went

Mediterranean in our routine, doing all the physical chores whilst we still had the energy, humping sacks of food and moving pigs before the sun had climbed too high. In the searing heat of the day, Frieda lay in the shade of the larch trees chewing the cud, rather than grazing the yellowing grass. Her milk yield dropped away. Only in the morning, when there was some dew in the fields, did she show an appetite. We carried twelve gallons of water to her trough twice a day. Every night we listened to the weather forecast predicting nothing but sunny days for the foreseeable future, with temperatures up in the eighties. Harry was keen to dig a well, convinced there were gallons of cold, clear water just beneath our feet. 'Hey, maybe we'll strike oil.'

For the first time in years Gethin Hughes climbed the stile, coming with Spider at his side. We had decided to dredge the stream. Jack and Harry loosened the stones with pickaxes, while Rob and I shovelled out the mud.

'Hope you're not going to blame me for this,' he said.

I had neither the time nor the inclination to make the effort for conversation with him. We knew where we stood with each other; we acknowledged one another's existence from a healthy distance.

'You need to dig at least two feet,' he said, removing his cap, wiping his sweaty face with a handkerchief. 'I'll tell you now, dig a trench, let the water run down to its lowest point. Then sink your holding tank beneath it.'

This was Gethin giving friendly advice, being helpful, making an effort. I eventually asked him the purpose of his visit.

'Only to tell you I'm getting a digger tomorrow to clear the stream.'

'Thanks for letting us know.'

'Well, the water will run dirty for the day. Don't want you turning on me.'

Then without a goodbye he made his way back over the stile, calling Spider who had been having fun with Moss. At least our dogs got on well together.

All week we dredged the stream, sinking a hundred-gallon circular tank at the top of the vegetable garden. The water poured in, and when the tank was full we closed it off. This was our lifeline during the months of drought. Only when there is a shortage of something do you realise how dependent you are on it.

Tom and Agnetta were coming the next day and I needed to confirm with Jack what he wanted to do. We went to the Quarryman's and over a bowl of chips and a couple of lagers I sounded him out.

'It's not for me, is it? I'm my own man. Best leave me out of it.'

'I knew that's what you'd say.'

'It's probably a good idea, but it would all be too complicated for me. Besides, I prefer my own company.'

Once Jack made up his mind, that was it. I had no intention of trying to sway him. I asked him what plans he had; we'd been at Dyffryn over six years. But he hadn't any, content to be out in the wild places with his sheep and Meg. He said he liked the arrangement we already had, was happy living nearby, up at Rose's cottage. He had no wish to change anything.

'Don't you want a woman?' I asked him.

'Sometimes I think about it, but not often. It seems to be more of a concern to our mother than to me.'

Ros wasn't surprised when I told her of Jack's decision.

That night, as I walked up to look in on the pigs, the sky darkened, heavy with cloud. The air had cooled. Was there a thunderstorm coming? No one had talked of it. Wind stirred in the trees, and as I entered the farrowing pens I felt the first few drops of rain. Often, no matter how quietly I moved among them checking on the litters, the sows would get to their feet grunting, coming to say hello. They knew the smell of me. Sometimes I would bring them treats, letting them chew a carrot, giving them a few extra nuts. I liked the feel of their wet snouts as I fed them. But whilst I lingered the rain got heavier on the asbestos roof and suddenly the night lit up. The thunder directly overhead crashed so loudly that it shook the building. All the sows were agitated and on their feet. It sounded as if the ceiling of the world had cracked open. Torrential rain was falling and unable to leave the building I opened the door and watched the zigzag lightning move across the landscape, sudden flashes of brightness silvering the raindrops. I hoped we wouldn't lose our power. But in twenty minutes all died down, and as quickly as it had come so it departed. The immediate effect was to clear the air; standing there I could smell the earth again. The freshness of grass, the dust taken out of the atmosphere, the sweet smell of pine reaching me from the larch trees. It was as if a dormant sense had returned. The whole place was still, dripping with water, rumblings of thunder fading away in the distance.

Sam and Lysta watched it all from their bedroom window. The electrical storm had charged their batteries, firing them up and they were far from wanting to go to sleep. Ros thought reading them a story might calm them down. It didn't; they were wide awake for an hour.

'Tell us a joke, Dad,' said Sam. 'I want to laugh myself to sleep.'

'That's impossible,' I said.

In the morning, when the sun had risen high enough to warm the damp earth, it seemed the fields were smouldering. Clouds of steam hung in the air and swallows were weaving through the mist, feeding on the wing. The soil was as hard as clay that's been fired in a kiln. We needed steady rain; we were desperate for it now. We ran a hose down from the holding tank into the vegetable garden. Now we could water in the mornings and again as the sun was setting. Still we carried water to the porkers, never letting their troughs run dry.

Rob heard on the news that some pigs housed in a shed in Norfolk got so dehydrated they went berserk, broke out onto a disused aerodrome and ran amok, eating the tyres of an old Dakota that the firemen used to practise on.

I walked Dave down to the lower fields where there were several muddy springs he could roll around in to cool himself down. I couldn't leave him there, although it took an hour out of my day; it broke the monotony of lying in his pen. The mud stuck to him, protecting him against sunburn. When we walked back he looked more like a bison than a pig. Dave always ignored the geese, which would suddenly appear in the midday sun to hassle us. It was never hot enough for them to take a siesta. Always on patrol, the only time they amused me was when I found them one afternoon swimming in Sam and Lysta's paddling pool. They had no regular routine, although during this prolonged hot period they would often drink from the same spot in the stream.

Meanwhile my mother was making plans; my sister was returning from Canada in two weeks. Dinah was looking for somewhere for them to live in Westbourne. She gave me the keys to Hendy, asking me to look after the place. It all happened very quickly, and we didn't know if she was going to return or put the house on the market.

It was July, and in two months Rob would be gone. I had no idea who would replace him. For sure it meant employing someone; I couldn't run the farm on my own. Should I ask Harry? He had always been a free agent; there was never a day when he was not turning his hand to something. It was a loose arrangement with no set hours. Every week after I finished the meat round I slipped him some cash. The amount varied, offset against the meat and vegetables he took. It didn't feel right to offer him a full-time job; it would have changed the dynamics of our relationship to become his employer. Harry working a forty-hour week with overtime would suit neither of us.

Changes were coming, and Jack, unaware of the plans I was making, was following his own independent life; although we were still partners in the farm, he drew off only what he needed. Nothing had ever been written down. It was an agreement between brothers, and had never caused any difficulties. Whatever we did would have to be OK with him. If not, I was in no position to buy him out. Maybe it was time to get Dyffryn valued. All this, while the earth baked and the endless summer remained hot and dry.

Again on the news we were shown pictures of tankers delivering water into the towns, people queuing in the streets waiting to fill buckets and containers. We were advised to use bath water on the garden, to save every drop. Washing your car was banned; all were covered in a layer of dirt. It felt as if we lived on the edge of a desert. When the wind blew, dust clouds rolled in like a sandstorm. The whole countryside was parched and fire crews were kept busy, warnings put out to picnickers not to drop a careless cigarette end. In those summer months of '76, all we got was the occasional thunderstorm, never enough to raise levels in the reservoirs, although the crops lifted their drooping heads for a while. Then the clouds would vanish and back came the clear days. No one had ever known a year like it.

An hour before Tom and Agnetta came to hear our final decision, I told Ros I didn't want to go through with it. I had made up my mind. Dyffryn was our way of life. It was me who decided what we were going to do on the farm. I couldn't hand that over to anyone else. For the first time in our marriage we were seeking separate directions. Ros was adamant she wanted a new beginning, something that took her away from Dyffryn.

'If you aren't interested, then I'll do it on my own.'

After we gave them the news that Rob was leaving and that Jack and I would not be getting involved, Ros still spoke enthusiastically, telling them she was keen to give the children an alternative education to the one the state offered. When she agreed to oversee their vegetable garden, I realised we were in danger of drifting apart. There was nothing left to say, and I could sense their disappointment. We all tried to lighten the mood, to pick ourselves up with other topics of conversation, but the decision I had taken hung in the air for the rest of the evening.

Progressing quietly in the background of our lives, and now coming to fruition after many months of trial and error, which was the only way you ever found out anything at Dyffryn, our first sheepskins were being delivered as finished garments. The cleaning and curing of them we now understood. But the problem had been how to get them made up into something that people would consider wearing. Then Ros had met Celia Foxton, a batik artist and fashion designer. She was well off and could pursue her creative desires without the stress of having to earn a living. She and her boyfriend owned a smallholding in Waunfawr. He bred shire horses and took black and white photographs of the Scottish highlands. Celia converted a barn into a studio, where she had an old-fashioned loom. She had whitewashed the walls, hung her batik blinds of coloured landscapes in the windows. When the light shone through them, they had an iridescence like stained glass.

It had been many months since she had taken up our challenge. Having filled some old whisky vats with different coloured dyes, she now had a range ready to show us. She pulled up in her Volvo estate with a pile of sheepskins in the back. Celia wore swirly, ankle-length dresses of her own design. She liked poppies on a dark background. She hennaed her hair, wore heavy black mascara. There were physical similarities to Mary Quant. What I didn't know was that Ros and Celia had organised a fashion show, and we were the models.

Celia had created various styles for both adults and children. Lysta, somewhat self-consciously as you would expect of a child, was the first to enter the sitting room, wearing a purple waistcoat with gold trimmings.

'Do a twirl,' said Rob.

'Oh yes, I do like that,' enthused Ros. 'It fits perfectly.'

'Those imitation tortoiseshell buttons are very fashionable at the moment,' added Celia.

'Thank you, Lysta,' I said. 'Very nice movement you have.'

'Dad, don't be silly.'

'Sam, walk properly. Don't shuffle your feet,' said Ros as Sam paraded before us in a dark tan jacket with silver buttons.

'Now this one has no breast pocket but . . . Sam, could you open the jacket for us? It has an inside pocket sewn into it. I think this style will appeal to the children of rock stars. It's very show businessy.'

Meanwhile Rob had been ushered out, returning in a tight-fitting waistcoat, jet black with three white buttons. He wiggled his petite little bottom and ran his hands up the inside of his thighs. 'I feel so liberated.'

'Rob, please take it seriously,' said Ros, not amused in the slightest.

'This is very casual,' went on Celia. 'It's really best suited to be worn over a T-shirt. I've aimed this at the young dudes market. I can see it being sold in the Portobello Road or Carnaby Street.'

Then Jack, with some reluctance, was pushed in by Ros wearing a dark green three-quarter length coat, with deep side pockets and a hood.

'Now this is my particular favourite,' said Celia. 'It really is for the outdoor masculine type. I was actually thinking of Jack when I designed it. Out there in those cold blasting winds, exposed to the elements. As you can see, I've trimmed the cuffs, finishing them with a leather band.'

'How does it feel, Jack?'

'Can't see myself wearing it, but I'm sure somebody will.'

'You'll be the best-dressed shepherd in North Wales,' said Ros. 'It really does suit you.'

'We'd sell this coat to ramblers and hill-walkers. Also I can see it being worn at outdoor concerts and football matches.'

That completed the fashion show. 'I wanted to model something,' I said, peeved not to have had the chance to strut my stuff.

'They will come in a range of different colours and sizes,' continued Celia, lighting up a Sobranie cigarette with a gold filter. 'So what do you think?'

'Very impressive,' said Ros. 'I'm so pleased; it's been so long in the making.'

'When are we going to talk money?' I said, at which point Ros dived in.

'It has nothing to do with you. Celia and I are coming to our own arrangement.'

I don't know why but I'd completely forgotten that Ivan Treadgold was coming to value Dyffryn. When I heard his Lancia scraping over the stony track I had no idea who he was. Thinking he must be a salesman turning up without an appointment, I went and hid in the farrowing building. You'd be surprised how many reps had driven into Dyffryn in unsuitable cars, always hoping to make a sale, leaving with their exhausts hanging off. Ivan's arrival certainly exceeded the legal decibel limit. But I came out to meet him when I heard him calling my name.

'That's going to cost a few quid,' he said, peering under the car. 'I was hoping I might get away with it. It's my son's. Mine's in the garage.'

As we walked around the farm we talked about the drought, what hay would be fetching soon on the open market. He knew his stuff, advising me to sell our surplus lambs now, saying that prices would continue to fall until the rain came and the grass grew once more. I told him the story of Dyffryn, that we were an organic farm free of chemicals. But he already knew about us, and without any sales talk from me said he would be keen to try a lamb; his wife believed in buying local produce. We walked and talked for an hour, and when we got back to his car he told me he thought the place was worth £30,000.

That evening, as the single stars appeared one by one in the darkening sky, with Moss by my side I walked the lower fields, subdued and silent, listening to the thinning song of invisible birds settling down for the night. Changes and decisions took up all my thinking. I knew I had to face up to them, but no matter how hard I searched within myself, I found no answers. Only the twilight and the glowing horizon that lit the distant sea offered any comfort.

When I returned to the house, I could hear Ros upstairs with the children. I went and turned on the record player and watched the black vinyl spin. It was Led Zeppelin climbing a stairway to heaven, something we certainly weren't doing.

13

Decisions Reached

Jack and I had never sat down together and talked about money. We just got on with farming; neither of us had ever been interested in building up a stash. Everything we made went back into the farm. Over a cup of tea and a bacon sandwich in the Beach Café I told him the valuation Ivan Treadgold had put on Dyffryn. He raised his eyebrows when I said £30,000, looked away across the beach, where a lilo carried by the wind somersaulted through the sunbathers. An Irish setter retrieving sticks from the sea shook out its coat over an old lady trying to snooze in her deck chair.

'Do you want to sell up?'

'No, I just thought it was time to have it valued.'

I tried to explain the whole Tom and Agnetta community idea in more detail, but the more I spoke the more complicated it sounded. Meanwhile, Gwyneth Thomas had brought over a bowl of water for Moss and Meg, both lying under the table. She was on all fours beneath us, tempting them with treats. 'Give me a paw . . . give me a paw . . .'

'Ros wants to get involved, but I've told them I don't want to be a part of it.'

'Where does that leave you and Ros?'

'I don't know yet. I'm a bit uneasy about it.'

'I do see a problem coming.'

'What's that?' I said.

'We need to find someone when Rob leaves.'

'Any ideas?'

'Harry seems the obvious person.'

'I'm not sure,' and I told Jack all the reasons why. That it worked well for Harry to come and go as he pleased. He would want to keep his freedom, be paid in cash.

'Maybe not any longer, now he's getting married, with the weight of a mortgage on his shoulders. I think you should put it to him. He could well be interested in taking a flat wage, rather than keep chasing a pound.'

'I'll sound him out,' I said. 'But I'm not keen. I'd be his boss.

Can you see Harry doing a forty-hour week?'

'Think of the mortgage, with a baby on the way. Bronwyn'll want to know where the money's coming from.'

We walked the dogs along the beach amongst the holiday-makers. You could hear the Brummie accents, some Liverpudlians too, no doubt renting the caravans on the farms that bordered the sand dunes. Children held on to kites, grandfathers paddled with knotted handkerchiefs on their heads. Working-class families from the north of England, who brought black inner tubes with them rather than buying rubber rings. Fish and chips, hot dogs and a bottle of Vimto were the holiday treat.

We skimmed stones, talked some more; it was easier than doing it face to face. At the far end of Dinas, where the sea flattens and the wind drops, Jack told me he had met someone. It was often only here, in this particular spot, that you could hear yourself speak. Elsewhere the wind was always a tiresome element, forever fighting conversation, buffeting the senses.

'Sorry, Jack, did you say what I think I heard you say?'

'Probably.'

'But you haven't had a girlfriend for years.'

'Well, nothing may come of it.'

'What's her name?'

'Corinna.'

'How did you meet?'

'She was hitching, making her way to Glynllifon to start an agricultural course.'

'Rose Tobias won't be pleased; the spurned lover.'

'Ha, ha!'

August, and still the long hot summer continued. On my Friday meat round it required all my ingenuity to get anyone to open their purses. People wanted light meals in these sweltering days, not the traditional Sunday lunch. I offered discounts at what I called 'drought rates' to those who would buy now to put away in the freezer. Some took me up on it, but most were buying cold meats from the Co-op to go with their salads. I told

Harry it was hardly worth coming up on a Thursday to butcher the meat, that maybe we should not bother until the weather broke, or get going again in September when the kids were back at school and the temperature had dropped a few degrees.

'I took eighty quid last week. There's no profit in that.'

Hughie appeared at the door shirtless, wearing a pair of trousers held up by braces, his fly half open, his body glistening with sweat.

'You're flying at half-mast,' I said, but he completely ignored me.

'Have you got five minutes?'

His sheep had broken out and were grazing in the cemetery. Jobber was walking on only three legs. Could I come with Moss and bring them back? There was a burial in half an hour; we needed to move quickly. By the time we got down there the hearse was already parked outside, minus the coffin. The sheep were grazing between the headstones, while in the far corner a group of mourners stood in a quiet circle. I knew this was going to be tricky with the sheep scattered all over the place.

Before I let her go, I warned Hughie that Moss was keen, but did not have Meg's experience.

'Duw, boy, get on, be damned with it.'

Not appropriate language for a cemetery. So with a hushed voice I sent Moss with a 'Get away, girl', hoping that she would sweep round behind them and lie down without my needing to shout and disturb the mourners, who as yet were unaware of us. So far, so good: as she crept forward the sheep, now alert to her presence, gathered together with an urgency that hadn't spilled over into the panic that an over-zealous dog can cause. Moss was showing a maturity I hadn't seen before, as if she were involved in her own game of grandmother's footsteps. Every time they turned she froze; they turned again, and she froze.

Hughie patted me on the shoulder, in acknowledgement of what a good job she was doing. They were lowering the coffin into the grave as the sheep formed into a tight group. I wished Jack had been here watching her. I'd given her no commands, but as the ewes moved forward she raised herself, stalking them, holding back far enough to let them come quietly between the gravestones. It was wonderful to see her like this, controlling the flock as a real working dog. She completed the job perfectly, steering them out through the cemetery gates onto the road. Only one renegade put a slight blemish on the whole operation by jumping into the hearse. On such a sweltering day, the back had been left open.

I scooped Moss up into my arms as we walked behind the flock, hugging and praising her all the way back to Dyffryn. After Hughie had turned down the track to Llwyndu Canol, I rolled around in the grass with her. I'd never felt so close to her. The trauma of that terrible beating that had so damaged her confidence was behind her now. Later Hughie came over to show his gratitude with a bottle of whisky.

'You did well.'

'Not me,' I said. 'She did it all on her own.'

I telephoned Harry and we arranged to meet in the Quarryman's at six. When he asked me why, I told him to discuss the future. He immediately became nervous, as if he suspected I would be bringing bad news.

'Can't we talk about it now?'

'No, it's best face to face.'

'What's going on?' he said. 'What's happened?'

'Nothing. What are you worried about?'

'It's in the tone of your voice. You're serious, man. I know that serious voice.'

'I've got to go. There's a bloody pig out.'

There wasn't, but there was a farm auction I wanted to go to. We needed to buy some fencing posts, to replace those rotting along the lower boundary.

Later that afternoon, as I was driving back to Dyffryn, the weather broke at last, a steady persistent rain soaking into the scorched earth, getting beneath the surface, where gnarled roots could drink again.

It was remarkable how quickly the parched land recovered, lifting the drooping heads of the barley, bringing a fresh greenness to the dry leaves. All that had withered and looked so forlorn revived, strengthening in both stem and root. It had been the longest dry period since records began. My windscreen was smudged with dead insects and I had to pull over, unable to see the road ahead. I took off my T-shirt to wipe the glass clean. The air was full of the smell of vegetation; a cooling breeze swayed through the crops. Birds flicked their feathers as water droplets ran down their backs. For this year's fledglings it must have been the first time they had felt this curious stuff falling on them. Moss too enjoyed herself, her head out of the window, biting at the rain, quenching her thirst.

I met Hughie at the gate carrying an empty churn in each hand, raindrops bouncing like little silver ball bearings on his bald head.

'Duw, boy, at last,' he said. 'It's behind us now.'

When I walked into the house Sam was feeding Seth at the kitchen table. They were both wearing Red Indian headdresses full of brightly coloured feathers.

'Dad, I'm Big Chief Running Water, and this is my brother Little Drip.'

'How! Pleased to meet you.'

Lysta came running into the room dressed as a squaw. 'How, Dad. We are Red Indians.'

'I can see that. What's your name?'

'Red Dove.'

'You didn't happen to do an Indian rain dance?'

'Why?'

'Because it's pouring outside.'

'Dad, help us put up our tent in the sitting room?'

'OK, but where's your mother?'

'She's outside in the garden.'

In the back bedroom I opened the window and watched Ros standing with her arms outstretched, her head back to feel the rain on her face, her mouth open to taste the wetness on her tongue.

After putting up a wigwam for the young tribe who now inhabited the house, I tied Red Dove to a standard lamp. Big Chief Running Water and Little Drip were going to rescue her. I drove to the Quarryman's Arms to meet Harry.

With the rain still falling under heavy grey clouds I turned on the headlights. Pools of water flooded the roads and round tight bends I could feel the Land Rover sliding on the greasy surface. With no grip, cars were skidding. No doubt there would be accidents on the winding roads of North Wales. Already, as I passed down Penygroes high street, the council workers were lifting the covers from blocked drains. Tom 'Tatoes was unloading his lorry, throwing sacks of potatoes to a line of people, carrying them over their shoulders into the shop. Outside the Paragon garage Trevor Ellis, undeterred, shouted, 'Hey! Perry, I've got the very car for you.'

Harry was finishing a pint when I walked into the saloon bar, his face anxious, his hair wet and combed. He was chewing on his favourite snack of pork scratchings. 'What are you having?'

'Just a lemonade, thanks.'

We sat at a table in the corner, waiting for him to finish his mouthful.

'You sound like a cement mixer.'

'What's all the trouble, then?' he said.

'Why do you think there should be trouble?'

'I've known you long enough, that tone in your voice.'

'You make us sound like an old married couple.'

'Duw, God! Is that what it's come to?'

'Harry, let me explain.'

So I began, not even certain myself that I was selling him a good idea. I told him about all the changes we were facing, Rob's imminent departure, the need to replace him. 'And you getting married with a baby on the way, needing to buy a place, taking on a mortgage.'

'To be fair to you, man,' he said, 'I thought you were coming here to tell me it was the end. But you're not. You're offering me a job.'

'I suppose I am. What do you think of that?'

'I've never been employed. It's too close to the taxman.'

'I don't think it would work, you working for me full time on the PAYE.'

'I don't do nine to five.'

'Harry, we feed the pigs at seven.'

'Well, seven till three. I need another pint.'

We talked through a maze of possibilities, haggling over money, Harry wanting sixty pounds clear every Friday.

'I need you to work Sundays, which means you can't get pissed on Saturday nights.'

We went on and on, didn't give up. We talked about the perks of the job, Harry to take some of his wage in meat and vegetables. 'Even milk, man, and that bread of yours, you can chuck that in.'

We seemed to be getting closer, within a whisker of agreeing a six-day week, including working some Sundays, fifty pounds in his back pocket, and two joints of meat, either pork or lamb; Harry didn't eat beef. Three loaves of bread a week, two pints of milk a day, a box of vegetables as and when.

'Agreed, man,' he said, walking to the bar to get his fourth pint. But when he returned he said, 'What about sick pay and holidays?'

'Of course you'll get sick pay, and two weeks' paid holiday. And a free packet of tissues if you want.'

At last the deal was done and we shook on it.

I went and rang Ros, telling her to start supper without me. She wasn't pleased, saying it had taken an age to release Red Dove.

'Sorry.'

I made my way back to Dyffryn through the rain, the worn windscreen wipers scraping over the glass, streetlights glowing in auras of mist. The chemist was still open for late-night prescriptions; the fish and chip shop oozed a cloud of steam. A soaked bale of hay fallen from a trailer lay in the gutter. Peculiar feelings passed through me. There were a lot of changes coming; not of my doing, but outer events breaking in on my life. I thought of my mother, wondering whether she would be coming back. Gwyn gone, Rob on his way. And what was going on with Jack, now he had met Corinna? Then there was Tom and Agnetta; the split that was happening between me and Ros. We were in a state of flux.

The time finally arrived for Rob to leave us. He'd been at Dyffryn more than five years. Jack turned up with Corinna for the 'Last Supper' as I called it. She was not what I had been expecting, having imagined her well built with short hair; she was, after all, going to agricultural college. How wrong I was. She was slim with shoulder-length dark hair, as tall as Jack. She had beautiful green eyes, and a smile that lit up her whole face. She immediately hit it off with Rob, for she too had travelled through India. Ros soon discovered a shared interest too, growing organic vegetables, living off the land. We still had half a bottle of Metaxa brandy, Rob's favourite tipple, left over from my mother's Cypriot holiday. Harry joined us, carrying a sleeping bag under his arm, 'Just in case I don't make it home tonight.' Brandy before a meal on an empty stomach is never a good idea, but we drank a toast to Rob and put on the Lovin' Spoonful. *What a day for a daydream.*

In the Aga Ros roasted a goose, one of our own that Dewi had finally run over. After all the near misses, the front tyre of the post office van had flattened its neck. No one mourned its passing, in fact the opposite: one down, three to go. We reminisced, drinking Ros's last bottle of pea-pod wine, remembering the most ridiculous incidents, the stupidity of imagining pigs would behave the way we wanted them to.

Rob said he would never forget the time we held fifty-odd weaners in the barn while we put an electric fence across a patch of fallow land. The plan was to get them to plough up and manure it for us. Pigs are good at this, cheap and effective. What we hadn't allowed for was what would happen when we let them out. The boisterous mob of young hooligans, pent up and frustrated, ran amok like lunatics escaping the asylum, taking the electric fence with them. Rob chased one through the larch trees, unaware that the slate that covered the cesspit had been partially removed. What happened next is beyond description.

Jack recounted the time we put six pig arks in a field for the sows after they'd been served. 'It was a simple mathematical equation: total number of pigs to be held in the area, thirty, six pig arks, five pigs per ark.'

'Correct,' we all said.

However, the pigs didn't follow Jack's logic. They didn't wish to sleep five to an ark. In fact, fifteen of them fancied sleeping in just the one. Result, the complete destruction of a wooden ark, split asunder in an incredible surge of exploding pig flesh, rolling over each other like a collapsing scrum. Then, finding themselves in a green field, they were off, galloping in the way only pigs can, slow and ungainly in a short-lived stampede. Luckily they soon ran out of puff. I remember Jack giving me that stony look when I told him, 'I don't think six into thirty goes, not in a pig's world.'

So we ate and drank and got stoned. It wasn't often we were all together reliving our lives. What a strange fate had brought us all together, to live out a stretch of time that was now coming to an end.

'So, how would you sum it all up, Rob?' I asked.

'Five went farming in the hills, because that's what we've been doing,' he said.

'Sounds like an Enid Blyton book,' said Jack.

'Don't mention Enid Blyton to me,' I said. 'Remember the WH Smith incident.'

'To be fair to you, Rob man,' said Harry, 'when I first saw you that day it was nearly five minus one. You with that holy-man look.'

'Couldn't cope with that, could you, Harry?'

'I'd heard of those Jesus freaks, never thought I'd come across one up here.'

In the morning, still feeling the effects of the night before, we drove Rob to Bangor station and waved him goodbye on the train to Chorley. It was a sad day for all of us.

With the weather having settled back into its seasonal pattern, late-September sales picked up again on the meat round. Harry now called me boss, tipping his cap when we met each morning. If I ever acted too much like an employer he would stand to attention saluting me, 'Yes sir,' then march off, goose-stepping, his arm at right angles, muttering 'Heil Hitler'. But nothing had really changed with the new arrangement. As we worked, he talked about becoming a father and husband, paying off the mortgage, which was now through from the Woolwich.

'Duw, man, I've never had to think about anybody else before, just myself.'

I nearly said, but thought better of it, that he was losing his freedom. He was waking up to his responsibilities. I wondered what sort of man he would become, and hoped he wouldn't lose his sense of humour. For that's how Harry and I worked together, laughing a lot even when life was hard.

Tom and Agnetta had bought a farm down on the flat lands of Pontllyfni, one hundred and fifty acres of rich arable soil and a six-bedroomed farmhouse, with barns and three cottages. They never mentioned the price; it was a private sale. It must have been well over a hundred grand. They still called in every week, always bringing news of the latest progress on forming the community. Ros, still keen, continued to show her commitment to the venture. Tom invited us down to walk around the farm with them.

Jack was tight-lipped about Corinna. Whenever I asked him how things were going, 'It's OK' was all I got from him. He'd spoken to our mother who had told him she was putting Hendy on the market. All news to me, but she rang that night to tell me she was staying in Westbourne with my sister, that there was no going back on her decision.

Harry asked for the day off, saying he was marrying Bronwyn in the register office in Caernarfon. He hadn't told anyone else. They had invited nobody, wanting to keep costs down. Not that his father would have struggled from the house, but he should have asked his mother. They were going to drag two witnesses off the street was how he put it.

When I saw him the next day and asked him how it had gone he said, 'Duw, man, it was great because it was so simple.'

'How did you celebrate the evening?'

'I took her to the cinema to see *A Hundred and One Dalmatians*. I sneaked in a couple of beers and we sat in the back row.'

'Wow! That's what I call going to town.'

'Then we got fish and chips in Penygroes.'

'Don't tell me your mother served you?'

'Yes, and she asked me why I was wearing a pink carnation. I said, "'Cause we just got married."'

'And what did she say?'

'She didn't. She said, "That's sixty pence."'

Harry did manage to redeem himself. He took his mother to the Vic, plied her with gin and tonics and told her that if the baby was a girl it would be named after her. Then Bronwyn went back to her parents, and Harry helped his mother home.

Recently I'd been having a recurring dream. I was walking through a dense wood, stepping over fallen trees, my clothes ripped, the path heavy with mud. I was not wearing the right footwear. Then at last, after stumbling along for hours, I came upon a clearing bathed in moonlight. Ahead of me was a bridge over a river, but every time I came to it I turned back, something stopping me from crossing over. I had dreamt this so many times, it was simple enough to interpret. The wood symbolised Dyffryn, the journey the relentless slog to reach a state free of financial anxiety, which was the clearing in the moonlight. Over the bridge was where Tom and Agnetta were waiting. And I couldn't walk across. I wrestled with it, because Ros was still so keen, but in truth it wasn't me. I knew it was all coming to a head.

Just after we had finished supper, while Ros was upstairs with the children, Jack turned up. I knew as soon as I saw his face he had something to tell me.

'Why don't you roll one up?' he said. Meg leapt on to the sofa to play with Moss.

'Not bad news, is it? Tell me.'

And he did, speaking seriously, as if a big decision had been reached. He was moving in with Corinna, going to rent a cottage somewhere nearby, probably in Penygroes. It was a big step for Jack, for he was used to his own company, and most of the conversation he'd had was with Meg. I thought it would be a good idea if they moved into Hendy until it was sold. It made sense, rather than leave it empty. It was only fifteen minutes from Glynllifon, so convenient for Corinna, and it would be easier for our mother to sell the place with someone living there.

Ros came in. 'Will you go and say goodnight to them?'

'Jack's got some news for you.'

Getting the children off to sleep wasn't the same any more. Sam and Lysta read their own books now and didn't need their father to create fairy stories. Seth gurgled quite happily in his dream world, gazing at the mobiles that twirled above his cot. Sam and Lysta had become rational in the twinkling of an eye, seeking logical explanations to life's mysteries. Such is the evolution of man's consciousness; we all thought like children once. Sam wasn't keen on being kissed by his father any more, offering me only his cheek, engrossed in his book. It's a masculine thing: probably somebody at school had said 'What! You still kiss your father!' But Lysta was affectionate, loving big hugs and kisses from her dad.

When Gitto knocked on the door asking for forty quid, which I counted out in ten pound notes, he said, 'I don't know how much longer I can hold this price. Petrol's gone up five pence a gallon. The cost of tyres, as well; all the basic things on the increase. There's no money in being a haulier. The take-home pay in those new factories makes me think I'm working for a pittance.'

'Lucky you're not married with kids.'

'You're right. Look at the mess Harry's got himself into. Can't even come out and play darts on a Friday night any more.'

To give Ros a break and Seth a change of scenery, Harry and I had him for the afternoon, taking him with us as we moved from job to job. Sitting happily in his buggy, watching us moving pigs from building to building, he played with whatever we gave him: a pigeon feather, a pine cone, stones from the stream. All held his attention as he examined them closely, with a look of heavy concentration. He got extremely excited when Moss appeared chasing a sow, snapping at its trotters, and expressed himself in a gobbledygook language, waving his arms frantically. We paid a visit to Dave, who stuck his head out through the bars, his tongue hanging from the side of his mouth. Moss was flat on her stomach, taking in every move Dave made. So much did Seth enjoy his afternoon, I told Ros we should do it more often. 'He's quite safe, as long as the brakes on his buggy work, and a pig doesn't charge into him.'

I hadn't noticed Jobber walking along the boundary wall, now sound on four legs, leaping down and running across the field towards me. Moments later Hughie came into view, closing the gate, moving slowly. He held his arm at a strange angle, as if he was carrying an invisible basket. He seemed to be leaning slightly to the right. It was some minutes after Jobber arrived that he eventually joined me. His hand and wrist were bandaged, his fingers a deep purple and supported by a plastic splint that fitted over the dressing. You could see in his face he was suffering the pain of what looked like a nasty injury.

'Duw, boy,' he said, removing his cap and running his forearm across his brow. 'I thought when I broke my leg lying under a drum of molasses was the worst I would ever feel, but this leaves that well behind.'

'What happened, Hughie?'

'Duw, boy, in all my years a freak accident, if there ever is such a thing. I hope you've got the stomach for it.'

'Tell me,' I said, motioning to him to sit down on the old wooden bench in front of the house.

'Jobber, leave that bloody bitch alone,' he shouted. 'Well, I was fixing up to the PTO [power takeoff]. I had a length of cable in my left hand, which I know I shouldn't have been holding, but I've done it for years, when I slipped and the thing got tangled up and tightened itself around my wrist, crushing my fingers. I screamed, boy, in agony. I thought I was going to watch my hand being torn from its wrist in front of my very eyes. I yelled until she came running, running she was in that bloody tight skirt of hers, my Myfanwy. It was she who turned it off and came with me in the ambulance to the hospital.'

'God, Hughie, you were lucky not to lose your hand.'

'Duw, you're right there, and now six months as an invalid ahead of me. I'm finished, you know that.'

'But surely Bryn can help when he comes home from the factory?'

'Him,' he said, raising his eyes to the heavens. 'He won't lift a finger. He would rather I sell the farm, be like the rest of them. Take a fancy bungalow on one of those estates.'

'Can you not buy in some help?'

'No, no,' he said, with a heavy sigh of resignation, bowing his head, staring at the ground. 'Do you know how old I am?'

'Sixty-odd?'

'Sixty-five, man. Not many years now before the grave opens up.' Then he started to laugh. 'You know, when she runs, it always reminds me of a fat goose running from the oven.'

'Who does?'

'No matter, boy, not your concern. Help me tomorrow, will you? I've two tons of hay to unload. There's no one else to turn to.'

'I'll help, but Bryn needs to lend a hand.'

When I got back after walking the farm that night and I'd finished milking Frieda, Ros was in the kitchen making supper. She didn't look up from the vegetables she was chopping.

'You'd better go up and say goodnight to the children.'

Upstairs Lysta told me, 'Mum isn't in a good mood tonight.'

There is nothing that festers like a cold silence. So during supper I said to Ros, 'Can we get on with it, what you need to say, even if it leads to an argument? Let's have it out and get on with our lives.'

After she finished her mouthful she took a sip of water and said, staring straight into my face, 'You are an inconsiderate selfish bastard.'

I wasn't ready for that, and had no immediate response. When somebody says something like that, you automatically wonder if it's true.

'Can I ask why?'

'Your whole attitude to Tom and Agnetta's plans. Not once have you supported the idea. You think only of yourself.' Moss hid behind the sofa whining, as she always did whenever she heard raised voices. We argued as quietly as possible, using venomous language but under our breath.

In the aftermath of emotional warfare, when the smoke clears, someone has to raise a white flag. It was me taking those delicate steps, needing to know how much damage I had done. That's when the repair work begins, admitting you might well have been in the wrong, hoping to find some middle ground. Ros heard me out, but told me she could not let the opportunity pass her by. Even without my involvement she meant to press ahead. Though our marriage wasn't over, we were going to go our separate ways. She would give up growing vegetables at Dyffryn; would no longer be a part of the farm. After the children had gone to school she would spend the day down with Tom and Agnetta, devoting herself to the community. She would have what she wanted and so would I. That was the decision we reached. It was two a.m. when I whispered to Moss, 'It's all right. You can come out now.'

I turned on the record player. How appropriate. Bob Marley's 'No Woman No Cry'.

14

Whiteout

We stood outside the Quarryman's Arms; once again Harry had thrashed Jack and me at darts. Every defeat was not just a whitewash, but a humiliation. I told him there was no point to it, not any more. It was my final game. I have no hand-eye co-ordination. I am short of certain faculties that Harry takes for granted. I also have no natural rhythm, I can't dance, and I can't read maps. I could never finish on a bull's eye, even if my life depended on it.

It was a late-November night. Bronwyn was shivering, holding their new baby, Irving, under her coat. The first flakes of snow fell silently, as if someone had torn up a velvet curtain and was scattering it across the face of the earth, the pavements in the high street whitening as we made plans for tomorrow. Jack was coming early to move the ewes to Henbant, where we rented the land on a six-month agreement from Arfon's cousin who now owned the place. He was no farmer, but worked in the power station over on Anglesey and would eventually sell the farm at public auction. We paid cash, which we sent to him in a registered envelope. As far as I knew the house had been condemned as unfit for human habitation. Since Arfon's death I had driven into the yard to have another look. Mother Nature was claiming the house back slowly, strangling it under an advancing army of branches from the trees that leant over it, stretching through the windows, out of the chimney. It looked like some macabre work of art, or a set in a horror film. Hard to believe that three years ago a farmer and his wife had lived there.

Harry would get to us at seven. With the run up to Christmas, prices were at their highest. We had another forty porkers ready to go to FMC. Gitto had promised he would arrive punctually at eight. No one held out any hope of that happening.

Jack and Corinna were renting Hendy from my mother, so I was going to drop him in Penygroes, get some fish and chips and make my way back to Dyffryn. That was the plan, but as the snow fell more heavily, with a northerly wind getting up, Jack and I had the same thought. If it was blowing this hard down here, it would be much stronger up in the hills.

'I'm coming to Dyffryn,' he said. We had thirty-odd ewes in the top fields.

So after getting his coat and waterproofs from Hendy, eating fish and chips out of a newspaper we drove into a blizzard, what they call a whiteout. We were already in three or four inches of snow as we opened the gate into Dyffryn.

Ros had left the kitchen light on. I changed and found a torch, one I'd bought recently that was as powerful as a car headlight, and the two of us, with Moss and Meg, went out to search for the ewes.

They could be anywhere: all the gates were open as they had the run of the place at this time of year. But Jack narrowed down the possibilities, knowing how sheep protect themselves in extreme weather. Keeping out of the prevailing wind, they gathered beneath the stone walls. But now the wind was directionless, swirling chaotically, and seemed to surround us. Finding a flock of white-coated sheep in a blizzard is a daunting task. You act on instinct, trying to think as they would to find a safe corner that offered shelter.

Jack shouted to me, 'You look lower down. Just walk the walls; they'll be together somewhere.' After half an hour we still hadn't found them. What made everything worse were the huge drifts banking up over the walls. There was no visibility; we couldn't see our hands in front of our faces. Nothing was going to survive out here tonight. I grabbed Jack and we crouched down behind a wall to get out of the wind.

'What are we going to do?'

'Keep bloody looking,' he shouted. 'If we don't find them they will suffocate under a drift. We've got to keep searching.'

'Look at the dogs. It's hopeless. Let's take them back to the Land Rover before the snow gets right over them.'

With the dogs in the Land Rover, we came up with another plan and carved up the fields between us, who would go where. We had a whistle each, which we'd blow only if we found them.

Just to slog through the snow was a battle in itself. The effort of walking, of lifting one foot then the other, drained us of energy, and our ears were on fire. I was coming to the point of giving up altogether when I thought I heard bleating. I stopped and listened and like a fool bleated back. What else would you do? It seemed a natural way to respond to a sheep. I heard it again, but couldn't tell from which direction. So I blew my whistle, waiting for Jack to give a blast on his. I waited, counting the seconds. After ten, I gave another longer whistle, blowing until my lungs were empty.

'Where are you, Jack?'

Nothing; and of course he couldn't hear me, in a howling wind that consumed every sound. Neither could I see his torchlight waving, so I went down into the snow on all fours, shining the torch. I crawled beside a stretch of wall, under a high bank of snow, feeling at last the woollen coat of a ewe, tight up against the stone. She panicked, leaping up, breaking the surface, shaking her head, drawing in deep snowy breaths, trying to run from me. But under the heavy weight of her coat and in the deepness of the snow she couldn't. It was impossible to move quickly, but I went along that wall scooping away the snow in my arms, digging down, knowing they were there, a long line of them, queuing quietly, waiting for death to come and take them.

At last I heard a whistle and some yards from me saw Jack's torchlight.

'They're here!' I shouted. 'They're here! What took you so long? Sorry, don't answer that.'

So Jack and I dug them out, he working from one end, me from the other, pulling them free one by one, their coats clagged with snowballs. Released from certain death, they stood around sniffing the white air, staring blankly at each other. We counted twenty-eight; two had not survived. They'd suffocated, their nostrils thick with snow.

It was three a.m. and still the blizzard raged. Now we were faced with getting the ewes safely to the barn. But Jack, who knew his sheep, walked ahead knowing they would follow him, while I hung back making sure we didn't lose any of them. That trek was long and arduous, for the snow swept into our faces. We'd been out there for over an hour. I couldn't feel my toes and my fingers were purple with cold. My face glowed and both my ears had little furnaces burning inside them.

By the time we had got them housed in the barn, broken up hay bales and put concentrates in the troughs it was 4.40 a.m. Deep down in a dry trouser pocket Jack found the Golden Virginia, and we smoked a couple of roll-ups.

'They're all in lamb, you know,' he said as we watched them, none the worse for what they had been through.

'Look at the colour of your fingers,' I said.

'Frostbite.'

'Well, Gitto's not going to be coming this morning.'

'Suppose we'll lose our power.'

'Jack, are we crazy? What a way to earn a living!'

'I don't know myself, not any longer.'

'What do you mean?'

'Corinna doesn't want to stay in North Wales after she's got her diploma.'

'Now you tell me. You certainly know when to choose the moment. So you'll be on your way?'

'Probably, who knows.'

We made our way to the house. A light still shone from the kitchen. The larch trees were buckled over, snow clinging to their branches. It was two inches over my wellingtons. There was no let-up, and after the longest drought it now seemed we were in for a long hard winter.

Having slept for only an hour, wearing bed socks and gloves, I felt as if I had just got into bed when Lysta whispered in my ear.

'Dad, wake up. It's snowing. It's very deep. We won't be able to go to school.'

It was still dark when I turned on the radio to listen to the news. The weather was bad everywhere, bringing the country to a standstill as it always did.

From the bedroom window I watched the sun come up into a clear sky, shining over the whitest landscape; it looked as though no man had walked upon the earth. I half expected a woolly mammoth to appear. An untarnished vision as far as the eye could see. Not a sound, utter silence, not a breath of wind. Nothing moved; complete stillness, two colours visible, a brilliant blue and an unblemished whiteness. All the roads were blocked, not a vehicle moved or engine started up. The machines lay silent as the sun dispersed its buttery rays over the crisp white hills.

Then it all came back, my life, pigs waiting to be fed, and I hurried and got dressed. There was no sign of Harry and of course there wouldn't be. I laughed at the thought, imagining him trying to cycle up from Penygroes.

Ros was worried about my fingers, and when I showed her my toes she said I should go to the doctor.

'I don't think I'll be going today.'

I told her about our night, that Jack was sleeping in the back bedroom.

'You really need to get your hands and feet looked at.'

But I was out of the house, needing to see how the pigs were after the night of the blizzard. Why we hadn't lost our electricity was beyond me. Having fed the pigs, I checked the litters. They had all survived; not a single loss. I always feared the worst after extreme weather, rain, wind or snow.

I walked Dave from his pen. Snow up to his shoulders, he ate mouthfuls of the stuff, burying his head in it as I threw snowballs at him. I left him to amuse himself and went down to get Frieda, who had spent the night in a sheltered corner, where the larch trees leant over, creating a protective canopy. She stood alone in a patch of green, an oasis in a white desert. She followed me reluctantly; it must have been uncomfortable to feel her udder swaying in the snow. I wondered if it would stop her milk flowing. Maybe I should wash her teats with warm water.

We were completely snowed in, and would be for days. We

cleared the drive by reversing the Land Rover up and down, compacting the snow. We drove the Fergie along the track to the Carmel road. The virgin snow was smooth and sparkled in the sun; nothing had come this far, neither up nor down, not a footprint from man or animal. Across the fields a breeze blew transparent powdery clouds like icing sugar, glittering against the blue background of the day. The only birdsong came from a blackbird. Overwhelmed by the whiteness, even she knew there would be no worms on the menu today through a foot of snow.

The children loved it, building snowmen from huge balls the size of large boulders that they rolled down the drive. They threw handfuls of bird seed down in front of the house, only to watch the geese scoff the lot. Jack couldn't get to Hendy, but telephoned Corinna to say we were cut off from the world. She told him snowploughs were already clearing the Caernarfon road, and those who lived above their shops had opened for business. Teams of people were sweeping the pavements. That old spirit of rallying round in times of trouble was alive and well in Penygroes.

Harry rang, Lysta answering in her impeccable telephone voice. 'Hello, Penygroes 441, how can I help you?' They were well trained by Ros, always speaking professionally in case it was a customer wishing to place an order.

'I'm not going to get up there today,' said Harry.

'Nor tomorrow,' I told him.

'I could come in by hot-air balloon.'

'It's all right, Jack's here. We can cope.'

Three days later the thaw set in, and everything began to melt. The sound of constant dripping could be heard everywhere, from gutters and trees. Great swathes of snow slid down roofs and gradually the grass appeared across the fields. The temperature continued to rise; only in the shadows did the snow remain.

At last, a week after the blizzard, Gitto managed to get his lorry up the hill to pick up the porkers. The school reopened, and life got back into its old routine. Ros left at nine every morning to go down to Tom and Agnetta. It felt strange to see her leaving; a gap had certainly opened up between us. Now no one tended the vegetable garden, and when spring came we would plough it up, put it back to grass. It felt as if life was shrinking, that some of the energy had gone from the place.

Our fingers and toes recovered. I never went to the doctor, but after two days they itched incessantly. It was worse in the night, lying in bed. I kept it hidden from Ros, who was annoyed with me for not getting medication. I had to do all my scratching out on the landing. I did get some cream from Owen Bethel, the chemist, who was more interested in my mother than in listening to my symptoms. His assistant, Maimee, who had once told me I stank to high heaven, suggested I put some 'oinkment' on my toes, which greatly amused her, astonishing Owen who was taken completely by surprise. 'Well, Maimee, in all the years I have known you that is the very first time I've heard you make a joke of something.'

'It's not of my own making, Mr Bethel. I read it in a Christmas cracker.'

'Humorous, none the less, and very appropriate.'

On the day before Valentine's Day I was in Caernarfon for two appointments. Before the dentist I went to the FMC offices to talk about the state of the British pig industry. It was under threat from the invading Danes, who were flooding the UK with their vacuum-packed bacon. They had a huge marketing budget, taking prime slots on TV, in the middle of *Coronation Street*, gaining an ever-increasing market share. Bacon producers were worried and needed to respond quickly. A 'Buy British' campaign was launched, everything labelled with Union Jacks. My grandfather once said the most effective way to invade a country is through its stomach, and he was right.

However, none of that was on my mind as I stood outside the newsagent's in Castle Street looking at the Valentine's cards. It was a miserable day, the blah of relentless drizzle, the kind that weeps over you without a breeze to carry it away, dampening the soul.

I had never sent Ros a Valentine's card before, nor had she sent me one, sharing the view that the whole thing was a commercial racket, invented by the greetings card companies, florists and chocolate makers. But today I wanted to. I thought it might stir up some romantic emotions that had sadly fallen by the wayside. As I looked through the cards, I suddenly remembered that Gwyn had sent Ros Valentine's cards. What was going through his mind, pretending to his daughter that he was her secret admirer? Maybe the psychothcrapists would have something to say about that.

In the post office with my pen poised over the card, wondering what I could write that wasn't sentimental or corny, I asked the old-timer with the fox terrier standing next to me if he would write it for me. He took it in his stride, asking if it was for a girlfriend.

'No, no . . . but can you write this message for me?'

'Yes, boy, tell me.'

'Just . . . I want us back the way we were.'

And he did, not in small shrunken writing, which is often the case with old folk, but in scrawling florid lettering that rose and fell like waves upon the sea. Ros would never have a clue whose hand had written it. He wrote the address on the envelope and I thanked him. It was one of those little encounters with a complete stranger that makes you ponder on its significance. As we shook hands, our eyes meeting, I asked him how he had made his living.

'A sailor for thirty years, a life on the ocean wave.'

So in Castle Street I posted my Valentine's card to Ros, probably from where Gwyn had sent his for so many years. Since Gwyn's death, I no longer went to Trefanai for Sunday lunches. There was no point in my being there, and it was easier for Eryl to relax with her grandchildren. All I ever did was sit in an armchair reading a Sunday newspaper. It was a pity, for Ros more than anyone. In her exasperation I once heard her telling Eryl, 'He's not a bad man. Why don't you give him a chance?'

I had half an hour to kill before my dental appointment, a curious half hour, aimlessly wandering the Caernarfon streets. I walked around the castle and along the quayside through the murk, the seagulls screeching on the masts. This wasn't my town, I didn't have any connection with it or its history, didn't speak the language. I was there because it was Ros's home, not mine. I don't know why all this came rising up in me. Then I remembered Gwyn's words: 'You're not a Welshman.' Probably it was stirred by the dreariness of the day, finding myself at a loose end, in a vacuous state of mind.

I went into Jim Breen Turner's dental surgery and sitting in the waiting room pulled out a magazine at random from the pile on the table. Distracted, I escaped into the pages of *Hidden Greece*, unknown places away from tourists where the traditional way of life was still alive. The old windmills on the hillside, the bearded priest going down to his church on a donkey, followed by a herd of goats. The making of olive oil, the olives carried in baskets by the villagers who had harvested them together. The old monastery built up on the cliffs above the blue, blue sea. I had transported myself to this nameless island when the nurse called me in. 'Mr Breen Turner will see you now.' I asked if I could take the magazine. She looked at the front cover and said, 'Of course. It's over two years old.' So I stuffed it in my jacket pocket and went in and had a tooth filled.

When Lysta answered the phone and said, 'Mum it's for you. I think he said his name is Phil Antler, or Adler,' Ros rushed from the table.

'Phil, how are you? What news?'

All of us, curious to know who was ringing Ros, sat in silence not saying a word, just listening as a smile grew ever wider across her face.

'Wonderful, wonderful. I'll speak to Celia and ring you tomorrow.' Then we watched Ros run around the room, her arms raised, shouting, 'Yes! Yes! Yes!'

'What's happened?' I asked.

'That was Phil Adler, the guy selling our sheepskins in the Portobello Road. He's sold out, and wants to order some more!'

'How much money have we made?' I asked.

'Don't you mean "How much have *you* made"?'

That evening Tom and Agnetta came to supper, talking with the energy and excitement that comes at the beginning of a new cycle, when everything is on an upward curve. Ros was animated too, putting forward ideas, talking about homoeopathic herbs, the cultivation of Russian comfrey, long held by the anthroposophists to be a medicinal plant. The architectural drawings for the school were rolled out on the table. They had sixteen families all prepared to sell their properties and join the community, mostly from England, but also three from Scandinavia whom Agnetta knew, all putting money in, giving up good well-paid jobs to buy into the dream. Tom was thinking of quitting his fish round to devote himself full time to working the land.

'What about you, Nick? How goes everything at Dyffryn?'

For the first time I found myself struggling to find anything positive to say about the place. How dull it must have sounded when I said, 'We labour on.'

He just smiled, sensing my flat mood. Ros's life seemed far removed from mine. Every morning now we kissed one another on the cheek, almost politely, saying no more to each other than 'See you this evening'.

Neither Sam nor Lysta ever said anything, unaware of what was happening between their mother and father. I kept it all to myself, while I watched Jack and Corinna's relationship flourishing. They went away at weekends, sometimes leaving Meg at Dyffryn if they were going to stay in a guesthouse that didn't accept dogs. The first time Jack asked me to look after Meg, I knew a big change was taking place in my brother. He and Meg had always been inseparable. They had slept out in the wild, in huts during lambing, under the stars in the summertime. Jack's days walking the bleak landscapes of North Wales were coming to an end. The hard times without a razor, carrying dirt under his fingernails, the smell of lanolin and formaldehyde hanging about him. The solitude, sitting in the bracken and damp heather, drinking from a thermos. Maybe now he could do without it, being up here in this stony landscape, amongst the elements, the raw features of a winter's day. In every step there is one's inner silence. That's the life of a shepherd: words a scarce commodity, just his own mutterings. I wondered if Jack in some way had been rescued; not from himself, but from a gradual withdrawal that befalls all who work alone, gathering sheep above the tree line. Who would not change their whole life for the comfort to be found in a loving heart and a cooked breakfast?

One Tuesday afternoon in the spring of '77, driving back from Bryncir market, I stopped to pick up a hitchhiker sitting on a boulder beside the road, his head down, thumb out. I had no idea it was Bryn, Hughie's belligerent son. He smelled of alcohol. If I had recognised him I would not have stopped. In all the years I'd known him, he had given me nothing but filthy looks and a curled lip. But he was next to me now in the Land Rover, so I asked him why he wasn't working at the Firestone factory instead of on the road hitching.

'I've quit the job,' he said. 'Not my choice, but for the sake of the old man.'

'You're working the farm?'

'I promised him one year, and if he can't take it on again we sell it.'

'How's your father doing? Has he got the use of his arm back?'

'No, he can't do anything. Can't lift a bale, can't put a cluster on an udder. He's a cripple.'

'Lucky he's got you to fall back on.'

As he put his feet up on the dashboard, I opened my window to clear the alcohol fumes. And because I resented his being there, found myself asking a question I'd wanted to ask for years.

'What makes you such an unpleasant human being?'

'What does that mean?'

'Well, I don't think I have ever heard you say a good word about anything.'

'Bollocks.'

'That's what I mean.'

I dropped him at the track down to Llwyndu Canol. Grabbing the two empty churns by the gate, he rolled them down the drive, both hands in his pockets, an arrogant swagger in his step. I shouted after him, 'Thanks for letting me give you a lift home.'

'Yeah, if that's what you call it,' he yelled back.

On my return, Harry, looking concerned, told me that in his opinion the stiffness in Dave's back legs was arthritis, that we should think about retiring him from his stud duties. He'd struggled to mount a sow that afternoon, and although the will was there he kept slipping out of her, his trotters giving way under his weight.

We had a young replacement boar, Kurt, whom we used to serve Dave's offspring, the sows who produced good healthy litters that we kept back for breeding. Kurt was from an underused bloodline Josh Hummel had recommended. All of Dave's descendants carried a blue ear tag, numbered with their date of birth; any inbreeding would have been a disaster.

Dave had been with us for over five years, boy and beast. I would never send him to the abattoir; he was one of the family. I planned to build him his own retirement home, a pig ark down in the lower fields where he could wander at his leisure and roll around in the mud on warm summer days. I would spend time with him, take down buckets of swill, cold porridge and carrots, pieces of toast, all his favourite treats.

And so in the first week of May I walked him from his pen, where he had served his time with an enthusiasm that had never waned. It was a poignant moment for me when I closed the gate behind him. He walked slowly, putting his back trotters gingerly on the hard concrete, alive to the aromas in the spring air. Moss didn't harass him as he took his time, lingering, distracted by the smells of the larch needles and pine cones. His back end swaying gently, he flicked his large floppy ears when flies landed on his pink flesh.

Down in the lower fields he followed me to the ark, where I had broken up a bale of fresh straw, but he was more interested in a gorse bush, rooting around, throwing up stones, his snout covered in dark mud. I watched him for a while, sitting with Moss as he amused himself, every now and then losing his back legs on the uneven ground. He looked a lonely figure, as if he had been sent into exile, no longer useful or playing a part. I felt sad for him as I remembered the days of walking him to the bus with the children and how much we owed to his incredible sex drive.

Most of my time now was spent with Harry, and on Fridays, when I was away doing the meat round, which gave us nearly half our income, he would be at Dyffryn on his own. It was on one Friday at the end of May that he ploughed up the vegetable garden. Ros knew, and a part of me hoped she would have second thoughts, suggest we keep it going, reduced in size. But she didn't, all her time taken up with Tom and Agnetta. When it was done and I told her, she dismissed it, saying, 'Well, that's one thing less we need to worry about.' I thought of all the effort that she had put into that patch of land. Now none of it seemed to matter.

Every morning Harry and I went about our work in good humour. Not many things got past him, those signs that a keen eye picks up from being with livestock, in amongst them, touching them. Something seen early is much easier to treat. He could sense my attitude had changed, noticed my keenness to get things done had diminished. I didn't let things slip back, but I didn't seek to make improvements. We just ticked over, keeping on track, running the farm efficiently. We weren't going to grow wheat this year, Ros now bringing bread back from the community bakery. We would put aside six acres for hay, grow two acres of spuds for Tom 'Tatoes.

On the surface we seemed like a happy family, and in lots of ways we were. Sitting round the kitchen table every night eating supper, the children full of stories about their school friends and Ros telling us what she had done in her working day. Everyone thought we were just the same. It was I who felt detached, unable to tell Ros that I was going round in circles.

There was no antagonism; outwardly we were a picture of a loving couple. But there was no depth and now no passion in our life. I never felt we were living a lie; it was just that we weren't who we appeared to be. In those quiet moments that precede sleep I was filled with a sense of irony, that the very thing that ought to have brought us together had driven us apart.

I knew Jack and Corinna must have reached a decision when Jack said 'Let's talk this evening. Come with me to Cae Rhys. I'm going to look at a ram.' This was so definite, so unlike my laconic brother, who would usually have muttered 'Let's think about it', that I knew at once he'd made up his mind. I guessed already what he was going to tell me.

The drive that evening from Nebo will long remain in my heart. We had been there to check on some late-born lambs, and, as the sun bejewelled the Irish Sea, high up in the breezes blossoms that could have been butterflies drifted in the soft currents of the spring air. Moss and Meg stood on the tailbar, their noses catching the sweet-scented waft of the hawthorn hedges as we took the tight bends down to Pant Glas. It was the time of day when the light is layered by cloud, gilding the cliff tops of Cwm Silyn. We took it all in, and words did not need to be spoken between brothers as we went down into that evening, our lives about to go their separate ways. As Jack put together a couple of roll-ups, we were absorbed by the luminous glow of twilight, listening to the cry of rooks. In the darkening western sky we could see the sharp summits of the Wicklow hills, whilst before us the road to Criccieth was spiked with the shadows of pine trees.

Jack looked at the ram penned in the rusting Dutch barn at Cae Rhys, a remote farm that overlooked the sea. 'Not for us,' he said, after he had checked its mouth and run his hands over it for five minutes.

In the pub in Llanystumdwy, just off the road between Porthmadog and Pwllheli, we sat with a couple of barley wines, taking small sips of the sickly-tasting black syrup, which we endured for the warm glow that followed. It went straight to the brain, and after you'd finished a glass you would feel pretty good. The dogs were curled up under the table and we were the only people in there, apart from the barman. And a parrot who repeatedly squawked out in Welsh something that Jack translated as 'Mine's a pint, shut that door'.

'Tell me then, Jack, what have you decided?'

Without hesitation he said, 'We're going at the end of September.'

'Where?'

'Gloucestershire . . . that's the plan, if I get the job.'

'What job?'

'Shepherd in North Cerney.'

'Never heard of it.'

'It's a village near Cirencester.'

'So what shall we do with the farm?' I asked.

'That's for you and Ros to decide.'

Well, at least I knew where I stood. 'Why are you looking for a new ram if you're going?'

'Well, I'm not taking the sheep with me, am I?'

'You're expecting me and Harry to look after the pigs *and* a flock of sheep?'

He shrugged his shoulders. 'Don't know. Who knows. We need to think about that.'

With our glasses empty we looked at each other, wondering.

'One more for the road?'

'Why not.'

That second one got me going. I'd never talked to Jack about personal things, but I gave him more than an inkling about the difficulties with Ros. I rambled, talking to a whitewashed wall, letting things spill from me about the chasm that had opened up between us. He didn't say anything; I didn't expect him to. It was more an unloading on my part, the release of letting someone know. Jack didn't need to give an opinion, but I think I conveyed to him my uncertainties; that I had no idea where I was going.

He shrugged his shoulders, Jack's reaction to most things. I asked him if he thought he would marry Corinna. 'That's a long way off,' he said.

'By the way, why didn't you buy that ram?'

'I could only feel one testicle.'

When I got back to Dyffryn, there was a note on the table. *Gone to bed early. Ros.*

The morning rose cloudless over the hills. Frieda bellowed with the exultation animals feel when the spring sun warms their backs and the grass tastes sweeter around their tongues.

Harry arrived in a T-shirt, a comb in his back pocket; he liked to run it through his hair after he had leant his bicycle against the kitchen wall. Bryn slouched over, complaining about a row with his father, a cow that had mastitis. He wouldn't be here unless he wanted something. Could we pick up ten bags of concentrates from Eifionydd Farmers? He handed me the cash.

'But you have an account with Spillers,' I said.

'Not any more,' he said. 'Tomorrow will do.' He stood looking at me, waiting for an answer, and said, 'You'll do it for my father, won't you?' knowing full well I wouldn't for him. I would have hated to be part of that household. How did Myfanwy put up with it all?

'Hey, boss.' Harry called me over. 'There's a couple of porkers that don't look right. When you've got a minute you should come and see for yourself.'

He was right to be concerned. Amongst the twenty porkers we were fattening in one large area, two looked very thin. As always, we stood leaning over the wall watching them, studying their behaviour, seeing if they were being bullied.

'Maybe they need worming,' I said.

'That's not worms,' Harry said. 'Besides, they were wormed two weeks ago.'

We observed them for fifteen minutes, detected nothing, no clue as to what could be wrong.

'Let me run some food along the trough, see if they come to feed with the others,' suggested Harry. As soon as they heard the rattle of the bucket they all ran squealing, for their appetites were never satisfied. The two skinny pigs were in there with the rest of them, hungry for every nut. It was a mystery.

'Maybe we should separate them, house them somewhere else, keep a close eye on them.'

So we penned them in an old stone sty, where a sow had been kept years ago, long before we came to Dyffryn.

When Sam and Lysta came home from school they loved to be outside in the lengthening evenings. What consumed them now was the idea of building a tree house amongst the larches. They showed us drawings, pleading with us that it could be finished in a weekend.

'You can cut the wood with your Husqvarna chainsaw,' said Sam.

'Harry will help if you ask him,' said Lysta.

'I think that's vital,' said Ros. 'I know what your father's like trying to cut things in a straight line.'

'All right, let's see if we can do it on Saturday afternoon. But we'll need Harry's help.'

After the children had gone to bed, I pulled the cork on a bottle of Mateus Rosé and told Ros that Jack would be leaving in September. It didn't surprise her.

'They're going to start a life together.'

'And what about us? Don't you feel as if things have changed between us?' I asked.

'We certainly are not how we used to be.'

'It's not the same, you no longer here with me.'

'Well, that's true, but that was your choice.'

'Come back, Ros. It's as though you only live at Dyffryn, aren't a part of it any more.'

At least we were talking, but she looked sad as I held her.

'We need to reach one another,' she whispered. 'Something has slipped away. I feel alone and I don't know why.'

'Is it Gwyn?' I asked. 'Isn't it he who has slipped away?'

And she wept tears of loss, and then I knew. It was not me who was the rock in her life; it had always been her father.

'I miss him,' she said. 'And I'm sorry, I know I've turned away and lost interest in the place.'

I went to the record player and put on *Goats Head Soup* by the Rolling Stones. Ros and I had always loved 'Winter' and it did feel at the moment that a lot of love was all burned out.

15

Death and
a Future

I woke from a worried sleep with a feeling of foreboding and, unusually for me, lay with my head on the pillow listening to birdsong, watching the shadows of a flapping curtain play upon the ceiling. I felt detached from the things around me, curiously removed from the essence of my whole life. I had got to that stage of going through the motions, putting on a brave face. Whatever was going to happen would come upon me whether I smiled or looked glum.

And I knew, before Harry arrived, what I'd find. Our two sick pigs had succumbed during the night to who knows what, dead on the flagstones of the pen. When I picked one up by its back trotters and held it like a fish it weighed nothing. It had just wasted away.

That morning we found that a litter that had been thriving the day before had lost their sheen, were showing a hollow look. I knew that some disease was in the herd. I didn't think it was *E. coli*, which could be treated with antibiotics. We had seen that through the years, and besides, they were not scouring. This was something else. I knew I would have to call out Barry Evans. He scratched his head too, taking one of the carcasses to carry out tests.

'I've not seen anything like this,' he said, putting it into a black plastic sack. 'It will take two or three days. I'll have to send a sample to a laboratory in Liverpool.'

But nothing dampened Harry's spirits. Out from his pocket he pulled a scrap of paper with a list of jobs to be done. As we carried bales of straw to the farrowing pens he tried to persuade me to come to the Quarryman's for a pint and a game of darts.

'I told you, Harry, those days are over. There really is no point in being constantly given a drubbing.'

With Jack now involved with Corinna and Bronwyn at home with the baby, Harry was beginning to feel housebound. She allowed him one night a week to go out for a drink. But there was no one he hadn't beaten at darts in the villages of Penygroes and Llanllyfni. He must have been desperate to challenge a serial loser like me.

I ate lunch down in the lower fields with Dave, having brought him the contents of the swill bucket from the kitchen. I sat eating a sandwich, with Moss happy to be next to me in the warmth of the sun. She watched me eat, and throw the odd morsel to Dave. Moss had never drooled in her life, or, like a Labrador, stared endlessly while food was around. She had a delicate appetite and always ate slowly, enjoying each mouthful, while Dave scoffed everything on offer and belched a lot.

It was here, while we were eating our lunch, that I dreamt up my escape route. A huge risk, I knew, but it excited me. I could sense that everything was coming to an end. All I had to do was convince Ros, show her there was some reality to it.

I wanted to sell up, take the children out of school and go and live on a Greek island for a year. Getting Ros to go along with it didn't seem like a tall order to me. Jack wouldn't mind; he'd get half the dosh from the sale of the farm. He wouldn't mind at all, living in Gloucestershire with Corinna. The children would love the adventure, a year out of school. We could take all the necessary books, teach them ourselves. It wasn't unheard of, parents educating their children. Harry would be the loser; there would be nothing I could offer him. That was something I was going to have to wrestle with. And what if Ros said no, an absolute no? Where would I be then? Was I looking at the end of my marriage?

When Sam and Lysta came home, Harry gave them the last hour of his working day to finish off the tree house. He hung up a rope ladder and as I watched them climb up through the branches Jack arrived. We sat in the kitchen and I told him my plan. He listened for ten minutes, not saying a word. And still hadn't said a word after I'd made a pot of tea and put together a roll-up. In the end I said, 'Well, say something.'

'I'm still reeling.'

'Do you think it's a ridiculous idea?'

'Extreme,' he said. 'Isn't there anything in between?'

'What do you mean?'

'Well, something nearer. Greece seems a bit farfetched. What do you think she'll say?'

'I don't know. I really don't know.'

'When are you going to tell her?'

'Tonight.'

'Well, good luck.'

But our conversation didn't end there. I told him about the death of the pigs, that we had the beginnings of a disease in the herd. I showed him the ailing litter, whose condition had now deteriorated even further, all of them looking thin, some with deep purple blotches on their snouts. They couldn't walk, but staggered about, still hungry for the teat. The sow would lie quietly as they suckled, but they had weakened, feeding for just a few seconds before they lost interest.

'We won't know anything until Barry Evans gets the results.'

Jack shook his head. 'They are very sick pigs.'

'I've got an ominous feeling about it.'

When Ros and I were alone that night, I came somewhere close to articulating my feelings, that it was time for a new beginning. I only touched on what was happening to the pigs. I couldn't tell her now the harsh reality of what we were facing.

'Couldn't we sell up and get away for a year?' I said. 'What have we got to lose? It would be exciting for the children. We can do a good enough job educating them. Tom and Agnetta will still be here a year from now. I might feel differently then.'

I opened a bottle of Blue Nun, which was all the Co-op sold; well, that and a gruesome Riesling. I poured Ros a glass.

'I'm asking for a year, Ros,' I said, 'not your whole life.'

'Where were you thinking of spending this year?'

'On a Greek island.'

'What?'

'A remote Greek island.'

'Why not somewhere closer to home?'

'Like, the Isle of Wight?'

'Don't be sarcastic.'

'Ros, I want a foreign land, a different culture, a foreign tongue.'

'Well, you had that here . . . you didn't do very well with it.'

'Only the Welsh can speak Welsh.'

'Sam and Lysta have picked it up.'

Unfortunately we didn't have a Demis Roussos record, otherwise I would have played 'Forever and Ever' to create a Greek atmosphere.

'Let's do it, Ros.'

'We would need to speak to the school.'

'Yes, of course.'

What was going on with her? It was strange. I had always thought I knew her, but not now, her hand trembling, holding the glass of Blue Nun.

'What have we done?' she whispered. 'I don't know what we're doing.'

She looked fragile, as if she was shutting herself down. In the morning she didn't leave Dyffryn. Over breakfast, before going back to bed, she said, 'This wouldn't have happened if Pa was still alive.'

Sam and Lysta could tell something was wrong with their mother and tried to cheer her up, telling her about Mrs Davies, their schoolteacher, who had slipped over playing rounders, 'showing her knickers to everyone'.

'Have you got a hangover, Mum?' asked Sam.

'Not from Blue Nun,' I said.

Then Harry knocked on the door. 'Hey! Come on, we've got some trouble out here.'

I hugged Ros and whispered, 'I'm sorry, I've got to go.'

Now we had our first sow showing symptoms of the disease. She stood in her pen, holding her head at an angle, her mouth open. When she tried to walk her gait was weak and stiff. So this mysterious illness affected pigs of any age. She had seemed in good health the night before; such was its virulence, it took hold so quickly.

'Wow, man, this could go through the whole herd,' said Harry.

'We're going to be keeping Cluttons busy.' Cluttons was the company that took away dead stock not fit for human consumption.

We'd never watched the pigs so closely, and now as we moved from pen to pen we disinfected our wellingtons, the least precaution we could take. Not that we thought it would make any difference. How could a remote farm be carrying such a virus? I thought it had to be airborne. We couldn't have brought it in with new stock; we hadn't had any for over a year. And besides, our gilts had come from just one source, Josh Hummel. We weren't insured, and were facing considerable financial loss.

As Ros withdrew into herself, my anxiety, which I usually keep well hidden, increased twofold, and not just for Ros. At eight thirty in the morning Barry Evans arrived at Dyffryn. He carried a large envelope that contained several pages of lab results. He had marked certain sentences in yellow felt-tip pen. He delivered the findings of the report as might a pathologist, clinically and unemotionally, reading to Harry and me word for word what had come upon the pig herd at Dyffryn. When he actually named it – Chicago Vomiting and Wasting Disease – I thought I was the victim of a bizarre joke. But Harry was next to me and at the same moment squeezed my arm so tightly I knew it was for real, that there was no escaping it. Barry went on to tell us there had never been a recorded case before in North Wales and that it originated in the pig herds of North America, in Chicago where there was a large population of factory farmed pigs.

'I've never been to Chicago,' I said, 'and I don't know anyone who has.'

'Who knows how it got here.' He kept on reading, reaching the damning conclusion 'There is no treatment for the disease'.

The symptoms were horrible. As the virus took hold the victims would lose the ability to suck or swallow. They would become thirsty and stand with their heads over water, unable to drink. They would then become severely emaciated and rapidly waste away. There was no vaccine. The only hope was that some sows would have a natural immunity and pass this on to their piglets. The virus could affect susceptible pigs at any age. Well, we already knew that. As the disease progressed there would be a partial paralysis of the legs and the abdomen would become bloated. They would tremble as if they were shivering from extreme cold and then lie down, go into convulsions, roll their eyes and die within two to four days of onset.

'So there is absolutely nothing we can do,' I said.

'It won't affect them all. Some will resist it,' said Barry, handing me the report.

'Man, it's all in the lap of the gods,' said Harry, looking to the heavens.

Barry said it was not a notifiable disease, but obviously there was no point in buying replacement stock until we were free of it. 'I'm sorry to be the bearer of such bad news.'

'How long will it take to pass through?' I asked. 'And when will we know for certain we are rid of it?'

'I can't say for sure, but two, three months and then no cases for a month should see you clear.'

I imagined Dyffryn over the coming weeks as a horror show. Now, in these summer weeks, when the weather was easy, and the pigs liked to siesta in the lazy afternoons, they were going to face the invisible onslaught of an evil microbe that would decimate them. Bloody Chicago Vomiting and Wasting Disease. I would have preferred it to have come from Mars, to be something extraterrestrial, but Chicago!

'I'll keep dropping by,' said Barry. 'You're not alone; I want to monitor the situation closely.'

'How much is it all going to cost?' I asked. 'Besides, there's nothing you can do.'

'There'll be no charge,' he said. 'If you've got it here it will spring up somewhere else soon. I want to study it.'

After he had gone, the first thing I said to Harry was, 'No one must know, absolutely no one. OK?'

'Yes boss.'

'These next few weeks are going to be the hardest we've ever faced.'

'We'll get through it.'

'You've always been an optimist, Harry, no matter what.'

There was something else I had to tell him, without too much drama: that Ros and I weren't seeing eye to eye about a few things at the moment. It was all a bit delicate. 'It will only make matters worse if she knows what we're facing on the farm. So play it down, Harry.'

'I won't say a word.'

'Just keep smiling like you always do.'

Of course I told Jack as soon as I saw him. No matter what came down upon Jack, he met it with equanimity, that shrug of the shoulders. I can't remember when I first noticed it in him, I'm sure not in London. He must have picked it up out here amongst the shepherds. So much of farming is in the hands of fate; it's a mannerism that says whatever will be, will be.

Ros hadn't left the house for three days. She didn't come down to breakfast, so I rang Eryl and told her how worried I was. As far as I knew we didn't have a GP; Gwyn had always been our doctor. But Ros needed to see someone. She was depressed, had lost interest in everything. Eryl came over within the hour and took Ros and Seth back with her to Caernarfon. That evening she telephoned to say Ros was staying the night at Trefanai. She was abrupt, and when I asked her how Ros was she said 'You've got a lot to answer for' and put the phone down.

The following day we found another three pigs, all of them sows, quivering in their pens. Bloated, they hung their heads close to the ground, their tongues hanging from the sides of their mouths. They stood dejected, lifting their trotters up and down on the same spot. We wouldn't have felt so bad if we could have helped, but just to watch them suffering, unable to ease the pain, tore into the heart. All we could do was try to offer some comfort, get them to lie down on some clean straw.

We brought them water, holding a bucket, trying to get them to drink, but they weren't interested. That afternoon the first gilt aborted her litter; the hopelessness of the situation dug ever deeper into us.

When Dewi came by, bringing a letter from Winford Hook reminding me I was a month late with my year-end accounts, I kept up the pretence that everything was fine. Harry's inexhaustible energy kept the charade going and he invited Dewi in for his usual cup of tea.

'Duw, good idea, don't mind if I do.'

Over the wide plain of the sea a heat haze shimmered. We sat outside, Frieda with her head over the gate. Dewi rambled on about the next election, the possibility of the Plaid Cymru candidate, Dafydd Wigley, winning a large majority. But my mind was elsewhere and I was paying no heed to the conversation going on around me. I didn't hear the telephone ringing.

'Aren't you going to answer it?'

But before I had raised myself it had rung off.

'Are you all right, boy?' said Dewi. 'You seem out of it.'

'He didn't sleep well last night,' said Harry.

'You should try this ginseng stuff. I take it every morning. Makes you buzz,' he said.

'Where do you get it?' asked Harry. 'I might try some of that.'

'Owen Bethel flogs it . . . expensive mind.'

'It can't be that good if it's legal.'

'It's highly recommended by Mrs Hughes. Try it, she said, you'll get the post delivered in half the time.'

'Has it worked?'

'Well, I'm half an hour early, aren't I?'

The telephone rang again. It was Vida Koeffman, whom I hadn't spoken to for some time. She told me I'd come into her thoughts. She asked if I was well; she had sensed I was in trouble. Did I need any help? She was somebody I could trust, so I told her what was going on, and listened to her reassuring voice. I had often asked myself, knowing her struggles, why life had never hardened her. It was as if she lived within the very centre of herself; she understood life's great enigmas.

'Sometimes it is necessary to bring about change through crisis, although you might not know why until many years later.'

Just listening to her lifted my spirits. 'An old woman in her eighties has seen a few things, you know.' She laughed. 'It's getting harder to remember them, though. I only rang to make sure you are coping with what's ahead of you. Anyway, we might not speak again. Thank you for looking after Frieda.'

'Why won't we speak again?'

'An old lady running out of time, that's all.'

How had she known I was in trouble?

Dewi was still talking politics with Harry when Sam and Lysta came running down the drive, satchels swinging, gym shoes round their necks.

'Dad!' they shouted.

'What's the hurry?'

'Nain's coming. We're racing her back.'

My first thought was here comes trouble, and with Dewi tucking into another slice of bara brith he wasn't going anywhere for a while.

'Mum, Mum, you're back!'

Harry stamped out his roll-up. 'I've got work to do.' Grabbing a bucket, he walked past Eryl with a quick 'Afternoon'.

Dewi got to his feet. 'Mrs Griffiths, how nice to see you. Thank you so much for the donation.'

'It was my pleasure.'

'Your mother-in-law,' said Dewi, 'has supported the eisteddfod for many years.'

Ros got out of the car, passing Seth to me. Our eyes didn't meet as I leant forward to kiss her. At least she didn't pull away, but after acknowledging Dewi she went into the house with Eryl.

'Dewi, I've got to go.'

'Go, boy. I'm on my way. Try that ginseng.'

I wanted to follow Ros in and talk to her, but I stopped at the front door as I knew it would be impossible while Eryl was in the house.

After Harry and I finished feeding, we painted red crosses on the pens where pigs were dying. We dragged out the carcasses, laid them in the lean-to and covered them with hessian sacks. Tomorrow Cluttons would take them away, and probably more.

We had a roll-up, sitting on the steps of the stile that bordered Cae Uchaf.

If Harry was feeling the strain he was showing none of it. As we smoked I looked down into the running stream. I could never name the water weeds that grew below the surface or along the banks. I knew the reeds and stiff grasses, but not those that flowered in clusters, no more than a finger high. Water flowing over flinty stones has a calming effect, as does a dragonfly that holds the eye as it hovers, its wings distilling the light of a fading sun, shimmering and transparent. It gave me respite while Harry and I, our shoulders touching, remained silent. I thought of Vida, her words having worked their way into my heart.

I made my way back to the house. Eryl's car was still parked outside. I sensed that a volcano was about to erupt. But when I walked into the sitting room Mozart's piano concerto in C minor was playing, my mother-in-law humming along as if she knew every note. Ros was spooning mashed banana into Seth's hungry mouth. Everyone seemed preoccupied, and I was politely ignored. Sam and Lysta were drawing at the table. Moss of course jumped straight onto the sofa. I waited for her to be shooed off, but Eryl seemed to be floating in a melodic world.

Supper was eaten with innocuous small talk, like strangers meeting for the first time. After the children had gone to bed, rather than endure an uncomfortable silence I asked Ros how she was feeling, but Eryl, bringing in a tray of tea, answered for her.

'You might well ask. She is on antidepressants.'

'Are you, Ros? Are things that bad?'

'Oh, my God! Only a man could say that, an insensitive man who has no idea how his wife is feeling.'

'Ma, don't make things worse.'

'Eryl, don't you think it would be a good idea if you left us alone?'

Her face showed so much anger at the suggestion that Moss growled, and instead of disappearing stood between us barking at her. 'The cheek of it!' she said. 'It would be better for us all if you were to go.'

And from Eryl's point of view, sitting on her matriarchal throne, it would have been. Let's get rid of the dreaded Englishman; she saw her chance now, with Ros and me divided.

After I'd calmed Moss, I picked up her handbag and offered it to her, saying, 'Please go.'

'Ma, go. It's for the best.' At last Ros had spoken.

'You are not well, and I have no intention of standing by while you get pulled in all directions.'

'Tell her again, Ros. Tell her to go.'

'Ma, please, Nick and I have to talk. I'll ring you tomorrow.'

She left, but not until she'd expressed what she'd always felt, her disappointment that Ros had married me in the first place. 'Why haven't you got a proper job? You're not even a qualified farmer, playing at this and that.' And, as she gathered her things together, she said, 'You were never right for this family of ours.'

I watched her get into the car and, rather than driving off immediately, putting on her headscarf and checking her face in the rear-view mirror, her appearance always kept up, the good doctor's widow.

If all that wasn't enough, before I could sit down to talk to Ros a pig wandered past the window. Lysta shouted from her room, 'Pig out, Dad.'

How many times had I heard that cry, and run from the house grabbing a bucket? Frieda was still on duty, leaning over the gate. Did it amuse her watching me chasing yet another pig?

When I got back to the house I went upstairs to make sure the children were asleep. There they lay, in amongst their toys, books still in their hands, felt-tip pens and half-finished drawings strewn over their eiderdowns. Children seem to fall asleep in an instant, as quickly as a camera shutter.

Now at last I was alone with Ros, with the calamity of our lives, the shipwreck, call it what you will. Two survivors looking for a raft, for that's what we were, lost at sea.

'Don't let's blame one another for anything,' I said. 'That would be a good starting point.'

'Well, be honest with me. What's gone wrong?'

'We have lost our way and need to find a way back.'

So we sat there, picking through the emotional mess, Ros admitting that since Gwyn had died she had not mourned her loss and instead had poured herself into the community adventure. Because I had not gone along with the idea, resentment towards me had been gradually growing. 'I miss him terribly. I think about him every day.' But now she realised that it was too soon to be getting so involved with Tom and Agnetta. 'Maybe you are right. It would be better in a year from now, when they are established. It was a distraction after Pa's death.' She had run herself ragged, feeling depleted. 'I've no energy left.'

Should I tell her what was happening on the farm? I did in a way, to a lesser degree than the whole truth. What purpose would it have served? I said a few of the pigs were dying of a mysterious illness called Chicago Vomiting and Wasting Disease. She smiled ironically. 'You haven't made that up, have you?'

I was glad she didn't take it seriously, that I'd said it anyway. The significance of it she would find out all too soon.

'Put on some music,' she said. 'That JJ Cale album.'

I asked about the antidepressants she was taking.

'I'll throw them away. They make me so lethargic.'

'Why did you ever start on them?'

'Ma said I was depressed, and I was. Maybe I still am; I don't know how I feel. Do you know, what I'd really like is a holiday. We have never taken a break ever since we've been here. But I know it's not possible.'

'But it is,' I said. 'We can sell the farm, take the Magic Bus from Victoria to Athens, get on a boat from Piraeus, find a remote island. I'll work if I have to.'

The two of us lay on the sofa and I told Ros, 'This cycle in our lives is coming to an end. We should move on. What have we got to lose?'

'I'll have to talk to Tom and Agnetta.'

'Of course. I'll ring Ivan, tell him we want to put the farm on the market.'

'And speak to Mr Parry, organise things with the school.'

As the music stopped all we could hear was that repetitive click of the needle stuck in the groove after the last track.

'Let's do it,' Ros said.

I knew then we were back together.

'By the way, thank you for the Valentine's card.'

'I don't know what you're talking about.'

'I must say, the handwriting intrigued me. Who wrote it?'

'I really don't know what you're talking about.'

'Say what you meant, then, those words you wrote in the card?'

I didn't. Instead I went and fetched the letter Gwyn had written, that I was to read after his death. Now was the right time, and maybe, although it was sad for her to hear, it might ease the pain. I was sure Gwyn had written it because he would have found it too difficult to say. For not only did he entrust me with the care of his books, which were his real friends, but said it pleased him to have me as a son-in-law. At the end of the letter he said, *You are no Welshman, here is not your home, soon you will be gone. Don't stay for the sake of others, continue your journey and be strong.* It made Ros weep, but I felt that night the healing had begun.

In the morning Ros slept in. It was a Saturday, and Sam and Lysta were excused the chore of laying the breakfast table so that they could watch *Tiswas*, their favourite television programme. It was Spit the dog who amused them, me too if I was around. I left the house, hearing them laughing, to join Harry, his head full of a summer cold, dragging the carcass of a gilt from its pen to be put with the others that had succumbed; a pile of death to be taken away in the lorry that Cluttons sent out every day. They had to be winched on board, a steel cable attached to a trotter. We watched them hauled up the ramp inch by inch, listening to the dull clunk of the cogs as the driver turned the handle.

So it went on for the next two months, decimating the pig herd at Dyffryn. Sometimes we lived in hope, that after three or four days without a death it was behind us. But back it would come; there was no pattern to it. Eventually we had only the odd isolated case. Until on 14 July Barry Evans declared us free of Chicago Vomiting and Wasting Disease. We had lost over thirty sows, fifty-five porkers and I don't know how many piglets. We would receive not a penny in compensation, and although the FUW gave us tremendous support there was nothing they could do to help us financially. The Ministry for Agriculture, Fisheries and Food were sympathetic, but as it was not a notifiable disease nothing was forthcoming from them.

And then, when you have reached that lowest point, your luck changes, just as you were about to give in.

Ivan Treadgold rang to say there was a Dutch sculptor in his office looking to buy a hill farm.

'He's in the area for a couple of days. Do you want to meet him?'

'Why not?' I replied. 'He sounds like an interesting guy.'

He and his girlfriend came by taxi all the way from Caernarfon. That must have been expensive. I wondered why Ivan had not driven them; surely not because of the damage done to his exhaust. He had shoulder-length hair and was wearing a collarless shirt with a pinstriped waistcoat and faded jeans. She had rings on her fingers, dark leather trousers, a loose flowery blouse. My first impression was of a glamorous hippy. As she shook my hand she smiled, showing perfect white teeth. He looked as if he'd had a heavy night. What is it attractive women find in roughened men with that unkempt look? Maybe I should ask Ros. Like all the Dutch, they spoke good English.

'Hi. I'm Ocker, and this is Yvonne.'

Before we walked to the lower fields I lent them each a pair of wellingtons. We had various sizes left by visitors through the years. Down the track under the larch trees I chased away the geese who were flapping their wings and coming towards us aggressively. I threw a handful of mud at them.

'Sorry. They see everyone as an intruder. I've been meaning to get them into the oven for ages.'

I opened the gate. Ahead of us I could see Dave lying in a bog. The poor boy was having great difficulty getting up when he heard us coming.

'That's his health spa,' I said. 'He's our old boar, living out his retirement.'

We walked the boundary wall, which met a ring of mountain ash curving the length of Dyffryn's border.

'There's not much grass down here, only what you see running through the middle, where you can graze a few cattle.'

In the hazy July evening they told me of their lives in Amsterdam. As we walked she touched him a lot, slipping her hand in his, putting her arm round his waist, loving where she was, taking in the view.

'I manage to make a living from my art, selling most of it in one exhibition a year,' Ocker told me. Yvonne was a painter, and they both wanted to 'hang out' in a remote part of the world. He was interested in how we lived, growing as much as we could on the farm. I told him I preferred to barter whenever possible.

'Hey, man, that's so cool.'

'We're not a bunch of hippies. We have to work hard.'

'Yeah, yeah, I understand.' But they weren't interested in buying Dyffryn for agricultural purposes. As we talked, I gathered they wanted to create a sculpture park, to exhibit their art in a natural landscape, letting the weather give it the patina that can only come from being exposed to the elements.

While Ocker and I waited outside, Yvonne walked round the house. 'Do you mind if I have a joint?' he asked, taking one ready rolled from a cigarette case.

Yvonne leaned out of a bedroom window shouting 'I want it, I want it!' And when she joined us she snuggled up to Ocker, saying, 'So what's the next step?'

'I take it you want to buy the place.'

'We do, we do!' she said, speaking for them both.

'When do you want to complete by?' I asked.

'Now,' she said.

Then, having already made up his mind, Ocker said, 'I'll give you your asking price, thirty thousand pounds.' He handed me a business card, showing a huge statue in a fountain of entwined birds.

I said, 'Is that your name?'

'Yeah, that's me, Ocker B. van Tits.'

'Wow, what an unusual name,' was all I could say.

They were keen to pin me down, wanted to move into Dyffryn in September, only a little more than a month away. They would have handed over a deposit there and then, but I said I had to talk to Ros. They were here for another three days; we would have an answer for them before they left. They gave me the telephone number of the guesthouse where they were staying in Bontnewydd, and I rang for a taxi to pick them up.

That evening after supper, when we finally got the children to bed, I told Ros.

'Thirty thousand pounds.' I said.

She said nothing, reaching for a bottle of Blue Nun.

'In a month, Ros. They want to complete in a month.'

These were tense moments. She could easily pull back and drop the idea, not ready for all the effort of a new beginning. Eventually, after keeping me guessing with a long pensive stare, she leant forward to fill her glass and lifted her head, our eyes meeting.

'Let's do it. Accept their offer,' she said.

In that very moment life suddenly flowed forward again. The psychological dam broke and energy found its right course; we were on the move.

There was only one thing left to do now. I picked up the phone and made the call to Ocker.

Since we were leaving anyway I did not replace any of the stock. Harry knew it was only going to take one pair of hands to run the place. The whole atmosphere of the farm had changed. It had lost its purpose, and in early August I went on my final meat round. It was a day of long goodbyes, telling them one by one that this would be the last Friday I would be calling on them. Some were closer than others, but all of them meant something to me. I had no idea it was going to be so emotionally draining. I kept telling myself they were just customers buying joints of meat, they didn't own my heart. But after so many hugs and kisses and watching them wave to me as I drove out of Talysarn for the last time, I was overcome with sadness. It was true; I had been the housewives' farmer.

With us now restored, plans continued to be made. Ros booked the coach tickets, sorted out things with the school, arranged the children's work for the next year. All her doubts, and the sense of guilt she felt about Tom and Agnetta, soon melted away. We had an evening with them when Ros bared her soul. She sought forgiveness for letting them down, while they blamed themselves for being blind to her grief over Gwyn's death. It was what you could call a cathartic clearing of the air. It was the final lifting of an emotional weight for Ros; you could see it in her face. That smile returned.

Ocker had paid his deposit, and the sale proceeded in solicitors' offices.

In mid-August I drove to Porthmadog to put Winford Hook in the picture. It was bound to be a messy affair, all those loose ends to be tied up neatly for the taxman. I walked past the Cob record shop into his office, up those creaking stairs, and knocked on the door, waiting for the sylph-like figure of Mrs Hook to turn the handle and let me in. My first surprise was how much weight she had put on; my second, how much Winford had lost. They had always intrigued me as a married couple. Everything gives way to its opposite is a definite law of the universe. Winford, who couldn't have been short of a penny or two, obviously did not care much about his appearance. He had shrunk inside his clothes, which were the same ones he was wearing when he was three stone heavier.

'Sit yourself down, Perry.'

I did, noticing the cat in the fireplace; where else would it be? Winford, with a poetic perception of my state of being, said, 'It looks as if the tides of life have left their mark on you.'

'Do you mean seaweed?'

'Boy, you have changed; you're losing your youth.'

'Well, you're no Lionel Blair yourself.'

Mrs Hook, now heavier in step, made her way towards me, rattling the teacups, clinking the cutlery. I felt a tinge of sadness, knowing I would never sit here again. I emptied the saucer just as I had always done. I was strangely fond of her; she was beyond type. After she had left us, I told Winford my plans. A look of astonishment moved slowly down his face, the fountain pen falling from his hand and rolling across the ledger. He was speechless. Eventually he said, 'You're . . . you're going to survive.'

'Well, I hope so.'

'The hills are not going to claim you.'

In that last half hour he showed another side of himself. I think he was genuinely pleased that I was escaping from a life that he had seen defeat so many. Now he stood up, and for the first and last time walked round to the front of his desk and shook my hand warmly.

'Send the paperwork in. I'll square it all up for you.'

I stopped outside the Cob, but didn't go in. Instead I looked at the large poster in the window advertising Bob Marley's *Exodus* and drove back to Dyffryn.

Harry was all on edge when we met in the morning. It took us no more than an hour to feed and muck out the pigs. After I'd milked Frieda he came to me, saying, 'I know it can't go on much longer.'

'What?'

'Me being here like this. I'm fed up with looking for things to do.'

As we walked down with a bucket of swill to see Dave I fought with myself, trying to find the right way of putting it. There was no point in delaying what had to be said to this man who had shown such loyalty, been working with me for so long. It was as difficult as those painful conversations with Ros. But he forced it from me and I was glad.

'We're selling up. I have to. There's no future here.'

'I know that, I've known it for some time. So when are you going?'

'In September . . . the fifth to be precise.'

We walked the next few yards in silence as it gradually sank in.

'I'm going to look after you, Harry.'

'How do you mean?'

'With some money. I'm not just going to walk away.'

'To be fair to you, man, I could do with it.'

'I know that. There will be enough to keep you going for a while, until you find something else. You're a survivor.'

'What will you do? Where will you go?'

'We're going to live on a Greek island for a year.'

'With the children?'

'Of course with the children!'

We talked no further of it, for when we saw Dave it was obvious the old boy was in trouble. He struggled to get to his feet as we called him, rattling the bucket. His back legs buckled as he tried to raise himself up. He could only manage a few yards before he went down again. I knew then he was in pain, the time had come. We fed him, holding the bucket in front of him as he sat on his backside. There was nothing wrong with his appetite. As he ate I scratched his ears. He sniffed the bottom of the bucket, throwing his head around, his bright blue eyes still vivid. He looked in good condition, his skin still had a sheen to it, and as he sat there licking his lips you would have thought he was a healthy pig. But his arthritis was now so severe it had reduced him to an invalid. We should not let him lose his dignity as well.

'It breaks my heart to see him like this,' I said to Harry. 'We should call out Barry Evans. Let's take him up and put him in the barn.'

'What, just the two of us?'

'I'll bring the Land Rover down,' I said.

'It will take more than you and me to lift him.'

'Jack's coming later. The three of us can do it then.'

On that warm summer morning dancing with insects, as the bees fed in the gorse flowers, I asked Harry if he would leave me to sit alone with the old boy who had been so much a part of my life. With Moss flat out in the bracken I hugged him, my arms round his neck, and talked to him as you would to a loved one, remembering the first time he tried to shag, the walks with Sam and Lysta to wait for the school bus. The days when he carried them and then stood at the gate, the children waving, their faces pressed to the bus windows. He was a pig with personality.

As I walked away, I looked back at him sitting there like a stone statue, solitary, his head tilted skywards into the blue beyond, unmoving, me weeping because I knew his fate. And when Barry Evans came the next day and shot the bolt into his brain I said to Harry, 'The king is dead, long live the king.' I didn't know what to do with myself, such was the sense of loss.

After Gitto had taken the last of the sows to Bryncir market, only Frieda remained. The porkers were sold to FMC as part of our contract. Sows with litters went to various local smallholders who fattened pigs on kitchen swill, not interested in producing a lean animal, having them killed by local butchers. When I gave

Tom the bees, he told me, 'You know you can come and join us at any time.'

Ivan Treadgold organised the farm auction, all the equipment laid out in the top field. The Massey Ferguson, the Land Rover, the plough and harrow, everything we owned was there. Fencing posts, barbed wire, troughs, shovels, the wheelbarrow. And now it was my turn to feel like those before me as the buyers came and picked over every implement. As each lot was sold a memory sprang up, the days working with it in the fields, even how the weather was, who had been with me. For Harry it was too much. I saw him walk away with Ros down to the house. Jack hung around, jotting down the prices in a notebook. We knew some of the buyers, but it was significant that Gethin Hughes was not amongst them, nor Hughie. Dewi bought the wheelbarrow, for sentimental reasons, he told me. 'That's how I'll always remember you, pushing that thing around.'

Jack and Corinna bedded down in Rob's old caravan for our last week at Dyffryn, the beginning of the long goodbye. Hendy was still on the market, despite my mother's dropping the price by £2,000. Whatever Jack didn't want was being sold to a house-clearance chap in Caernarfon, apart from Gwyn's books, which were crated up and being held in storage. After banking not far short of £3,000 from the farm sale, I wrote a cheque to Harry for a thousand pounds. I put it in an envelope, saying he wasn't to open it until we'd gone. He knew it was a cheque. 'It will see you all right for a while.'

'To be fair to you, man, you're a good 'un.'

All the sheep up at Caesarea were to be sold in two weeks at Bryncir; the farm was now deserted. Frieda had the place to herself, and being literally an old cow and beyond having another calf she was without value to anyone. I bribed Dewi into taking her, giving him fifty quid, and the twelve bales of hay that remained in the barn. It was on the understanding that he would not have her slaughtered, that she would see out her last days with him. I trusted him; what else could I do?

That last week at Dyffryn we got to know Corinna, a girl like ourselves, close to the soil. She was ambitious, had plans for Jack and herself that I knew would take my brother away from shepherding. Unlike Jack, she was sociable, loved the company of others. She expressed her point of view, quite unlike Jack, who preferred to show indifference to the world. What a relief that they would take Moss; she wouldn't have been happy with anyone else.

It was one thirty in the morning when I staggered downstairs to answer the phone. It was Rose Tobias ringing from California, telling me she had just opened Jack's letter. She hadn't come over this year, staying in America to look after her elderly mother.

'Gee, I'm going to miss you guys. And as for that brother of yours, not waiting for me, taking another woman!' She was joking, I'm sure. 'And who's going to look after the place for me?'

I said I'd talk to Harry about that, and added that we were only going for a year; it was more than likely we'd return.

Then the phone went dead. I waited ten minutes but she didn't ring back. I remembered her out in her garden, painting, shouting to us whenever we passed, 'Come on, guys, come on in for a beer.'

Ros had mentioned nothing to Eryl, only telling her mother our plans three days before we left. It was a good idea. We couldn't have lived with the fallout for any longer. Her comment, Ros told me: 'The act of a man who has no direction in his life.'

When my mother heard what we were up to she spoke from her own personal experience, concerned about practical matters.

'I hope you've got proper medical insurance. You know they will not have a hospital on a remote island. If anything horrible happens, they will have to get a helicopter and fly you to Athens. They only have the odd bandage and a bit of sticking plaster, believe me. Take plenty of aspirin with you . . .'

'Don't worry, Mother. Ros has already packed a medicine chest.'

'And as for dentists . . . well, I could tell you a story or two.'

'I'll write as soon as we're settled.'

'And watch out who you work for. Each island has its own mafia.'

'Yes, Mother.'

'And remember to beware of Greeks bearing gifts.'

'Yes, of course.'

'Don't take cash, take travellers cheques.'

'I'd better go now. Just off to have an injection against yellow fever.'

'What?'

'I'll be in touch. Goodbye.'

How strange it was, those last few days walking around Dyffryn. Everything seemed to blur into one great sunset, dispersing colours over the vast Irish Sea. The solitude I felt, having farmed these fields and poured myself into a way of life that was now behind me. My belief in everything we had tried to do at Dyffryn remained the same. Organic farming had to be the future if the planet was going to survive, but many more would have to take up the cause than a few little groups on remote hillsides. I remembered again the note Mrs Musto had left, warning me to watch out for those neighbours of mine. How right she was. Somewhere I still had that envelope.

I wandered around the buildings, the empty pens, the chewed doors, the stained concrete walls where the pigs had rubbed themselves. It was the hush, after so much physical energy had been spent. All the effort involved in controlling a pig herd. I could hear them whining in the silence, as if it was the end of term, the dormitories now quiet, all the boys gone home. A surge of sadness came over me for all of them, not just for those who had succumbed, but for all who had been here, including the dearest of them all, Rattlerow King David the Fifty-seventh.

On the night before we left, Hughie came over with Myfanwy to say goodbye.

'Duw, boy,' he said, 'it's goodbye then, something I'm not too good at saying.'

'Well, you've said it.' Myfanwy handed us some boiled sweets

for the children. 'And here's some penny ducks for your journey.'
Welsh meatballs she had made herself; still warm in the paper
bag. 'They're just as nice cold, you know.'

'Thank you.'

'Won't see you again, not at my age.'

'Goodbye.' I bent down and kissed Myfanwy's white cheek,
smelling her cheap perfume.

I had talked everything through with Jack, given him the
cheque book, Winford Hook's telephone number. I told him I
would ring when we reached our final destination, wherever
that might be. 'See you then, brother. Who knows when.'

'You could say we've been on a journey together.' We hugged
one another.

'Thanks for looking after Moss.'

In the morning Harry drove us to Bangor station in a hire car
from Trevor Ellis at the Paragon garage. Ros and Lysta were
tearful, Sam shook Harry's hand, wanting to appear grown up,
but Harry threw his arms around him anyway. He squeezed
Seth's cheek, whispered in my ear, 'You should never have given
me that much.'

'You bugger, I told you not to open it until we'd gone.'

'Dad, no need to swear,' said Lysta.

'Oh bollocks, sorry.'

'Dad!'

I watched Harry as the train pulled away and to be fair to the
man he stood there waving until I could see him no more.

And so we went on our way to a Greek island. But that's
another story.

Acknowledgements

I would like to thank the following people who have all helped in different ways. Especial thanks to my wife Arabella – without her dedicated help and enthusiasm this book would never have been completed. Heartfelt thanks to many friends, particularly Ingrid Lacey and Leslie Smith who gave the book so much time and consideration, Rob and Kate Marshall, Paul Sharpe, Judith Mather, Nathaniel Mobbs, Elsa Peters, Barbara Hennell, Marc Wilson, Mike and Jo Saffell, Pat Booth, Ruth Cleaver, Lucia Dhillon, Tom and Sasha Sykes, Claire Kenward, Candida Hubbard, Melanie Wilde and Lucinda Knight, some of whom read every draft and came back for more, and all kept the wheels turning. To Jan, Martin, Corinna and Gavin Perry and my sister Dale for their support. Andrew Hobden of the Welsh Assembly Government and Andrew Gurney of Farmers' Union of Wales for animal and hay prices in the 1970s. Ros Monteiro, not only for her illustrations, but also her unerring encouragement. And a huge thank you to Teresa Monachino who always believed in the book, gave it style, and found its rightful home with Neville Moir and Alison Rae at Polygon – and of course editor Nancy Webber who made my day.